The Aleut Internments of
World War II

The Aleut Internments of World War II

Islanders Removed from Their Homes by Japan and the United States

RUSSELL W. ESTLACK

Forewords by DIMITRI PHILEMONOF *and* BLACKHAWK WALTERS

McFarland & Company, Inc., Publishers
Jefferson, North Carolina

LIBRARY OF CONGRESS CATALOGUING-IN-PUBLICATION DATA

Estlack, Russell W.
  The Aleut internments of World War II : islanders removed from their homes by Japan and the United States / Russell W. Estlack ; forewords by Dimitri Philemonof and Blackhawk Walters.
    p.   cm.
  Includes bibliographical references and index.

  ISBN 978-0-7864-7638-1 (softcover : acid free paper) ∞
  ISBN 978-1-4766-0587-6 (ebook)

  1. Aleuts—Evacuation and relocation, 1942–1945. 2. World War, 1939–1945—Alaska. 3. World War, 1939–1945—Concentration camps—United States. 4. World War, 1939–1945—Concentration camps—Japan. 5. Prisoners of war—United States—History—20th century. 6. Prisoners of war—Japan—History—20th century. 7. Alaska—History, Military—20th century. 8. Alaska—Ethnic relations—History—20th century. I. Title.
  D810.A53E88 2014
  940.53'17798—dc23   2014007217

BRITISH LIBRARY CATALOGUING DATA ARE AVAILABLE

© 2014 Russell W. Estlack. All rights reserved

No part of this book may be reproduced or transmitted in any form or by any means, electronic or mechanical, including photocopying or recording, or by any information storage and retrieval system, without permission in writing from the publisher.

On the cover: *top* Attuans await transport to an internment camp in Japan, June 1942. Chief Mike Hodikoff is in the suit; *bottom* Aleuts from St. George and St. Paul sail aboard the USAT *Delarof* to their new home in southeastern Alaska, August 1942 (both National Archives)

Printed in the United States of America

McFarland & Company, Inc., Publishers
  Box 611, Jefferson, North Carolina 28640
    www.mcfarlandpub.com

To the loving memory of my parents, Elmer and Ethel Estlack,
who through their examples taught me
about love, life and rules to live by.
They are gone, but never forgotten.
To my wife, Luisa, who believed I could write this book.
Her loving support makes life worthwhile.
To my wonderful grandchildren,
Joseph W. Peckumn, Aubrey Rose Peckumn, Amanda and Samantha Estlack,
and to my children, Allison Peckumn and Russell Estlack, Jr.
May they always enjoy the freedom and blessings of America,
the Land of the Free and the Home of the Brave.

Table of Contents

Acknowledgments ix
Foreword by Dimitri Philemonof 1
Foreword by Blackhawk Walters 3
Introduction 5

1.	Clash of Cultures	11
2.	The Russian American Company	28
3.	American Century	44
4.	Missionaries and Miners	57
5.	Alaska, the Last Frontier	68
6.	Prelude to War	77
7.	War Comes to Alaska	80
8.	Blood on the Sand	88
9.	Prisoners in the Land of the Rising Sun	98
10.	Aleuts in Japan	105
11.	War and Evacuation	113
12.	Atka	118
13.	The Pribilofs	123
14.	The Voyage of the *Delarof*	128
15.	Strangers in a Strange Land	134
16.	Burnett Inlet	140
17.	Ward Lake	144

18.	Funter Bay	150
19.	Killisnoo	159
20.	Employment Opportunities	165
21.	Fur Seal Operations, 1943	169
22.	Home Is Where the Heart Is	174
23.	Homecoming	183
24.	Restitution	198

Appendix	205
Notes	223
Bibliography	229
Index	231

Acknowledgments

This book is the result of the collective efforts of a number of people
who gave me the freedom to tell the story of the Aleut people.
I am especially indebted to the Aleutian/Pribilof Island Association
for their generous and untiring efforts
to assist me with my research
and to the president and CEO of the APIA, Dimitri Philemonof,
who believed in this project from its inception.
My thanks to my good friend and fellow author,
Douglas Brough of Barrow-in-Furness, Cumbria, England.
His suggestions were invaluable
in the preparation of this manuscript.
Without their help and support,
this book would never have been written.

Foreword
by Dimitri Philemonof

Russell W. Estlack's historic account in this book is a story close to my heart in that it speaks of my family, my friends, and above all my Aleut people whom I humbly serve as president and CEO of the Aleutian Pribilof Islands Association Inc. (APIA) in Anchorage, Alaska.

After Russell wrote his Pulitzer Prize–nominated book *Shattered Lives, Shattered Dreams,* he learned about a little-known fact—that of the Aleut internment in southeastern Alaska and Japan during World War II. He called APIA to gather more information on the subject in order to write another book that he felt, and I agree, needed to be written.

Russell enthusiastically deciphered hundreds of pages about World War II reparations and documentation stored in APIA's Cultural Heritage Library and Archives and consulted our CD, *The Relocation and Internment of the Aleuts During World War II,* and DVD, *The Untold War Story,* which received an Emmy nomination in 1992 and a Bronze Telly Award in 1994.

Russell's manuscript accurately describes the horrific experiences Aleuts suffered from the federal government and others. Accounts during World War II tell of being herded off their beloved Aleutian Islands to spend years living in abandoned buildings in various locations in southeastern Alaska, arriving with few of their personal belongings. They suffered many hardships, such as rebuilding dilapidated buildings, hunger, ill health and the deaths of family members. They returned to their burned-out or ransacked homes to discover the pilfering of precious items by military personnel. Accounts tell of the suffering and death of half the population of Attuan Aleuts while interned in Japan; by order of the federal government, the survivors never returned to their beloved island. This book also describes the St. Paul fur seal industry—how the enslaved men were ordered to slaughter millions of fur seals to generate money for the federal government, including restitution settlement to the Aleut people by the United States government.

Very little is known about the Aleut people of the Aleutian Islands. This book is only a chapter capturing the many atrocities my beloved Aleut people have suffered—starting with the first discovery of Alaska by Russians in 1741 to further sufferings endured at the hands of the Americans after the purchase of Alaska in 1867.

Many thanks to Russell for his insight and energy to document this story and enlighten the public so that others may know. This book is a must read!

I will say "fortitude" is a good word in describing the Aleut people who throughout history have endured all the horrific impositions of suppression, oppression and almost annihilation from this earth.

It is said, if you never ask, you are never told. Therefore, I, along with the other Aleut people, thank you, Russell, for asking. Ancient Aleut oral stories always end with "It is said."

Dimitri Philemonof is president and CEO of the Aleutian Pribilof Islands Association and a representative for the St. George Village Corporation, the Alaskan Housing Authority, the Alaska Federation of Natives, and the Aleut Corporation. He was instrumental in helping pass World War II reparations and establish the Russian Orthodox Church Restoration Trust Fund.

Foreword

by Blackhawk Walters

I remember well my first meeting with Russell and the beginning of our friendship. It was ten years ago after the publication of my first book. We both attended a Southern Utah Book Writer's Convention. I listened to the naysayers about how hard it was to get published. I raised my hand and said, "If you have a story to tell, then write it and publish it yourself. If the story is good then it will sell. I did this myself, sold the initial printing of one thousand copies in one day, and have republished twice more, making $30,000. If you are interested, see me after the meeting and I'll explain more." Of fifty people, one was serious: Russell Estlack. When he approached me, he asked questions, listened, took notes and called me several times on his journey to become a writer. Since that day, the student has surpassed the teacher.

Russell's book is a story close to my heart. My people were illegally taken from our homes by the Army of the United States and forced to march across the wilderness. The Creek, Choctaw, Chickasaw, Seminoles, and Cherokee were forcibly removed from their ancestral tribal homes. Thousands of Native Americans died on this forced march, which has become known as the "Trail of Tears." A similar incident happened to the indigenous Aleuts of Alaska. Because the United States military did not want Americans to know the Japanese had invaded Alaska, a news blackout was imposed.

The history books, colleges, and universities have ignored this incident. Thanks to Russell's research from U.S. government documents, Japanese soldiers, and personal stories of the Aleuts themselves, this story lives on. It is hard to believe that a tragedy such as this has not become a part of history.

Over eight hundred Aleuts who were American citizens were held prisoner by the United States military, supposedly to protect them from the Japanese. They lost their homes, which also were looted by service personnel and civilians; they lost their works of art, tribal crafts, and religious icons. Conditions were so horrendous that ten percent of the Aleuts perished under the supposed protection of the United States military. This was truly a racial incident. Authorities ordered the removal of anyone with one-eighth Indian blood; all others were allowed to remain in the Aleutians. Thanks to Russell, this story will survive and hopefully become a part of our history.

Blackhawk Walters is a four-time kick boxing world champion and was the first martial artist to teach karate on a nationally syndicated television show. He is a popular motivational speaker and the author of four books on success. He has appeared in numerous action films and has written and recorded five award-winning country and western albums.

Introduction

The story of the internment of the Aleut people is almost totally unknown outside the confines of Alaska. Because it has been largely forgotten by the American people, it isn't taught in colleges or universities, and there is no mention of it in the history books. Thanks to the desire of the Aleuts to preserve the history and personal stories of the people who lived through these events, a limited number of records still exist.

To understand the internment of the Aleut people and the reasons behind these tragic events, it is important to understand the history of Alaska. In 1741, the Russians came to Alaska in search of new lands to expand the fur trade. They encountered unknown native peoples and they subjugated them and enslaved them. To their Russian masters they were nothing more than serfs to be exploited.

When America purchased Alaska in 1867, the government, the military, and the white population of the territory were indifferent to the needs of the native population. They saw them as a problem to be dealt with. Manifest Destiny was alive and well and the Indians were pushed aside to make room for the white man's settlements. The Indians of Alaska endured greater cruelty and suffering at the hands of the white man than any other native tribes in North America.

The evacuation and internment of the Aleuts in Alaska was far different from the internment suffered by ethnic groups in the continental United States and Hawaii. The term "military necessity" did not apply to the Indians. Granted that the Japanese invaded Attu and Kiska in the westernmost part of the Aleutian chain, there was no military justification for the relocation and internment of the Aleut people. Government actions toward the Aleuts weren't influenced by wartime hysteria or fear of sabotage. Unlike the Germans, Japanese, and Italians who were interned in the name of national security, the Aleuts were relocated and interned for their own protection, according to the government, from the Japanese military forces that invaded Attu, Agata, and Kiska.

Each group of internees suffered economic loss and personal hardship, but for the Unangan (We the People), their suffering was far greater than any other ethnic group. The irreparable loss of much of their traditional culture and the tragic decline in the number of Aleuts still alive at the end of their ordeal was a direct result of their removal from the Aleutians and the Pribilofs and the harsh treatment inflicted on them by a wartime government.

The World War II odyssey of the Aleuts began with the Japanese invasion of the Aleutians in 1942. Torn from their villages and interned in camps in southeastern Alaska, as well as in Japan, they were subjected to horrible living conditions and saw their loved ones die in alarming numbers. They endured death and disease in abandoned canneries and gold mines with dilapidated housing, unhealthy water supplies, and almost nonexistent medical care or equipment. Conditions were more humane in Japan than they were in Alaska, but the Aleuts imprisoned at Oar City, Hokkaido, Japan, also suffered starvation and death.

Once the Aleuts were removed from their isolated villages, their homes were looted by service personnel and civilians alike and used to billet troops. In almost every instance, the people received a few hours' notice to evacuate and were permitted to take only what they could carry in a single suitcase. Personal possessions, religious icons, family albums, traditional works of art, and tribal crafts were lost to them forever. As they lined the rails of their ships and sailed away from their beloved islands, they watched in horror as American sailors burned their homes and churches to the ground and destroyed their culture and a way of life they had enjoyed for centuries. For many of them, this was the last time they would ever see their ancestral homes.

Unlike other internment camps in the United States and Hawaii, the internment camps in Alaska did not have guard towers, barbed wire or armed guards, but they were as much a prison as any of the others. They bore a strong resemblance to the Japanese POW camps for American prisoners. Conditions in the camps were so horrendous that ten percent of the internees perished. Epidemics, inadequate shelter, lack of medical care, and the deprivation of basic human needs took their toll. Throughout their ordeal, the Aleuts never lost their patriotism and love for America, their faith in God, or their dream of returning to their beloved islands once the war ended.

After three long years of hardship and suffering, the Aleuts returned to their villages debilitated and exhausted, only to find destruction and devastation. The homes they left no longer existed or had been trashed by American military personnel. Rehabilitation of their homes was paid for with funds from the president's emergency fund, but the Aleuts had to do most of the rebuilding of their communities and their lives on their own. To the Department of the Interior, the military, and other government agencies, the Indians were of little consequence. These agencies failed to recognize the sacrifices and losses the evacuees suffered and the selfless contributions they made to the war effort.

Racism appears to have been a major factor in the decision to remove the natives from their homes. When the authorities ordered the removal of anyone with as little as one-eighth Indian blood, they permitted non–Indians and whites to remain.

Even before the war, racism was a problem for native and other non-white populations in Alaska. Their social position was equivalent to that of Negroes in the American South. Hotels, restaurants, and cafes prohibited natives and non-whites from entering their establishments. It didn't matter that hundreds of natives enlisted in the U.S. military and were fighting the Japanese on distant battlefields. Discriminatory signs were prominently displayed across Alaska, with messages such as "Native Trade Not Solicited," or "No Natives or Filipinos Wanted."

Even though they were American citizens, they were wards of the federal government. Their lives were controlled and regulated by a government whose main interest was not the welfare of the indigenous natives of Alaska but a way to exploit them for profit. Rights granted to all Americans under the Constitution were denied to the Aleut people.

Mildred Greenhagan of Salt Lake City, Utah, learned firsthand how the United States government denied these American citizens the freedoms that all Americans take for granted.

Salt Lake City, Utah
October 19, 1942

Mr. E.C. Johnston
706 Federal Office Building
Seattle, Washington

Dear Mr. Johnston,

Mrs. Grover has been with us for some little time now and we have learned to think a great deal of her and to have considerable respect for her opinion.

She has talked many times about Sophie Procopius and her many good qualities, so we decided to see if arrangements could be made to bring her to the states to do housework for us. We would be willing to wire you money for her bus and boat fare here and then Sophie could pay it back to us at $5 a month. We would like to have her come down on the next boat if arrangements could possibly be made.

I remain respectfully yours,
Mildred Greenhagan
1415 So. 5th. East
Salt Lake City, Utah[1]

Edward C. Johnston was the superintendent for the Fish and Wildlife Service at Funter Bay, Alaska. Two weeks later, he wrote to Mildred giving her his answer.

Funter Bay, Alaska
November 2, 1942

Mrs. Mildred Greenhagan
1415 So. 5th East
Salt Lake City, Utah

Dear Mrs. Greenhagan:

We have just received your letter regarding the employment of Sophia Procopius. Sophia Procopius is already filling a position in Juneau at a salary of $50 per month with room and board. She expects to return to the Pribilof Islands when the Emergency is over.

It is the policy of the Fish and Wildlife Service to refuse to allow Pribilof natives to accept work in the states.

Very truly yours,
Edward C. Johnston
Superintendent[2]

Financial considerations also played a role in the government's decision to intern the Aleuts. The fur seal harvest was a major source of revenue for the U.S. government. They needed the Indians to harvest the seals or risk the loss of millions of dollars. Targeted by deceptive practices and threats, the Aleuts were forced to work long hours and not permitted to rejoin their families in the camps until the seal harvest was finished. The evacuation, internment, and inhumane treatment of the Aleut people were grave injustices perpetrated by government officials and military officers who saw an emergency where none existed. In an effort to keep the news of the Japanese invasion from the American public, the U.S. military instituted a news blackout on the war situation in Alaska and the internment of the Aleut people.

Memories of the invasion of the Aleutians in 1942, and the evacuation, relocation, and internment, continue to haunt the few remaining survivors and their families. In a speech to the Alaska War Symposium in 1993, Dean Kohloff, the author of *When the Wind Was a River*, recounted a homecoming of a family that suffered the deprivation of the evacuation and internment:

As Bill Tcheripanoff, his wife, and four children approached their Accutane home in 1945, a nightmare lay before their eyes. It had begun in 1942 when they were "whipped away" from their home "like dogs—to some strange place," Wrangell, and yet again "to another place wet with constant rain called Ketchikan." They had been Aleut evacuees and now found that all their "possessions were gone or destroyed." A determined Tcheripanoff said, "I knew I had to salvage my house for my family and I worked till my hands bleeding with pain made the wood red." But he concluded, "I cannot go on thinking about my sad experience as it only makes my heart want to cry."³

The Aleutian Islands rise out of the ocean like an oasis of green in a world of gray. Summits of a submerged volcanic mountain range, the treeless islands served as a formidable World War II battleground from 1942 to 1943. Impenetrable fog and wild gusts of wind called "williwaws" were a common enemy of both American and Japanese forces and often determined the success of military maneuvers. The Aleutian campaign involved tens of thousands of U.S. land, sea, and air forces advancing progressively westward along the 1,100 mile Aleutian arc to reach and successfully defeat Japanese troops occupying Attu and Kiska islands. The Japanese, befriended by a protective fog, secretly evacuated Kiska Island prior to the U.S. invasion. Today five National Historic Landmarks commemorate the Aleutian campaign of World War II and the lives and events that forever changed these desolate beautiful islands.

National Park Service map of the Aleutian Islands. From *World War II National Historic Landmarks: The Aleutian Campaign*. U.S. Government Printing Office, 1993 (673rd Air Base Wing History Office, Joint Base Elmendorf-Richardson, Alaska).

1

Clash of Cultures

Ten thousand years ago, the ancestors of the Aleuts migrated over the Bering Strait from Asia to North America. Traveling south along the ice-free coastline to the lower Alaskan peninsula into the Aleutian chain, they built their villages on these treeless, tundra-covered volcanic islands and proudly called themselves *Unangan,* "We the People."

Surrounded by the storm-blasted waters of the northern Pacific and the Bering Sea, the Aleutians curve in an arc like a 1,200-mile string of pearls from the Alaskan mainland in the east, to Attu in the west, to the Pribilofs in the north. A partially submerged continuation of the Aleutian Mountain Range, the archipelago separates the Pacific Ocean from the Bering Sea.

Northward-flowing air currents from Japan and frigid, dry Arctic winds clash like ancient warriors to produce "williwaws" that scream through narrow valleys and steep cliffs. Shrouded in fog and swept by vicious storms throughout most of the year, these islands are known as "the birthplace of the winds." Wind, rain, and snow from the most brutal stretch of the northern Pacific affect the weather of western Canada and the Pacific coast of the U.S. mainland. With 45 active volcanos, the Aleutians are a major part of the Pacific Rim "ring of fire."

Archeologists have determined that many of the Aleut villages have been continuously occupied for more than 8,000 years. From 1741, when the Russians first visited the islands and discovered an unknown people, to 1942, when the Japanese invaded the islands, the Aleuts lived in their villages and were treated as slaves. Their history shows that their suffering was far worse than any other indigenous people since the white man first set foot on the North American continent.

The Unangan were a communal people and from the earliest times generations of families lived in one dwelling. To help them survive the harsh winters, their semi-subterranean pit homes (*barabaras*) were covered with sod and grass over a wood frame. Entry into the *barabara* was accomplished by climbing a pole ladder and dropping down through a hole in the roof. Many families often lived in a single dwelling that was divided into smaller rooms attached to a large group room in the center of the structure. Villages consisted of a number of houses and were characterized by three social classes: wealthy, common, and slaves.

Like many Native American tribes, the Unagan wore wooden masks during their annual winter feasts to invoke the presence of powerful spirits. They believed in a creator who was related to the sun and whose good graces were necessary for success in the hunt. Reincarnation of souls and their migration between earth and the worlds above and below were major tenets of their religion. Animals played a large part of their belief in the spirit world and represented good and evil spirits. Hunters wore amulets and charms to ward off evil and appease the spirits to guarantee a successful hunt.

The Aleuts ate their food raw or uncooked and they didn't store or harvest food for winter. They dried fish and meat and combined it with mammal fat to flavor the fresh foods they gathered from the land. They subsisted on sea lion and built their camps close to the rookeries to give them easy access to one of their chief sources of food. The Aleuts of Akutan engaged in whale hunting, which they considered the most noble of all the Aleut hunts. Only the bravest and most fearless among the Aleuts of the village were permitted to hunt these leviathans of the sea.

To protect themselves from the freezing temperatures, incessant wind, rain, and snow, they donned a hooded robe (*kamleika*) made from sea-mammal skin. This garment was light and waterproof and sewn together with tundra grass. Each robe took about a month to make.

The Aleuts were master seamen and they learned how to conquer the sea and the elements. They designed and built boats (*baidarka*) that were known for their seaworthiness and maneuverability over rough seas in any kind of weather. After a long sea voyage, it was necessary to drag the craft out of the water to allow the skin to dry.

One, two, or three-hatched *baidarka* could remain at sea for extended periods of time. Each one was constructed to a specific size to match the size of the paddler. The hunter knelt or sat while he dipped his paddle in frigid waters, and it has been historically recorded that if appropriately dressed in a kamleika, an Aleut paddler could roll the *baidakra* completely over in rough seas and become upright again without being tossed from his craft. The Unangan conquered their environment, but were woefully unprepared to face the cruelty, servitude, and greed of a despotic Tsarist government.

At the end of the seventeenth century, the geography of the North Pacific was virtually unknown. The discovery and exploration of the Aleutian Islands, the Pribilofs, and the coast of mainland Alaska can be directly attributed to Peter the Great, one of the most significant, enlightened and accomplished leaders in Russian history. He was extremely intelligent and a strong believer in progress for his country.

One of Peter's first important acts as ruler of Russia was to wage a victorious military campaign against the Turkish bastion of Azov. As the strongest military power in the world at that time, the Turks refused to accept the loss of Azov. Peter was faced with the prospect of a long and costly war and he needed allies if he was to prevail against his enemy.

In 1697, Peter left Russia to seek military assistance from the crowned heads of Europe. He was greeted with pomp and ceremony befitting a visiting head of state, but little else. Since the crowned heads of Europe had no desire to go to war with the Turks, they refused to accede to his request for money and troops.

When not meeting with the monarchs of Europe, or attending diplomatic functions and dinners, Peter spent his time studying the latest technology and methods then in vogue on the continent. In each country he visited, Peter hired engineers, shipbuilders, architects, craftsmen, and merchants to come to Russia to help drag his country out of its unenlightened medieval past and educate his people.

For eighteen months he traveled through the Swedish Baltic provinces, Prussia and other northern German states, Holland, England, and Saxony. He spent four months in Holland learning how to build ships. Contrary to royal protocol, he picked up a hammer and actually worked as a ship's carpenter. In England, King William III presented Peter with a twenty-gun yacht and afforded him the opportunity to study the Parliament, Oxford, the Greenwich Observatory, the Royal Arsenal, the mint, and the Tower of London. William had no interest in joining him in his fight with the Turks, so Peter moved on to Austria.

During his reign, Peter instituted major reforms that affected all levels of Russian society. Despite opposition from the country's medieval aristocracy, he abolished an archaic form of government and appointed a viable Senate, which regulated all branches of administration as well as bearing the responsibility for Russia's foreign policy. He concentrated on developing commerce and industry and on creating a culture that mirrored the culture of Europe. Peter also modernized the Russian alphabet, introduced the Julian calendar, and established the first Russian newspaper.

Peter centralized the government and established new schools specializing in medicine, science, and math. He secularized the country's education system and exerted greater control over the Russian Orthodox Church. To improve the economy and to bring new wealth into Russia, he imported European goods and western mercantilism.

Peter's next task was to reorganize the military from a slovenly army and navy into an effective fighting force. He made the Russian army into an impressive force of professional soldiers who were ready to take on any enemy they might be called on to fight. By using his skills and experience as a seaman and carpenter, Peter modernized the navy and molded it into a formidable sea power.

While on a visit to Amsterdam, Peter learned that a Dutch scholar, Nicholas Witsen, had proposed that there was a connection between the Kamchatka Peninsula and the American mainland by way of a large island or a peninsula that jutted out from the North American coast. Though he was incorrect in his assumption, Witsen placed the location of this island where the Bering Sea and the Aleutian Islands are located. He described this peninsula as bulbous in shape and projecting westward in an area north of the Aleutian Islands, with its western edge within a few hundred miles of the Kamchatka Peninsula.

Maps drawn by Russian geographers showing the American peninsula even closer to Kamchatka convinced Peter that the distance from Kamchatka to North America was quite short. *Promyshlennki* (fur traders) recently returned to Russia recounted stories from Siberian natives of a great land to the east. Spanish mariners who used the Japanese Current to sail across the North Pacific on their return voyages from the Philippines to the west coast of Mexico also told of this land. Their ships were often caught in vicious storms and driven northward, where the sailors thought they sighted a large land mass. Since it did not appear on any of the maps or charts of the day, the mariners named it Gamaland, after Portuguese navigator Juan de Gama. He was one of the first to report the possibility of a large land mass in that part of the North Pacific.

On his tour of the European capitals, Peter met with many scientific leaders to consider the implications of the discovery and exploration of the Kamchatka Peninsula and the Kurile Islands. They discussed the question of the North Pacific and asked Peter to settle once and for all if Asia and America were connected. On his return to Russia, he ordered two of his officers, Fedor Luzhin and Ivan Evreinov, to proceed to Kamchatka to sail not only north and south, but east and west and draw a map of their discoveries. They left Russia in 1719 and reached Kamchatka one year later. After exploring the sea around the Kurile Islands, they returned to St. Petersburg in 1721. They drew maps and made a verbal report to the emperor, but it is not known what they reported to him.

A few months before his death in 1725, Peter the Great drafted a docu-

1. Clash of Cultures   15

ment outlining detailed instructions for the exploration of Kamchatka and the waters to the east of Siberia. World-famous mariner Vitus Bering was selected to lead the expedition. Peter wanted Bering to explore the coast and determine if Asia and America were connected. Peter's instructions to Bering read as follows:

> 1. There should be built on the Kamchatka [River], or at some other place adjacent, one or two boats with decks.
> 2. With these boats [you are directed] to sail along the coast that extends northwards and which is supposed (since no one knows the end of it) to be continuous with America.
> 3. And therefore [you are directed] to seek the point where it connects with America and to go to some settlement under European rule, or if any European vessel is seen, learn of it, what the coast is called, which should be taken down in writing, an authentic account prepared, placed on a chart and brought back here.[1]

In the winter of 1725, Bering led a group of eighty men across 6,000 miles of Siberian wilderness, exploring river valleys and plateaus as they went. On reaching the Sea of Okhotsk, he had a small ship, the *Fortuna*, constructed to carry his party across the open water to the western shore of Kamchatka. Once ashore, they dismantled the boat and carried it across the peninsula to the eastern shore. Despite the information provided by Luzhin and Evreinov, and the Chuikchi natives who inhabited the area, Bering concluded that there was no land to the east anywhere near Siberia. He now interpreted his orders to mean that he was to sail northward along the Siberian coast. If there was a land connection to America, it would have to be in the north.

Bering decided that he needed a larger ship than the *Fortuna*. He constructed the *St. Gabriel*, and then charted the coast northward along Kamchatka, around the Gulf of Andyr, and through the Bering Strait, which now bears his name. Convinced that the land connection he sought did not lie to the north, and because of the dense fog and heavy weather, he never sighted the North American mainland. Transiting the Bering Strait, he sailed back and forth, east and west, searching for a land that apparently did not exist. He returned to St. Petersburg and reported his findings to the Empress of Russia.

The following document is an excerpt from the log of Bering's first expedition.

> The vessel was provisioned (in Kamchatka) with everything needful for forty men for a year.
> On the 14th day of July we went out of the mouth of the Kamchatka River into the sea in obedience to the autographic orders given me by his imperial Majesty Peter the Great, as the map constructed for that purpose will show.
> August 8th, having arrived in north latitude 64° 30,' eight men rowed to us

from the shore in a skin boat, enquiring from whence we came and what our business was there. They said they were Chuikchi (whom the Russians of these parts have long known), and as we lay to they were urged to come to the vessel. They inflated some floats made of sealskin and sent one man swimming to us to talk, then the boat came up to the vessel and they told us that on the coast lived many of their nation; that the land not far from there takes a decided turn to the westward, and they also said that at no great distance from where we were, we should see an island. This proved true, but we saw nothing valuable upon it but huts.

This island in honor of the day we named St. Lawrence, but we were not able to see any people upon it, though an officer was sent in a boat from the vessel on two occasions to look for inhabitants.

At the 15th of August we arrived in the latitude of 67° 18' and I judged that we had clearly and fully carried out the instructions given by his Imperial Majesty of glorious and ever deserving memory, because the land no longer extended to the north. Neither from the Chuikchi coast nor to the eastward could any extension of land be observed.

The expedition returned to Kamchatka, and later arrived back in St. Petersburg on the 1st of March, 1730.[2]

Bering returned to Russia and made his report to Empress Anna Ivannovna, the officers of the Admiralty, and the members of the Senate. When he tried to persuade them that Peter's instructions had been carried out, some cheered and clapped, while others merely shrugged their shoulders. Bering's doubters maintained that as long as certain areas south and east of Kamchatka had not yet been explored, the question of a link between Asia and America had not been resolved. To bolster their claim, Bering's doubters pointed to numerous Siberian rumors that a large body of land did indeed exist south and east of Kamchatka.

Though the doubters were dissatisfied with Bering's answers, there were those in that illustrious gathering who believed he had done a good job, even if he didn't do it as well as he should have. Though he was partially discredited, they believed that with his skill as a navigator and his knowledge and experience of the sea, Bering would do much better if he were given a second chance.

Bering also wanted a second chance. He submitted a proposal for a second expedition to the Empress, and in December 1732 it was approved by the Senate. Known as the Great Northern Expedition, it became a massive enterprise unlike any previous expedition of exploration and discovery by any country in the history of the world. More ambitious than the first expedition, the proposal called for a survey of Siberia's major rivers along their course to the Arctic Ocean, the mapping of the Arctic coast as well as the coast of the Sea of Okhotsk, finding a favorable trade route south to Japan, exploring the Shantar Islands, and making contact with Spanish America. The proposal called for

Bering and Alexeii Chirikov to command the second Kamchatka expedition and sail southeasterly from Kamchatka to "Gamaland" and beyond to find the connection between Asia and America.

Russian documents of the time clearly indicate that Bering's explorations of Alaska were not primarily for the purposes of surveying and mapping, but for political and economic reasons. Russia wanted a permanent presence in North America and exploitation of furs and minerals found there. Bering and Chirikov were directed to claim the unoccupied North American coast for Russia and to identify resources and native populations for exploitation.

Bering and Chirikov crossed Siberia with the main body of the expedition. On June 5, 1741, Bering took command of the *St. Peter* and Chirikov took command of the *St. Paul*. The two captains sailed from Kamchatka in a southeasterly direction in search of "Gamaland." They sailed as far south as 46° north latitude before giving up this fruitless search.

During the voyage, the ships became separated and were forced to proceed independently of each other. Chirikov sailed off in a northeasterly direction, and on July 15 he sighted land near Cape Addington on the west side of Prince of Wales Island. He anchored his ship in the bay and sent his first mate, Abraham Dementief, and ten sailors armed with muskets and small brass cannon to shore in the longboat.

When, after several days, they failed to return, the boatswain, Sidor Savalief, took the remaining boat and went to look for them. Neither party was heard from again, but the next day, natives paddling skin-covered canoes came out to the ship. From a short distance away, they shouted at the crew in their own language, turned and returned to shore.[3]

After three days of waiting, Chirikov gave up all hope of ever seeing his men again. With the last of his boats gone, he had no choice but to set sail for Petropavlovsk. As he sailed northwest, he sighted high mountains near the entrance to Cook Inlet. He continued south past the east side of Kodiak Island and west along the Peninsula of Alaska. On September 20, 1741, Chirikov entered an unknown bay and met with the natives of the islands.

Chirikov and most of his crew were sick with scurvy. Without delay, they pressed on to Avacha Bay. They had good sailing weather and they were fortunate to miss the violent storms that had separated the two ships. On October 9, they reached the port of Petropavlovsk. Twenty of the crew had died and most of the living were disabled by the disease. Only one officer was fit for duty. In May of the following year, Chirikov went in search of Bering's ship. He passed near the island where it had been wrecked. Failing to find it, he traveled to St. Petersburg to make his report to the government.[4]

When the ships first became separated, Bering spent the next three days searching for Chirikov. He reluctantly gave up the search and sailed east northeast until about noon on July 16, when a lookout reported a large peak towering above a snow-covered mountain range. It was located on the North American mainland north of the Alexander Archipelago. Bering named it Mt. St. Elias.

Bering dropped anchor between Kayak and Wingham Islands on July 19, and named the former St. Elias Island in honor of the saint. On the 21st, Bering prepared to return to Siberia, but the ship's officers opposed him. They argued that they were on a strange and dangerous coast with scant provisions, and twenty-five hundred miles from their base of supplies. The decision to sail may well have been a wise decision for Bering. Unbeknownst to them, this anchorage was one of the worst storm centers in Alaska. There wasn't a safe harbor within a hundred miles of their anchorage, and they were unaware of the dangers the long chain of reefs and rocks along the Aleutians chain to them.

Bering was determined to sail westward. He was now at the mercy of the high winds and incessant rain that battered his ship. Because his crew took regular soundings, they escaped Sea Otter Rocks and other dangers that lay in their path. They skirted the eastern side of Kodiak Island and sighted a point of land Bering called St. Hermogenes. They drifted through Douglas Passage and on August 2 discovered an island they named Tammanoi (Chirikov Island). The next day they sighted twin peaks on the mainland and discovered the Semidi Islands. On August 30, they landed on Shumagin Island, named for a crewman who was the first on the ship to die of scurvy. Bering was also down with scurvy and too ill to leave his cabin. From that day until they reached their home port in Siberia, this dread scourge of the seven seas pursued them incessantly.

The *St. Peter* continued to sail westward when a major storm drove them southeast three hundred miles, back into the Pacific Ocean. For seventeen days they were battered and buffeted by a "williwaw" (hurricane-force winds that blow out of the north Pacific) off the south shore of the Aleutian Islands.[5] As the storm abated, they resumed their westward course. On November 4, 1741, they saw a large land mass that they wrongly identified as Kamchatka.

Bering called his officers together to decide if they should land or if they should try to reach Petropavlovsk. Their ship was in a deplorable condition and might sink at any time. The weather had turned freezing cold and the rain had turned to sleet and snow. The decks and the tackle were covered in ice and the rigging was rotting and breaking away from its fastenings. Most of the crew were too sick to man the watches. Bering argued for making port at Avacha Bay, but his officers stubbornly opposed him. They decided to land, and this fateful decision was to prove fatal for Bering.

Two of the officers went ashore to reconnoiter. They found a barren, snow-covered land with no wood except for driftwood from the sea. On October 8, 1741, they brought the sick ashore, but some of them died upon being brought up on deck into the open air. Others died upon reaching the land. Blue foxes crowded around them in such large numbers that the Russians had a difficult time keeping them away from the dead or from injuring those who were too sick to protect themselves from the onslaught. The few who were strong enough dug pits or caves in the side of a ravine and covered them with canvas and driftwood to protect the sick from the elements.

Bering was carried ashore and rapidly grew weaker. He needed food and medical care, but neither was available. His shipmates did everything possible to keep him alive, but it wasn't enough. Bering and thirty-one of his men perished from sickness, starvation, and exposure to the elements. Bering was buried with his men in a pit in the ravine on the island that bears his name.

With the coming of the New Year, the spirits of the survivors rose. They had escaped the fate of their shipmates and now they found new activities to keep them busy. George Steller, the naturalist Bering brought with him on this ill-fated voyage, found the island a rich field of study. It abounded with fur seals, sea otter, and fox, and the beaches were lined with sea cows. Their meat became one of the chief sources of food for the starving men.

The storms of the previous year had wrecked the *St. Peter*, but fortunately for the castaways, strong winds pushed it up on the beach. In the spring the survivors constructed a forty-foot boat from the wreckage, and loaded it with the belongings they salvaged and the furs of the animals they killed. On August 12, 1742, forty-six of the seventy-seven men who had sailed from Petropavlovsk the previous year returned to a hero's welcome. Not only did they return home with pelts from the sea otter, the fur seal, and the fox, they returned home with tales of the abundance of fur-bearing animals.

Bering's discoveries opened the door for hunters and fur traders to reap fabulous fortunes. When the news reached Europe, it spurred the Spanish and English to seek out new claims in the North Pacific. Bering and Chirikov had discovered headlands and islands from Sitka to Bering Island. They had solved the mystery of the link between Asia and America and blazed a trail across three thousand miles of uncharted ocean.

The arrival of the Russians sounded the death knell for the traditional way of life for the Aleuts. It is estimated that when Bering discovered the Aleutians, the islands were home to 20,000 natives. Decimated by massacres, servitude, deprivation, disease, and Russian cruelty, by the time the United States purchased Alaska from the Russians in 1867, the native population had dwindled to approximately 2,000 Aleut natives.

In expectation of huge profits, from 1740 to 1799, more than forty companies and merchants sponsored expeditions to Alaska and the surrounding islands. Under the direction of Grigory Shelikhov, the Shelikhov-Golikov Fur Company sponsored one of the first major expeditions and built the first permanent settlement in Alaska. In August 1783, three ships carrying 192 men, Shelikhov, his wife Natal'ia, and their two children sailed from the Russian port of Okhotsk. One ship was lost in a storm, but the other two ships, *Three Saints* and *St. Simon*, sailed south to Bering Island. One year later the expedition landed at Three Saints Bay at Kodiak Island.[6]

The colonists set to work building a fortified compound that included storehouses, living quarters, offices, and a large building to be used as a factory. Shelikhov sent conciliatory messages out to the Alutiqs inviting them to come into the settlement to trade. In a defiant manner, they refused. Angered by their response, Shelikhov decided to teach them a lesson they would never forget.

With the mistaken idea that they were safe from the Russians, a number of Indians gathered on a large rock overlooking the ocean. Shelikhov loaded his men into the ship's longboats and surrounded them. He demanded their surrender. They refused, and he opened fire with his cannon. He swept the rock with grapeshot, killing dozens of Indians. The terrified natives, panic-stricken at the unfamiliar sound of the cannon and the devastating firepower, jumped into the sea. Many drowned, while the survivors were pulled out of the water and held as hostages.

Angered by Shelikhov's actions, the Indians fought back, determined to drive the invader from their land. After a protracted battle that lasted for more than a month, the Russians succeeded in defeating their enemy. They pressed the Alutiqs into servitude for Shelikhov's company. Women and children were taken hostage and held in a long cabin on the shore of the bay to force the men to gather pelts. The Russians demanded ever greater numbers of pelts, and before long they had nearly depleted the sea otter population in and around Kodiak. Fearing for the safety of their families, the Indians were forced to travel far out to sea for longer periods of time in perilous weather conditions. Though they were experienced sailors, many of them drowned.

The Russians were unable to subdue the Alutiq as they had the Aleuts. It was impossible for the Unangan, living on islands, to escape their oppressors, but on the Alaska Peninsula, Cook Inlet, and Prince William Sound, the Alutiq and other tribes simply abandoned their villages and escaped into the forest. There were too few Russians to follow them, and since they could not subdue them, the *promyshlenniki* were forced into an uneasy truce with the tribes.

Food and other staples needed to maintain the settlement were often in short supply. It became necessary for the Russians to enter into a trading relationship with the natives if they were to survive the harsh environment of the untamed Alaska wilderness. They traded cooking pots, utensils, knives, animal traps, and especially heavy woolen coats, beads and calico in exchange for much-needed food until supply ships reached the colony. Due to the long and arduous voyages that often took more than a year to complete, few ships ever put in to Kodiak.

The settlement was not self-sufficient. The Russians needed a wide assortment of manufactured goods, including guns, tools, brick-making molds, building materials, clothing, books, writing paper and pens, and large numbers of candles to maintain their colony, and all of these items had to come from Europe. Food was their most pressing need. They lacked flour, tea, dried meat, salt, beans, barley and other grains, rice, chocolate, and vodka. By the time the ships reached Kodiak, if they ever did, much of the food had been stolen by the crew, had rotted, or was filled with worms.

The fur traders and the Indians on the mainland maintained a nervous peace, but not so in the Aleutians. The traders' control of the Aleuts was absolute. Cruelty rather than kindness was the rule. The *promyshlennki* killed the men and raped their women. Gunners and marksmen on the ships used villagers for target practice as they sailed past their villages. They required the natives to provide them with food and other supplies, and the women were forced to provide sex and companionship. While the men were away, Aleut women continued their traditional duties, but now they had to perform the tasks that were previously done by the men of the village. They scrambled to gather enough food for their families, which meant a greater reliance on fish and shellfish from the surrounding waters. During the first winters of Russian occupation, the people almost starved. Neither men nor women had the time to properly gather provisions to meet their needs.

The Russian government instituted *yasak* (tribute) on the native peoples of Alaska, and the fur traders were required to collect. When Czarina Elizabeth was crowned ruler of Russia in 1741, she ordered a royal tax collector to sail on every vessel to ensure that the natives paid the tribute demanded of them. The natives resented the *yasak*, but they had little choice but to pay it. They would soon learn that bows and arrows and spears were no match for Russian guns.

The Russian occupation devastated the Aleuts. Smallpox, measles, tuberculosis, venereal disease, and pneumonia that the Russians introduced into the islands decimated the people and helped to reduce the population from an estimated 20,000 to fewer than 5,000 natives. The Russians resettled many of the Unangan on other islands to meet their insatiable demands for hunters and laborers.

There were other changes in the daily life of the Aleut people. The traditional underground *barabaras* were replaced with above-ground structures, and the design and nature of clothing and utensils changed to meet the altered living conditions of the Aleut people. A number of villages were depopulated and disappeared entirely.

This harsh treatment often resulted in violent resistance and confrontation by the Aleuts against the Russians. The natives retaliated by destroying ships and killing the crews. On one occasion, a captain bypassed one of the Andreanov Islands when he spotted more than a hundred angry natives waiting for them to come ashore. A short time later, the natives killed a number of *promyshlenniki* because they believed the fur traders were guilty of improper conduct and ill treatment of some of the islanders' wives. In 1762, Aleuts from the Fox Island Group staged a coordinated attack on four ships and several shore parties, killing more than three hundred Russians.

By 1784, a crisis situation had developed for the people of Amchitka and the fur traders. The otter population on Amchitka had decreased to a point where few furs were taken. Since there were few pelts available for trade, the ships stopped coming to the island, leaving the fur traders to shift for themselves. Short on supplies, the Russians wanted the natives to return some of the necessities they had received for the otter pelts.

Tension escalated when negotiations between the Russians and the Aleuts failed to resolve the problem. The situation erupted into open conflict when the leader of the *promyshlennki* ordered two of his men to murder Oniishin, his mistress, who was also the chieftain's daughter. When the people heard what the Russians had done, they demanded revenge. That evening, hundreds of angry Aleuts gathered on a mountain and marched on the Russian settlement. The first attack was repulsed when the Russians opened fire and drove them away. A second attack also failed and the Indians retreated to the mountain.

The Russians soon realized that while the men were on the mountain planning their next attack, they had left their women and children alone and unprotected in the village. The fur traders entered the village and took forty women and children hostage. To save the lives of their dependents, the Aleuts surrendered. The Russians took their revenge by executing four of the tribal leaders. After the failed revolt, the natives began to move from Amchitka to neighboring islands. When Russian officials heard about the conflict, they ordered the arrest of the leader of the fur traders.

This was not the end of Russian brutality. They retaliated by instituting a twenty-year suppression of the Unangan. They sent out punitive expeditions to the Aleut villages and enacted harsh measures upon the villagers, killing many. As their ships sailed past inhabited islands, the sailors would use the natives for target practice. They took some or all of the women and children from different villages and held them hostage until their men accompanying the fur traders brought in enough furs to fill the holds of their ships.

The motivation for exploring and settling Alaska was the commercial expansion of the fur trade. When the *promyshlenniki* first introduced sea otter furs into their trade with China, they discovered that these pelts could generate greater profits than any other type of fur. Like the California gold rush of 1849, news of the huge profits to be reaped sparked a rush of fur traders across the Kurile and Commander Islands off the coast of the Kamchatka Peninsula.

In Siberia, the fur traders participated in collecting pelts, but hunting fur-bearing animals on vast stretches of snow-covered open land was much different from taking them from the sea. The Russians had no knowledge of marine harvesting, so they forced the natives to do their hunting for them.

Depleting the fur-bearing animal population almost to extinction, the fur traders extended their hunts to the Aleutians. Overhunting by Russian traders had all but eliminated sea otters as a source of pelts. To maintain their source of furs, they sought out the next most valuable furs, the fur seal. A three-year search by more than sixty Siberian trading companies for the breeding sites of these animals ended in 1786, when Russian navigator Gavriil Pribilof discovered the first two of the four islands that came to bear his name. Later discoveries included St. George and St. Paul Islands, collectively known as the Pribilofs.

The discovery of the Pribilofs extended the Russian fur trade in America for another one hundred years. The islands were the summer breeding ground of the largest concentration of Northern Pacific fur seals in the world, and they remain so today. Harvesting the seals was hard work and the Russians soon realized they could reap greater profits for their efforts if they could import skilled native men to do the work for them. Millions of seals were ruthlessly killed each year until the numbers of fur-bearing marine animals were almost depleted from the rookeries. The plight of the Aleuts continued to worsen in direct proportion to the declining number of seals. They were taken to the islands against their will on a seasonal basis, forced to go out to sea for greater periods of time to hunt for new populations of seals and otter to meet the demand of their Russian masters. Thanks to the Russians, the Aleuts suffered and died by the hundreds from diseases they had never encountered before.

In 1780, major changes were in the wind that would affect the fur trade and transform the lives of the Aleuts forever. These changes were brought about by the expansionist activities of Grigory Shelikhov, a Russian merchant who succeeded where others had failed. He would accomplish what no one else had done: the establishment of the first permanent Russian outpost in North America. As an agent for Ivan Golikov, Shelikhov traveled to Okhotsk and other ports to oversee the fur trade for his employer. In the next eight years he was involved with ten fur trading companies.

Early on, Shelikhov realized that competition between investors was wasteful, inefficient and costly. As the number of fur-bearing animals decreased, the *promyshlennki* were forced to go further east, thereby driving up the cost of each voyage. Shelikhov believed that a monopoly would eliminate these issues while creating huge profits for the investors. In the next few years, his vision would become a reality. In the meantime he formed a company with Golikov and his nephew Mikhail to hunt furs in North America and the Kurile Islands. While investments in other fur trading ventures were intended for one voyage and one cargo, Shelikhov's company was chartered by the government for ten years.

Shelikhov wasn't interested in simply sailing to the islands, collecting furs, and bringing them back to market; he wanted to establish settlements. Even though he invested in several different voyages with a number of partners, it wasn't until 1783 that Shelikhov was able to undertake his grand enterprise. His first settlement was about to become a reality.

He hired a large number of laborers and purchased the necessary tools and equipment, loaded them on three ships and sailed from Okhotsk. This voyage of fur-gathering and settlement-building adventurers carried 192 officers and crew and Shelikhov's wife, Natal'ia. One ship was lost in a storm in the seas off the Kurile Islands, but the two remaining ships proceeded to Bering Island for the winter. In the spring, they sailed to Unalaska and then on to Kodiak Island off the coast of mainland Alaska. Shelikhov established a post he called Three Saints Bay, the first permanent Russian post in North America.

Like so many who came before him, Shelikhov brutalized the native population. In a report to Empress Catherine, he wrote of the fierce resistance in his efforts to subdue the natives, forcing them to pay tribute and to trade with the Russians. The indigenous Alutiiq Indians retaliated by harassing the Russians. Shelikhov responded by killing hundreds of tribesmen and taking hostages to enforce obedience to his orders. Thanks to the efforts of missionaries of the Russian Orthodox Church, some of the harsh treatment meted out by the Russians was alleviated. At the request of Shelikhov and Golikov, in 1793, Empress Catherine approved a Russian Orthodox mission for the fledgling settlement. This was the first official attempt to convert the Indians to Christianity.

The Russian Orthodox Church played a major role in the early Russian settlements. In 1794, Archimandrite Ioasaf, eight clerics, and two servitors (laymen) arrived in Kodiak to convert the natives to Christianity and to minister to the religious needs of the Russians. They reported thousands of conversions among the natives in and around Kodiak in their first year.

Even though the company supported the efforts of the monks to Christianize the Indians, it soon brought them into conflict with the manager of the settlement, Aleksander Baronnov, and his assistants. The Russians felt that the monks were interfering too much in the affairs of the people and their treatment of the natives. The conversions had helped to reduce promiscuity and the number of common-law relationships between the Russians and the Indians.

The missionaries objected to the harsh treatment Shelikhov's people meted out to natives. They complained to no avail that the Indians were held in slavery and constantly persecuted by the Russians, and they went so far as to take their case to the Russian court. In 1796, Hieromonk Makarii and six Aleuts traveled from Unalaska to St. Petersburg to meet with Emperor Paul. They carried with them a letter signed by the leaders of the Aleut people listing their grievances against the Russians. One of the Aleuts died in the Kurile Islands, two others had to turn back because of illness, and another Aleut died when they reached Moscow. The Emperor received the priest and the remaining Aleuts and listened to their complaints, but their grievances fell on deaf ears. The royal court had heard it all before and refused to do anything to end the harsh treatment the Aleuts received at the hands of their masters.

Makarii and the Aleuts now had the sad duty to return home and tell the Indians that the Russians would do nothing for them to alleviate their suffering and raise their standard of living. They crossed the Siberian wilderness, and upon their departure from Irkutsk, the two Aleuts died. The priest also died before reaching his final destination when his ship was lost at sea. Ironically, Archimandrite Ioasaf died with him when the ship went down. Ioasaf had been ordered to travel to Irkutsk to be elevated to the rank of Bishop of Kodiak and was returning to the settlement on the same ship that carried Makarii home. Their deaths left the mission temporarily without a suitable leader.

Of the original party of priests and monks who arrived at Kodiak in 1793, after two years in the settlement, the only survivor of the group was a monk named German or Herman. With the deaths of Makarii and Ioasaf, Herman packed up his meager belongings and settled on Spruce Island off St. Paul Harbor near Kodiak. He lived a solitary life of prayer and contemplation, and often defended the rights of the Aleuts against the managers of the Russian trading company. In 1820, an epidemic swept the Kodiak settlement. Without giving any thought to his own health, Herman nursed the sick and dying, and raised funds for the colony. After his death in 1836, the people prayed to him for intervention and a number of miracles are attributed to him. He was canonized by the church in 1970, and is now known in the Russian Orthodox Church as Saint Herman of Alaska.

Another exceptional churchman who probably did more to build the church in Russian America and bring religion to the Aleuts than almost any other priest or monk was Ioann Veniaminov. Born Ioann Popov in Irkutsk in 1797, at nine years of age he entered the Irkutsk Theological Seminary to study for the priesthood. He was an exceptional student and he excelled in both theological and practical studies. When he turned seventeen, he was renamed Ioann Veniaminov in honor of Bishop Veniamin, a much-loved bishop who had recently died.

In January 1823, Bishop Michael of Irkutsk received instructions from his superiors to send a priest to Unalaska in the Aleutian Islands. A pious man and a devout follower of Jesus, Ioann accepted the assignment, and accompanied by his aging mother, his wife Catherine, his infant son Innocent, and his brother, he departed Irkutsk. After a long and difficult journey that lasted for more than a year, they reached Unalaska on July 29, 1824.

Father Ioann soon earned a reputation as an outstanding pastor and was respected and loved by Indians and Russians alike. With his grasp of practical skills, he taught the Aleuts and Russian laborers bricklaying, stonemasonry, carpentry, blacksmithing, locksmithing, and other basic skills. With their help, he built a modest home for himself and his family, and a church for the islanders. He opened a school to combat illiteracy among the islanders and the Russians, and he kept a daily record of the weather, the first known records of the weather in the Aleutians.

Father Ioann's diocese stretched over a vast area that included Unalaska, the Fox Islands and the Pribilofs. To visit these far-flung villages, he often traveled between islands by *baidarka* (canoe), battling the wind and waves of a stormy ocean in the Gulf of Alaska. His pastoral tours and his prowess as a paddler became legendary. On one such trip, he visited the Pribilof Islands, Akun Island at Unimak Pass, and the new Russian settlement on the Nushagak River some distance beyond the neck of the Alaska Peninsula. Spending time with the Aleuts, he became familiar with the local dialects, and in a short time he was fluent in six of them. Working with elders in each village, he developed an alphabet and translated the Russian Short Catechism and the gospel of St. Mark into the Aleut language. Father Ioann moved to Sitka in 1834, where he continued ministering to the Aleuts. He made clocks, furniture, and an organ for the church he helped to complete. A smallpox epidemic in 1836 and 1837 brought him in close contact with the Tlingit Indians living in the area. As he ministered to the Tlingit, he studied their customs and soon became fluent in their language.

In 1839, Father Ioann left Sitka and returned to Russia to report on his activities among the native population in the Aleutians and to request an expansion of the Russian Orthodox Church in Russian America. While there, he received word that his wife had died. He wanted to return to Sitka, but his superiors had other plans for him. On December 15, 1840, Father Ioann was consecrated Bishop of Kamchatka, the Kurile Islands, and the Aleutians. As was the custom in the Russian Orthodox Church, he took a new name. He was now known as Bishop Innocent.

He returned to Sitka, and for the next nine years he took long missionary journeys over the entire length of Russian America, from Sitka through the Aleutian Islands, to Kamchatka, to the Kuriles, to Aian. In 1850, he was elevated to the rank of archbishop, and in 1867 he was appointed the Metropolitan of Moscow, the highest post in the Russian Orthodox Church. He died in 1879, and in 1977, he was consecrated Saint Innocent.

2

The Russian American Company

With the success of his first settlement, Shelikhov wanted to expand his operations into other spheres of influence. At that time, his company was not the only one in Alaska. Pavel Lebedev-Lastochkin, Shelikhov's chief rival in the fur trade had also attempted to establish a permanent post in North America. Shelikhov sent hunters to Cook Inlet and Prince William Sound, but his competitor had already established a post at the mouth of the Kenai River. From 1794 to 1797, when Lebedev-Lastochkin was taken over by Shelikhov and Golikov, the two companies competed for the furs of Cook Inlet.

With his major rival out of the way, Shelikhov returned to Okhotsk for supplies and reinforcements. In Irkutsk, he made his report and outlined his plans for expansion. He wanted to send hunting parties along the Pacific coast as far south as the Spanish colony of San Francisco, and to create a monopoly to develop and control trade with Japan, China, the Philippines, and India, while at the same time conducting trade with the English, Spanish, and the Indians along the North American coast.

Shelikhov traveled to St. Petersburg to ask Czarina Catherine for a government ship, a detachment of one hundred soldiers, and a loan of 500,000 rubles. He also requested a number of priests to minister to the needs of the settlers and fur hunters and to build schools for their children and the native population. His requests were modest considering the potential for profits from trade in Siberia and North America, and Catherine was committed to the principles of free trade. But she was in no position to give him what he wanted. The impending war with Turkey and Sweden would drain the treasury and require troops for the Army and Navy and she had neither solders nor money to spare.

While wintering in Irkutsk, in 1790, Shelikhov had the good fortune to meet Aleksandr Andreevich Baranov, a merchant and veteran fur trader from

Kargopol. He persuaded him to go to America and manage the activities of Shelikhov's enterprises. This fortuitous meeting was to have a major impact on the settlement and expansion of Russian America.

This opportunity couldn't have come at a better time. Baranov had lived and worked in Siberia for more than twenty years, and he owned a glass factory, a vodka distillery, and other businesses in Irkutsk, and a fortified post on the Anadyr River. Whether from bad business decisions or other reasons, his fortunes had suffered some major blows. Baranov reluctantly accepted Shelikhov's offer, and in August 1790, he sailed from Okhotsk. Kodiak became his home for the next twenty years.

Baranov had a difficult and dangerous time traveling to his new post. As he was leaving Unalaska, his ship, the *Three Saints*, was wrecked. Baranov, the ship's crew and his fellow passengers reached shore with little more than their lives and the clothes they wore. They were forced to spend a harsh winter on the island, enduring freezing temperatures and winter storms. The island was devoid of trees. Using driftwood they found on the beach, the survivors built underground huts that were similar to native huts. They boiled sea water to extract the salt, and for food they gathered shellfish and dug roots from the vegetation that grew on the island. A week before Easter they supplemented their meager diet from the carcass of a dead whale that the washed up on the beach. Later that same week, they killed three sea lions.

Not one to remain idle for long, Baranov had the Aleuts build three *baidarkas* from the skins of the sea lions. In late spring, he sent two of the boats out to explore and seek new fur hunting grounds on the north side of the Alaska Peninsula. With the remainder of his crew, he set out in the remaining boat, and after a six-hundred-mile voyage over storm-battered seas, he reached Shelikhov's settlement on July 27, 1791.

As a manager, Baranov was aggressive and determined, well-organized and ruthless. One of his first acts was to move the settlement from Three Saints Bay to St. Paul Harbor on Chiniak Bay, the present location of Kodiak. He considered Three Saints Bay indefensible and therefore a poor location. From this new base of operations, he sent out hunting parties to the Alaska Peninsula, Kenai, and Kugach Bay.

Over the next few years, Baranov was kept busy establishing new fur trading centers. In 1793, he established a post at Resurrection Bay, the present-day site of Seward. In response to a request from Baranov, Shelikhov sent the *Orel* with materials to construct a ship, along with a shipwright named Shields. Upon inspecting the meager supplies Shelikhov sent, Baranov wrote, "We have only half a keg of tar, three kegs of pitch, not a pound of steel, not one nail, and very little iron for so large a vessel."[1]

Planking for the ship was cut in a rude sawmill constructed over a small stream which furnished the water power to saw the wood. Iron was collected from various sources, but it was of poor quality. For tar, Baranov substituted a mixture of spruce gum and whale oil. He distilled turpentine from pine trees and manufactured the paint from whale oil and other ingredients.[2] Completed and launched in August 1794, the ship was christened the *Phoenix*. This 180-ton ship had three masts and two decks, was seventy-three feet long with a twenty-three-foot beam, and was thirteen and a half feet deep.

Canvas for the sails was in short supply in Russian America. Sails were sewn from fragments gathered along the coast from Kamchatka to Kodiak, and were of such poor quality the ship had difficulty sailing into the harbor at Kodiak. In his letter to Shelikhov, Baranov wrote, "Over this achievement the rejoicing was great, and it was celebrated with solemn mass and merry feastings; only the sheep in the colony was killed to grace the occasion. What gluttony."[3]

In 1794, Baranov's chief lieutenant, Egor Partrov, and a party of Russians boarded the *Phoenix*, and accompanied by a fleet of five hundred *baidarkas* they sailed along the coast to Yakutat, Lituya, and Icy Bays. After founding a settlement they called Novorossisk (New Russia), they returned to Kodiak. Baranov returned to Kodiak in time to greet Archimandrite Ioasaf and the ten clerics from Okhotsk. A few days later, 130 *promshlennki* and thirty settlers and their families sailed into the port.

The bitter cold temperatures and the winter storms made life difficult. The clergy were unhappy and dissatisfied with conditions in the settlement and they created major headaches for the manager. Baranov's ideas were antagonistic towards the churchmen and they disliked him intensely. They wrote bitter and vehement letters against him to their superiors and fomented discord among the fur traders and settlers at Three Saints. As they saw it, there were too many nonproducing colonists in a settlement that was struggling to survive in a country that was so far removed from their source of supplies.

Shelikhov occasionally co-invested with Lebedev-Lastochkin in joint ventures, but their competition often resulted in violent clashes and pitched battles. From the time of his arrival in Alaska until he absorbed his rival in 1797, Baranov was engaged in a continuous running battle with his competitors. When Putrov and his party returned from Yakutat, they were attacked by hunters working for Lebedev-Lastochkin.

In addition to harassing Baranov's hunters, Lebedev-Lastochkin's foremen meted out harsher treatment to the Indians than Baranov did. The natives refused to accept this maltreatment of their people without a fight. In 1796, the Indians attacked and killed every member of a large Lebedev-Lastochkin

2. The Russian American Company

hunting party as they traveled over the pass between the Matanuska Valley and the Copper River. Two years later, they attacked one of Lebedev-Lastochhkin's posts on Kodiak Island.

Even though Baranov was ruthless in his treatment of the natives, surprisingly, Shelikhov's settlements did not suffer the same fate. One of the missionaries reported to his superiors that Baranov treated the natives in a most barbaric manner and that the hunters took the women as sexual partners, and killed any man who refused to hunt the sea otters.

When Russian fur hunters had killed off most of the sea otter and exhausted their supply of furs, they moved on to a new hunting ground. This periodic lack of furs forced Lebedev-Lastochkin's hunters to pull up stakes and transfer their operations from Kenai Bay to Prince William Sound. This brought them into direct conflict with Shelikhov's people and the Indians who inhabited the area.

Though they had been in Alaska for many years, time was running out for Lebedev-Lastochkin in Russian America. With the constant Indian attacks on their hunting parties, a lack of supplies, and conflicts with Shelikhov's hunters, Baranov dislodged them from the area. After 1792, Lebedev-Lastochkin stopped sending much-needed supplies to their men. By offering better wages and living conditions, Baranov was able to hire many of his rival's men. To make matters worse for his competitors, Shelikhov obtained a limited monopoly from the government that prohibited any other fur company from operating in the vicinity of his posts and settlements.

Rich and powerful from his trading ventures and other business enterprises, Shelikhov continued to plan for the expansion of his operations in North America. He was planning a major expedition to the Kurile Islands when in 1795 he mysteriously died. The cause of his death remains a mystery, but according to the rumors of the day, he may have been poisoned by his wife Natal'ia and her lover in an attempt to take over his enterprises.

Lebedev-Lastochkin saw an opportunity to oust his rival's widow and dismantle her husband's company. They attempted to organize the principal merchants in a takeover scheme against her, but Natal'ia was a strong, intelligent woman with an indomitable spirit. They had underestimated her resolve to keep her husband's investors together and fend off the conspirators' scheme to destroy his enterprises.

Fortunately for Natal'ia, she had friends in high places. Shortly before Shelikhov's death, his daughter, fifteen-year-old Anna, married thirty-year-old Nikolai Rezanov, a chamberlain in the court of Catherine the Great. Thanks to influence from friends, he was promoted to the position of Secretary for Senate Reports, writing important legislation and tax regulations for the government. On a court mission for the Empress in 1794, he met Shelikhov and became an enthusiastic supporter of his plans for expansion of the fur trade and the establishment of permanent settlements in North America and the Kurile Islands. Rezanov became the chief protector of the family interests.

With the death of Catherine in in 1796, and the ascendancy of her son Paul to the royal throne, Rezanov was appointed Secretary of the Senate. Unlike many of his contemporaries, he understood the potential for profits from North America, and he vigorously supported Shelikhov's vision for a monopolistic commercial enterprise. He also realized that without the support of the royal court, Russia's fur trade would be lost to their European competitors.

Rezanov prosecuted the plans for North America with a greater zeal then his father-in-law did. He argued his cause before the Czar, but Paul was antagonistic to the scheme and reluctant to grant the charter. Finally, in 1799 the Czar relented and gave Rezanov what he wanted: a trading monopoly modeled on the British East Indian Company and the Hudson's Bay Company, it was called the Russian American Company (RAC). The initial capitalization was 724,000 rubles divided into 724 shares of 100 rubles each. One third of all profits were to be paid to the Czar and the remainder split among the investors. This was Russia's first joint stock company and it came under the direct authority of the Ministry of Commerce of Imperial Russia.

The terms prohibited any other company from conducting business in any of the Russian possessions in America, the Kurile Islands, and islands situated in the northeastern ocean. The charter permitted the company to use and profit by everything which had been or would be discovered; to use the timber; to purchase powder and lead at cost from the government magazine at Nerchinsk; and various other rights and privileges for a period of twenty years.

Rezanov had supreme control over the affairs of the RAC in the colonies. His duties required him to visit all the company's outposts and to advise and direct the future management of the enterprise. He visited the Seal Islands, where he felt compelled to order the discontinuation of the killing of the seals to prevent further depletion of the herds. He established a school on Kodiak and founded a library with books he brought from St. Petersburg. Before he left Kodiak, he called the monks together and reprimanded them for their lack of attention to their duties. He admonished them to work harder to cultivate the land and educate the young men and women of the settlement.

Arriving in Sitka, Rezanov found the post in an appalling state. The living quarters were crude and primitive, and food was of the poorest quality. In his official report he wrote, "We fared poorly, but worse than all lives the founder of this place, in a miserable hut, so damp that the floor is always wet, and during the heavy rains the place leaks like a sieve."[4]

2. The Russian American Company

On inspecting some of the hovels of the fur traders, Rezanov wrote, "The people live in perpetual fear of the Kolosh Indians. Our cannon are always loaded, and not only are sentries with loaded guns posted everywhere, but arms of all kinds constitute the principal furniture of the rooms." The lessons learned from the destruction of old Sitka had not been forgotten.

The Russians had good reasons to fear the Kolosh. In his last report to the Russian government, Captain Pavel Golovon wrote a detailed description of these warlike savages:

> The Kolosh have been the constant enemies of the Russian entrenchment along the northwest coast and the adjacent islands. It is said that their hostility to the Russians was fostered by foreign merchants who feared that the entire fur trade would fall into the hands of the Russian Company. Whatever the reason, our first settlement encountered in the Kolosh fierce and relentless enemies. The Kolosh captured and destroyed the fort at Arkangel Michael on Sitka Island and the settlement of Slava Rossii in Yakutat, and they killed nearly all the inhabitants and garrison personnel.
>
> They are all superb shots, and thanks to the foreigners, they are armed with quite good rifles, pistols, revolvers and blades. A Kolosh will never part with his knife; at the first sign of an argument he will stab his opponent, but always if possible from behind in a treacherous manner.[5]

The Russian American Company was created to secure areas in America that were under Russian control and to expand the fur trade in those areas. The board of directors appointed Baranov to the position of chief manager and governor of Alaska. The Czar was so impressed with his success in organizing Shelikhov's enterprises that he awarded him the Order of St. Vladimir. Baranov was now a member of the lesser nobility.

The board of directors were looking for ways to increase their profits. To keep the information from the Czar, they secretly instructed Baranov to extend the colony as far south as possible while avoiding a confrontation with foreign powers. Unknown to his superiors, he did exactly that. With hundreds of native kayaks, one Russian ship, a hundred Russians, seven hundred Aleuts and three hundred Koniag Indians, Baranov sailed from Kodiak and across dangerous waters to a large Kolosh village at Sitka. With such a large force of armed men behind him, he negotiated with one of the chiefs to allow him to establish a post on the west side of present-day Baranov Island. He named the post Novo Arkangel (New Archangel). From his heavily fortified compound, he sent hunting parties southward toward California.

Many theories have been advanced as to why the Indians attacked the post. It may have been caused in part by the Russian traders' custom of taking native women as wives and sex partners or mistreatment of the Indians. There may have been serious disagreements with the chiefs of the tribe, or the Russians may have misunderstood the terms of their agreement with the Kolosh. Whatever the cause of the hostility, the Russians believed it was caused by English and American traders who wanted to drive the intruders out of what they considered their trading grounds.

Kirill Khlebnikov, a company clerk who had lived in Sitka for a number of years, stated that at the time of the attack, there were twenty-nine Russians, three Englishmen, two hundred Aleuts, and some Kodiak women who were married to Russians and Aleuts, living in the fort. Reports from English and American traders indicated that there were four hundred and fifty people there, including eighty Russians.

Before he returned to Kodiak, Baranov warned the chief of the post, Medvyednikof, that some Aleuts had been killed the previous year, and advised him to take all precautions against possible Indian attacks. To complicate matters, the Indian women who had been living with the Russians may have informed the Kolosh of conditions in the fort and the most favorable time to attack. On June 20, 1802, Medvyednikof sent some of his men to catch fish or to look after their traps in the creek while a few of the women went into the forest to collect berries. It was the calm before the storm.

On a signal from their chiefs, a horde of painted warriors wearing wooden masks carved in an animal likeness, and armed with guns and spears, quietly emerged from the forest and headed toward the fort. Before the Russians could raise the alarm, the Indians were over the walls and inside the compound. While the chief, Skayeutlelt, directed his tribesmen from a hill near the fort, a fleet of war canoes with hundreds of painted warriors frantically paddled across the bay to join the fray.

The Russians fought back with muskets and small cannons, but in a short time, most of the buildings were on fire. The women and children were terrified and tried to escape by crowding into an upstairs room. The trapdoor they were standing on gave way from their weight, causing them to fall into the waiting arms of the attacking warriors. With shouts of triumph, the warriors carried them away in their canoes to the Indian village and kept them as slaves. The defenders fought valiantly, but they were soon overwhelmed by the firepower of the enemy. Those who tried to escape were impaled on spears. The Indians erected poles around the perimeter of the burning fort and mounted on them the severed heads of the Russians.

A few of the Russians and Aleuts were hiding in the woods when the attack commenced, but they managed to escape to American and English ships in the bay. The Indians took prisoners and held them for the most horrendous tortures they could devise. Captain Ebbets in one of the American ships rescued some of the prisoners. He ordered his men to unlimber their cannons and open fire on the pursuing canoes. The cannon fire killed the pursuers and sank their canoes.

The American ship *Alert* and the British ship *Unicorn*, commanded by Captain Henry Barber, rescued additional survivors. Later that day, some of the Tlingit chiefs came on board the *Alert*, demanding Captain Barber turn over the survivors to them. He refused and held the chiefs hostage until their captives were brought on board and released. He then confiscated the furs they had looted from the fort.

Captain Barber saw an opportunity to profit from the misfortunes of the survivors and captives the Indians turned over to him. The survivors included three Russians, five Aleuts, and eighteen women and children. Before he would release them, he demanded that Baranov pay him a ransom of fifty thousand rubles. The two men haggled over the amount while the survivors waited anxiously for their release. With great reluctance, Baranov paid ten thousand rubles' worth of furs for their release.

The massacre at Old Sitka wasn't the only massacre the Indians inflicted on the Russians and the Aleuts. Baranov sent out a party of hunters to Sea Otter Bay. They had a successful hunt and were returning to the post when they stopped to camp for the night. Unaware of hostilities with the Indians, they took no unusual precautions. The Tlingit were watching them as they set up camp. Without warning, they attacked, killing everyone but the leader of the hunting party and seven Aleuts who escaped into the forest. The marauders destroyed the hunters' kayaks and set out for their village carrying the skins they'd plundered from the camp. The survivors waited for several hours to pass until they were sure the attackers had left. They crawled out of their hiding places and constructed *baidarkas* from the destroyed boats.

Traveling at night along the rocky shore, they made their way to Sitka. They found only the smoking ruins of the settlement, so they continued on to Yakutat. A few days later fifteen Aleuts who had escaped the massacre at Old Sitka wandered into the settlement. In these two massacres, more than 200 men were killed. Of the 450 individuals reported to occupy the fort at Old Sitka, only forty-two men, women, and children were rescued. Over the next several years the Indians would continue to inflict heavy casualties on the Russians, and the Russians would continue to fight back.

The Kolosh knew the Russians would return to the area in large numbers to avenge their defeat and rebuild the settlement. Anticipating the attack, the Indians built a large fortification six miles south of Old Sitka on a hill overlooking the Indian River. It has been described as an irregular square with its longest side facing the sea. It was constructed of wood and had a door and two gates on the side facing the forest. Behind its walls, there were fourteen *barabaras* (native houses). The Indians placed the captured cannons from Old Sitka in strong defensive positions, and they were armed with American guns that they had acquired through years of fur trading.

The Indians had placed their fort on the site of present-day Sitka. Little in the area has changed since they built their fortifications in 1802. A low-lying peninsula juts out into the sound and more than a hundred tree-covered islands protect it from the sea. At the north end of the sound, an extinct volcano known as Mt. Edgecumbe towers over present-day Sitka. To the east and south, majestic forest-clad mountains encircle the sound and protect the city from harsh winter winds. Like the fjords of Norway, bays and inlets reach into the land from the sea.

Baranov was determined to destroy the Indians' defenses and rebuild the settlement. In the summer of 1804, he called on the Aleuts and the natives of Kodiak to join him in an expedition to retake Sitka. He mustered 300 *baidarkas* manned by 800 men and 120 Russians on two small ships. The flotilla sailed for Sitka and Baranov followed a short time later with the *Ekaterina* and the *Alexander*. The *Neva*, commanded by naval officer Lieutenant Lisianski, sailed from Kodiak and joined Baranov's fleet on August 20.

The battle to retake Sitka commenced on September 28, 1804, and lasted into the early days of October. The Russians moved their ships into position, but the largest of the ships, the *Neva*, had to be towed into place upriver by one hundred *baidarkas*. Behind the walls of their fortifications, the Indians were dancing their war dance while their shamans invoked their gods to give them victory over their enemies.

The next morning, Baranov came ashore and placed cannons on a hill overlooking the fort. To avoid further bloodshed, he opened negotiations and called for the Indians to surrender. They refused and he ordered an immediate attack. The Aleuts destroyed all of the Tlingit canoes on the shore, and searching the surrounding forest, they found and burned large caches of food. Baranov attempted to lead an infantry attack against the fort with a handful of Russians and hundreds of Aleuts. The firepower of the Indians was so fierce that the attackers withdrew with a loss of ten killed and twenty-six wounded. Baranov was among the wounded.

The ships moved in closer to shore and bombarded the fort with heavy cannon fire. An Indian canoe loaded with powder attempted to sneak through the Russian blockade. It was struck by cannon fire and blown up before it reached the defenders. On orders from Lieutenant Lisianski, the guns of the *Neva* reduced the fort to rubble. On October 3, the Kolosh hoisted a white flag and released some of their hostages.

Negotiations dragged on for three days without results. When the Kolosh refused to surrender, the Russians opened fire again. The bombardment was too much for the Indians. In the dark of night, they abandoned the fort, retreated over the mountains to the northeast point of Baranov Island, and crossed over to Chichagof Island.

The next morning the Russians entered the ruined fortifications. They found two old women and a little boy the Indians had left behind. They also found the bodies of thirty Indians killed in the battle and five dead children. The children had been murdered to prevent their cries from alerting the Russians to the retreat. The Russians removed everything of value and set the remains of the stronghold on fire.

The lost ground was regained and Russia's farthest outpost reestablished. The task of rebuilding the settlement began immediately. Timber was cut from the nearby forest for a storehouse and other buildings. They named the new settlement New Archangel, enclosed it within a large stockade, and protected it with a fort they called Redoubt Archangel Michael. To proclaim the work of the Russians in this harsh new land, Baranov composed a song he called "The Song of Baranov." It was sung at the dedication of every new post established by the Russians and became a part of their ceremonies.[6]

Even though conflicts with the Indians continued to flare up, the Russians made plans to extend their settlements to the southeast along the Pacific Coast as far south as Northern California. In addition to increasing their supply of furs, they sought to satisfy the strong need for breadstuffs in the settlements of Alaska. Because the weather wasn't favorable to the ripening of cereals, their attempts to grow grain in Alaska were met with near total failure. The *promyshlenniki* were averse to farming, and the Aleuts were hunters and fishermen who had no interest in planting wheat.

To solve the problem of providing foodstuffs to the northern colonies, to gather the furs from that part of the coast, and to provide a port for ships employed in hunting in southern waters, Baranov decided to establish a settlement on the southern coast. In 1808, he dispatched two ships, the *St. Nicholas*, commanded by Captain Bulagin, and the *Kadiak* under Captain Kuskof to survey the coast from Washington to California. They sailed separately and were scheduled to rendezvous at a predetermined point, from which they would then proceed together.

The *St. Nicholas* never arrived. It was wrecked on the coast near Destruction Island. The wife of Captain Bulagin and some of the crew were captured by Indians. Captain Bulagin and the remainder of his crew wandered in the forest until hunger forced them to surrender to the Indians. Bulagin, his wife, two Russians and two Aleuts died. An American trader found some of castaways on the Strait of Juan de Fuca, ransomed them from their captors, and returned them to Sitka. When the *St. Nicholas* failed to keep the rendezvous, the *Kadiak* continued southward to Bodega Bay in California. Upon Kuskof's return to Sitka, he reported that the region north of San Francisco was unoccupied by Europeans and was ideal for agriculture and the grazing of cattle. One year later, the Russians returned to Bodega Bay and purchased the land from the Indians. The southernmost colony in Russian America was about to become a reality.

The best farmers in Russian America were selected to farm the land. Tools, equipment, and building materials were loaded aboard the *Chirikof*, and 95 Russians and 80 Aleuts sailed south. Located on a one-square-mile tableland and bounded on the ocean side by a 70-foot-high bluff, the site was about eight miles north of the Russian River in Sonoma County. The settlement known as Fort Ross was dedicated on September 10, 1812.

The stockade was constructed of redwood and was in the shape of a quadrangle. Blockhouses were built at each angle with cannons pointing in different directions. The commandant's quarters, barracks, chapel, storehouses, and offices were situated behind the walls. Farm buildings, cattle yards, a tannery, workshops, and living quarters for the farmers, fur hunters, and Aleuts were situated outside the walls on the plateau in proximity to the fort. On a nearby beach, the Russians erected a wharf, a building for the protection of the lumber and *baidarkas*, and a bathhouse. Unsafe anchorage at Fort Ross forced the Russians to build a wharf and a warehouse at Bodega Bay.

Agricultural endeavors were generally not very productive. Grain, fruit, and beef that were produced were sent to the northern colonies. The settlers planted grapes, and peach trees from Chile, and gardening of all kinds was pursued on a year-round basis. The Russians manufactured tile, pitch, leather goods, rowboats and other products they sold to the Californians. They made barrels and kegs to cure beef and ship it north to Sitka. Other industries included shipbuilding and hunting the sea otter for their pelts. Within a period of five years the animals were nearly exterminated. From that time forward, agriculture was the chief industry at Ross. Captain Golovin stressed the importance of agriculture at Fort Ross:

> Currently the Governing Board allows the colonial administration to bring in flour from California, and there is no doubt that this flour is secured less expensively than that brought in from Russia: first, because agriculture is developing each year in California to such a degree that at present a considerable amount of grain is being sent to Europe and thus the price of flour is gradually decreasing; second, it is cheaper to bring grain from California on Company ships than it is to bring it from Russia, especially since gran can be delivered to the colonies on ships that carry ice to California and previously had to return in ballast, for which it was necessary to pay a considerable amount of money with

no return. Of course it must be understood that in order to have an adequate source of grain supply from California, the Company will have to have a warehouse there, so that the agent who purchases grain when prices are low may store it until ships arrive, without having to pay additional money.[7]

The Californians opposed the construction of the settlement on the grounds that it encroached on their territory. The Russians ignored their protest and continued to occupy the land. With the near extermination of the sea otter and declining profits, the Russians sold the site to John Sutter and James Marshall in 1841 for 30,000 piastres. The last colonists from Fort Ross boarded the brig *Constantine* and sailed for Sitka on December 30, 1841.

Baranov had a bad year in 1813. On a stormy day in early January, a Kolosh canoe came into Sitka with a cargo of Russian sailors. Half dead from exposure and hardship, they were from the *Neva*. Battered by a winter storm, the ship had struck the rocks near the entrance to Sitka Harbor and broken up in the heavy surf. She sank with the loss of forty-one sailors, including the captain, as well as Baranov's replacement, Collegiate Advisor Bornovlookof. The survivors were camped on a beach near the scene of the disaster. They were in dire need of assistance, which was sent to them at once. From the survivors, Baranov received word that the brig *Alexander* had sunk off the Kurile Islands with a cargo of furs valued at $250,000.

The loss of these two ships dealt Baranov a serious blow. To replace them, he purchased two American ships that came into port to escape from the British warships, the *Atahualpa* and the *Lady*. The first ship he renamed the *Bering* and sent it to the Seal Islands to pick up a cargo of furs, then on to Okhotsk and then to the Sandwich Islands (Hawaiian Islands). The ship was wrecked off Kauai and her cargo stolen by the natives.

The second ship, renamed the *Ilmen*, sailed to California on a successful trading voyage. Later, while it was hunting along the coast, the Spanish took the ship's doctor, some Russians, and thirty Aleuts prisoner. An attempt to extend trade to the Philippines through an American agent also ended in failure. The good fortune that Baranov had enjoyed in his earlier years was fast turning bad.

Baranov wasn't ready to give up. He made one more attempt to extend the company's empire southward. For many years, he had dreamed of gaining a foothold in Hawaii. He saw the importance of these islands as a way to help make the colonies in Russian America self-sufficient. Food raised on an island plantation could easily be shipped to the settlements in Alaska. In 1808, King Kamehameha sent Baranov a proposal to exchange breadfruit, coconuts, pigs, rope and other products for Russian textiles, timber, and iron. Due to a shortage of personnel, Baranov was unable to follow through on the proposal.

Baranov's situation seemed to change for the better in 1813. An Austrian surgeon, Doctor Georg Schaffer, arrived in Sitka aboard the Russian ship *Suvorov*. After a dispute with the captain, he left the ship in a huff. Baranov met with the doctor and persuaded him to undertake an important mission to Hawaii. He was to get help from Kamehameha to retrieve the furs from the wreck of the *Bering* and to trade Russian products for food.

At the time Schaffer arrived in Hawaii, the islands were split into two kingdoms. Kamehameha had united most of the islands under his banner, but Kauai and Nihau were ruled by his rival, King David Kaumualii. Relations between the two kings were tense and the success of the mission required diplomacy and patience. Unfortunately for Baranof, Schaffer was the wrong man for the job. He possessed neither of these qualities.

Almost immediately, Kamehameha became suspicious of Schaffer's activities on Oahu. The doctor had made an alliance with Kaumualii, making him an officer in the Russian navy and promising to send him an armed vessel to provide protection from his rival. In return, the king gave the Russians land on Kauai for a plantation, permission to build a fort, and the right to the sandalwood trade. Encouraged by American and British traders, Kamehameha threatened to invade his rival's kingdom if Kaumualii continued his alliance with the Russians. Kamehameha feared his rival's growing strength and the danger the Russian presence in the islands might have on the autonomy of Hawaii. Kamehameha's ultimatum had the desired effect. Kaumualii forcefully expelled the Russians from his islands and they fled to what they thought was the safety of Oahu. Kamehameha took them prisoner, loaded them on to an American trading vessel, and sent them back to Sitka.

Kamehameha wanted favorable relations with the Russians, but now he no longer trusted them. On his round-the-world expedition in the *Rurik* in 1816, Captain Otto Kotzebue visited with Kamehameha. He sought to restore the king's relations with the Russians by assuring him that Schaffer did not have the authority to make promises to Kaumualii, and that those promises were not sanctioned by the Russian government or the Russian navy. Schaffer's failure to establish a colony in the islands cost the Russian American Company two hundred thousand rubles.

The Hawaiian debacle and a substantial decrease in the annual dividends to shareholders caused the company's directors in St. Petersburg to distrust Baranov. The original charter Peter granted them for twenty years was due to expire. He was chief manager for all those years and the company was ready to replace him. For twenty-seven years he'd managed the company's enterprise in Alaska, first for Shelikhov and then for the Russian American Company. The failure of his Hawaiian adventure had broken him in health and spirit.

The navy had a strong interest in Russian America. They felt that the Baltic was too small to adequately train their officers and crews for future wars. The vast Pacific Ocean offered them an opportunity to remedy this situation and to demonstrate efficient administration of the colonies. Since the directors had a less than complete understanding of the conditions and needs of the colonies, and didn't feel as fully in control of the colonies as they thought they should, this was an attractive alternative for them. Naval officers were used to the discipline of taking orders and following a chain of command, and they would be more effective in the implementation of the company's policies. Given the fact that most naval officers came from the upper nobility, the idea that they would be subservient to the merchant class was problematic for the directors.

In 1817, the directors appointed a naval officer, Lieutenant Leontii Hagemeister, to investigate conditions in the colony and to replace Baranov if he thought it was necessary. The directors granted him the authority to take whatever actions he felt necessary and they knew he would use it. Because the directors had limited knowledge of conditions in the colonies, and because they were unable to solve the problem of adequately supplying them, the navy took control of supply and administrative functions, a move the directors were powerless to oppose.

Czar Alexander and the navy were in complete agreement on the matter. The Czar was convinced that in light of the renewed interest in Alaska and the Pacific Northwest, it was imperative for the government to exert greater control over the company's activities in the colonies. He pressured the directors to appoint Hagemeister chief manager of the company to replace Baranov.

Hagemiester's first action upon reaching the colony was to inform Baranov that his services were no longer required. Baranov's lax management, the failure of the Hawaiian venture, and declining fur shipments and reduced profits suggested to some of the company directors that Baranov might be pocketing some of the company's resources for his own gain. As the new chief manager, Hagemeister took over Baranov's duties and appointed Kirill Khlebnikov, acting as an agent for the company, to audit Baranov's business records and to check on the financial status of the colony. After more than a year and a half, Kirill concluded that under Baranov's management, the colony had produced three hundred million rubles from furs and other ventures. He also discovered that Baranov could have profited many times over from crooked schemes, but instead had donated most of his own money to the company and to friends. His personal records showed that he was not a wealthy man.

While Kirill conducted his audit, the new chief manager went to work reforming the colonial administration. He made major changes in how the *promyshlenniki* were paid. They would no longer receive a share of the furs, but would be paid a salary and a clothing allowance. He sent a ship to Hawaii to recover as much of Schaffer's supplies as possible, and he led an expedition north along the Bering Sea coast to search out new sources of furs and walrus tusk. To ease the anxiety the colonists felt toward the notion of a naval administration, Hagemeister encouraged one of his officers to marry Baranov's fifteen-year-old daughter.

During his administration, Baranov had continuously wrestled with the problem of supplying the colonies with adequate supplies. As chief manager, Hagemeister was now faced with the same problem. On July 22, he sailed southward to Fort Ross to obtain supplies. Returning from California, he decided that due to his deteriorating health, he couldn't spend another winter in Sitka. Appointing one of his subordinates, Lieutenant Ianovski, as acting manager, and taking Baranov with him, he sailed for Europe.

Baranov was now seventy-two years old and had spent the last twenty-eight years of his life in North America. The failure of the Hawaiian venture had broken him. Decrepit in body and spirit, he rose from his sickbed to begin the task of transferring the company's property to the new manager. He had long been looking for a successor, but when Hagemeister summarily dismissed him, he felt betrayed by the company directors and the government.

Baranof's wife had been dead for years and his former home was like a foreign country to him. He debated whether to return to Russia or to build a home in the land he loved. The captain of the *Kamchatka*, Pavel Golovinin, was on a mission to survey the condition of the colonies and to report on the advisability of the renewal of the company's charter for another twenty years. He persuaded Baranov that he should return to St. Petersburg, that the company needed his advice and experience and would be glad to have him there. Swayed by Golovinin's advice, Baranov took passage on the *Kutusof*. He said goodbye to his friends, Russian and Indian alike, and many of the Kolosh came to see him off. After seeing his fifteen-year-old daughter Irene married to a naval officer, on November 27, 1818, he sailed from Sitka and left Russian America behind forever.

Before they sailed, Hagemeister left one of his subordinates in charge as acting manager, and took command of the *Kutusof*. The ship entered the harbor of Batavia on March 7, 1819, and remained there for thirty-six days. Baranov disembarked from the ship and took lodgings on shore. Traveling from the colder temperatures of Alaska to the tropical climate of Indonesia was too much for his feeble body. Before the ship sailed, the sailors carried him back on board. He died on April 16, and on the following day was buried at sea in the waters of the Indian Ocean.

Russian dominance of North America would continue for another forty-eight years. With declining profits from the fur trade and the high cost of maintaining their colonies, Russia decided to unload Alaska. On March 30, 1867, Secretary of State William H. Seward, concluded a treaty with the Russians to purchase Alaska for $7,200,000.

3

American Century

The purchase of Alaska in 1867 marked the end of Russian efforts to expand trade and colonization of the Pacific coast of North America and was an important step in the United States' rise as a great power in the Asia-Pacific region. The Russian American Company's financial troubles, and the realization that in case of war with England, Russia would not be able to defend its territory in North America, prompted negotiations that led to the sale of Alaska.

England was Russia's greatest rival. After losing the Crimean War to England in 1856, Russia now feared that in a future war, their rival would seize Alaska and add it to their empire. With the discovery of gold in 1850, prospectors poured into neighboring British Columbia. The increased population of this remote land compelled the British government to declare it a crown colony.

With their financial difficulties, the heavy cost in men and money required to defend their American possessions, and the fear that the British might take Alaska by force, Emperor Alexander II decided this might be an excellent time to sell. In the hopes of starting a bidding war, Russian envoys approached both the American and British governments. Knowing that they could take it by force, the British had little interest in buying Alaska.

Russia had many reasons for wanting to rid themselves of their North American holdings. They had borrowed 15 million pounds sterling from the Rothschilds at an annual interest rate of 5 percent. Now that it was falling due, they didn't have the money to pay it back. They also saw the sale of Alaska to the United States as an opportunity to further isolate and weaken British naval power in the Pacific. The Royal Navy base at Esquimalt in British Columbia would be surrounded by American territory and possibly annexed by American interest.

Russia offered to sell Alaska to the United States in 1859, and while the

United States government was interested in the proposal, the onset of the Civil War in America brought an end to negotiations. Following the Union victory over the South, in March 1867, Czar Alexander instructed the Russian minister to the United States, Eduard de Stoeckl, to renegotiate with Secretary of State William H. Seward. Stoeckl approached Seward through an intermediary, the journalist and politician Thurlow Weed, and the two statesmen began private discussions on March 11, 1867. They completed the first draft of the treaty ceding Russian North America to the United States, and concluded their negotiations at 4 a.m. on March 29. The purchase price was set at $7.2 million dollars and the treaty was signed the next day.[1]

The treaty needed the approval of the Russian and American Senates before the transfer could take place. When it was introduced on the floor of the U.S. Senate, where it needed a two-thirds majority to pass, there was little discussion on the bill. The government was embroiled in a constitutional crisis that pitted the Congress against President Andrew Johnson over his handling of Reconstruction of the South after the Civil War. While negotiations between Seward and Stoeckl were under way, an extraordinary session of Congress passed a bill designed to curb the president's power. At the same time, the House Judiciary Committee spent the summer debating articles of impeachment. With the impending battle between the two branches of government, the acquisition of Alaska was of little interest to the members of the Senate.

Senator Charles Sumner is often credited with making Alaska America's newest territory. He was a major player in the effort to convince the Senate to ratify the treaty when it came up for debate. As chairman of the Senate Foreign Relations Committee, Sumner would decide if the purchase would go forward or not. Before the treaty went to the full Senate for a vote it was up to his committee to approve or reject it.

When the treaty was submitted to Sumner's committee, the senator was skeptical of the project. He could have killed it, but as he thought about it, he became intrigued with the idea of expanding America's borders in the Pacific Northwest. Reading everything he could find on Russian America in the Smithsonian Institution and the Library of Congress and talking to knowledgeable people, he soon became convinced that it was in America's best interests to purchase Alaska from the Russians.

In a three-hour impassioned speech before the Senate, Sumner cited a list of Alaska's resources that the Russians had identified and argued that there were more riches yet to be discovered. He told the assemblage that the Russians estimated that 2,500 nationals and mixed-races persons and 8,000 Indians lived in Alaska, with 50,000 Inuits and natives living outside their jurisdiction.

The inventory included 23 trading posts placed on accessible islands and coastal plains. Four or five Russians were stationed at the smaller posts to collect furs for storage until the company's boats arrived to take them away. There were two larger towns, Sitka on the coast of Alaska and St. Paul in the Pribilof Islands. Sitka housed 968 residents in 116 small log cabins. With 283 residents and 100 homes, St. Paul was the center of the fur seal industry.

Sumner argued that this vast unknown land that had been under Imperial Russian rule should be blessed with the tenets of American democracy. The Senate was swayed by his impassioned plea. In a procedural vote to determine how the members of the Senate felt on the issue, by a vote of 27 to 12, on April 9, 1867, the Senate adopted the terms of the treaty. The bill to appropriate the funds for the purchase was held up in the House of Representatives until the summer of 1868 while the Senate was conducting President Johnson's impeachment trial.

Seward was convinced that Alaska would play a major role in America's future, but he had a much broader view of the world than many of his contemporaries. Like so many politicians and business leaders of the day, he believed that America's economic future depended on new world markets for American industrial goods and agricultural products. As a proponent of the doctrine of Manifest Destiny, he was convinced that the acquisition of Alaska would be a major step in extending America's border to the Pacific Ocean and the Bering Sea. He was keenly aware that the ratification of the treaty would cement stronger ties between Russia and America.

As he studied the maps of the region, Seward quickly realized that the great circle route between North America, Japan, and China would make a voyage across the Pacific shorter by a third than a direct route across the Pacific. Since the Pacific merchant fleet had converted to steam power, the ships would need coaling stations and provisioning ports along the northern Pacific coast. Seward attempted to purchase territories in St. Thomas and St. John in the Virgin Islands, and in Greenland and Iceland, to build port facilities for merchant and U.S. naval ships.

Many Americans were ambivalent about acquiring Alaska, while others supported it and saw the decision as an important step in the annexation of British Columbia. Upon first learning of it, journalists had a field day poking fun at the idea. Forty-five percent of the nation's newspapers supported it, but some newspapers, particularly Horace Greeley's *New York Tribune*, vehemently opposed the purchase, calling the new territory "Seward's Icebox," "Seward's Folly," and " Walrussia."

Historian Ellis Paxson Oberholzer summarized the position of American newspaper editors who opposed the purchase:

Already, so it was said we are burdened with territory we had no population to fill. The Indians within the present boundaries of the Republic strained our power to govern aboriginal peoples. Could it be that we would now, with open eyes, seek to add to our difficulties by increasing the number of such peoples under our national care? The purchase price was small: the annual charges for administration, civil and military, would be yet greater and continuing. The territory included in the proposed cession was not contiguous to the national domain. It lay away at an inconvenient and dangerous distance. The treaty had been secretly prepared, and signed and foisted upon the country at one o'clock in the morning. It was a dark deed done in the night.... The *New York World* said that it was a "sucked orange." It contained nothing of value but fur bearing animals, and these had been hunted until they were nearly extinct. Except for the Aleutian Islands and a narrow strip of land extending along the southern coast of the country it would not be worth taking as a gift.... Unless gold were found in the country much time would elapse before it would be blessed with Hoe printing presses, Methodist chapels and a metropolitan police. It was "frozen wilderness."[2]

The official transfer ceremony took place in Sitka on the early afternoon of October 18, 1867. Three American ships, the *Ossipee*, the *Resaca*, and the *Jamestown*, lay at anchor in the harbor. Blue-coated American soldiers marched through the streets of the town and up to the governor's mansion on the summit of Baranov Hill. Russian soldiers fell in next to them to await the lowering of the imperial flag of Russia. At 3:30 p.m. the Russian ensign was lowered to the accompaniment of artillery fire from both nations.

As it was lowered, the flag got caught in the halyards and a marine was sent aloft to release it. He tore it loose and dropped it on the heads of the Russian soldiers. The Stars and Stripes were then raised to the booming of cannons and the representative of the Czar, Alexi Pestchouroff, spoke a few words. "General Rousseau, by authority from His Majesty, the Emperor of Russia, I transfer to the United States the territory of Alaska."[3] General Lovell Rousseau accepted the transfer for the United States. The land dominated by imperial Russia for so many years now passed into the domain of the United States.[4]

T. Ahlund, a blacksmith recruited by the Russians to work in Sitka, wrote a somewhat different version of the ceremony:

> We had not spent many weeks at Sitka when two large steamships arrived there bringing things that belonged to the American crown, and a few days later the new governor also arrived in a ship together with his soldiers. The wooden two story mansion of the Russian governor stood on a high hill, and in front of it in the yard at the end of a tall spar flew the Russian flag with a double-headed eagle in the middle of it. Of course this flag now had to give way to the flag of the United States, which is full of stripes and stars. On a predetermined day in the afternoon a group of soldiers came from the American ships, led by one who carried the flag. Marching solemnly, but without accompaniment, they came to

the governor's mansion, where the Russian troops were lined up and waiting for the Americans.

Now they started to pull the Russian double-headed eagle down, but—whatever had gone into its head—it only came down a little bit, and then entangled its claws around the spar so that it could not be pulled down any further. A Russian soldier was therefore ordered to climb up the spar and disentangle it, but it seems that the eagle cast a spell on his hands too—for he was not able to arrive at where the flag was, but instead slipped down without it. The next one to try was not able to do any better; only the third soldier was able to bring the unwilling eagle down to the ground. While the flag was brought down, music was played and cannons were fired off from the shore; and then while the other flag was hoisted the Americans fired their cannons from their ships equally many times. After that, American soldiers replaced the Russian ones at the gate of the wall surrounding the Kolosh village.[5]

Under the terms of the treaty, the Russian government had sold the land and government property to the United States, but since the Russian American Company was a private enterprise, its holdings had to be sold separately. The last chief manager of the company, Prince Dmitrii Maksutov, was directed by the stockholders to sell it for whatever he could get. Everything sold at bargain basement prices. A wealthy merchant from New England, H.M. Hutchinson, purchased the company's entire inventory of merchandise, including a number of ships, for the paltry sum of $155,000. The inventory consisted of sheepskin coats, brass cannon, barrels of rum and casks of wine, leather goods, sheet copper, lead, tea, and hundreds of other articles of value. With a true value of $250,000, the goods were shipped to San Francisco. The sale also included the Russian ships in the harbor.

Shortly after the merchant completed the purchase of the goods from the Russians, he formed a company known as Hutchinson-Kohl & Company. Hutchinson was a shrewd businessman and his company realized tremendous profits from these transactions. One example of how profitable the purchase was is the transfer of the fur trading ship, the *Poloitofski*, to the merchant's company. He had purchased the ship for $4,000 and sold it six months later for $10,000.

Most of the Russians who had the means of transportation departed for Mother Russia on the first available ship. Those who remained were promised the rights of citizenship. The transfer went off without a hitch, but Indian troubles for the new landlords were just over the horizon. When Seward and Stoeckl were busy drawing up the treaty, they never took the time to consider the native population of Alaska or to ask them how they felt about the proposed sale of their country to the Americans. The Kolosh in and around Sitka were quite vocal in expressing their views on the treaty. They often confronted the U.S. Army commander to state their displeasure at not having been consulted about the transfer. The callous treatment and disregard for the rights of the Indians mirrored the American government's policies toward native Americans elsewhere in North America. They were viewed by the government and the military as a problem to be controlled in order to allow for white settlements and capitalist development. The Russians had ignored the sovereignty of the native tribes in the region, and the United States did likewise. Because they had occupied the land for a relatively short time, the Americans' dealings with the Indians were limited and they had little notion of who the natives were.

The Hydahs, Tsimphiens, and Tlingits inhabited the southeastern part of the country. The customs and habits of the three tribes were similar, but they spoke different languages. They were a maritime people who earned their livelihood from the sea, wove beautiful baskets, and carved canoes from a single log. They erected totemic emblems in front of their houses or on posts of the dwellings to indicate the family of the owner of the house. They were warlike and independent in spirit, and according to the Russians, the tribes numbered about six thousand Indians.

A mild and inoffensive people, the Aleuts lived along the Aleutian Chain that stretches in a 1,000-mile arc across the Pacific and reaches out toward the cost of Asia. Like the Indians on the mainland of Alaska, they depended on the sea for their survival. Fighting the elements of the Aleutian winters, they went to sea in skin-covered boats. They suffered the under the cruel hand of their Russian masters more than any other indigenous tribe in Russian America.

The Eskimos inhabited a large area of land along the western shores of Kodiak Island, to Point Barrow in the north, and east to the Canadian border. Like other native peoples of Alaska, they hunted the sea for the whale, walrus, seal, and fish, while on land they subsisted on caribou, wild reindeer, and birds and small animals. The Eskimos who had the most frequent contacts with the Russians inhabited the southern villages. An official census of the Eskimos was never conducted, but indications are that there may have been a greater number living in Alaska in 1867 than at the present time.

The valleys of the interior were the ancestral home of the Athapascan. These Indians were hunters and fishermen who in summer traveled the rivers in birch-bark canoes, while in winter they moved over the ice and snow in sleds pulled by teams of dogs. They depended on the salmon to feed their families. To catch these large fish, they built their cabins at the best fishing places along the streams and rivers. Because they lived in the interior, it is doubtful that they had any contact with the Russians.

Sitka was a magnet for adventurers, con artists, speculators, land grabbers, politicians, gamblers, and prostitutes. Americans, Russians, Germans, Jews,

Finlanders, Aleuts, and Tlingits walked the mud-filled streets at all hours. Houses of prostitution, gambling halls, and saloons opened for round-the-clock business and real estate prices on Sitka's one and only street climbed through the roof. A few merchants like Hayward M. Hutchinson earned huge profits, but for most fortune-seeking adventurers, Sitka was a bust.

Hutchinson came north with General Rousseau and thanks to his influence with Prince Maksutov, he was able to buy the entire inventory of the Russian American Company. When Hutchinson insisted that competition would result in lower profits than the expense of carrying on business, Congress awarded his company, Hutchinson, Kohl and Company, a twenty-year lease monopoly on the Pribilof Island fur seal fishery.

The newcomers who flocked to Sitka were not as fortunate as Hutchinson. They had expected to get rich quick, but they soon learned that the community that had once been sustained by the Russian fur trade did not have an independent economic base. Other than the gambling halls, the houses of prostitution, and the saloons, there was no way for them to make money. The Russians had effectively depleted the source of easily accessible commercial furs. Because the timber from the trees of the Pacific Northwest was closer to its markets and shipping costs were too expensive, lumber from the surrounding forest could not compete. A few prospectors searched for gold, but failed to find any. The fishing industry offered some potential, but the high cost of development and the difficulty of transporting the fish outweighed the profits that could be earned.

In the early years following the transfer, the only laws that existed in the territory were those that General Jefferson C. Davis imposed. Congress had failed to pass any laws relating to criminal and civil matters in Alaska, and in a short time, crime was rampant. Murder, attacks with dangerous weapons, theft and other outrages were not prohibited and seldom prosecuted.

A number of citizens attempted self-rule when they formed a provisional government in their town. With General Davis's blessing, they framed a charter, elected a mayor and city council, drew up city ordinances, and levied a subscription to build a school and hire a teacher. The first mayor was the collector of customs, William S. Dodge. The saloon crowd was opposed to any restraints on their freewheeling way of life, and since there was no law allowing the council to collect taxes, by 1872, the organization was dissolved for lack of funds.

Drunkenness among the native population was a major problem in the territory. The laws of the United States prohibited selling liquor to the Indians, but adequate provisions for enforcement in the territory didn't exist. The revenue laws of the day provided for the licensing of the sale of intoxicants, and customs officers were supposed to prevent the importation and sale of illegal whiskey from British Columbia. The profits from this criminal enterprise were so great that military officers and customs officials engaged in smuggling this contraband into Alaska.

To make matters worse, the Indians in the villages distilled a native brew from imported molasses that they called "hooch." Usually they were peaceful and well disposed toward their white neighbors, but under the influence of the "hooch" and other strong drink, they became resentful of what they perceived as ill treatment by the white man and the violation of their rights. They would go berserk and start fights on the smallest provocations. The women were worse than their men. Much to the sorrow of the soldiers in the post, they were experts with a skinning knife.

Jurisdiction for prosecuting criminals was given to a court in Portland, Oregon. Criminals were transported to this city to stand trial for their crimes twelve hundred miles from the territory. In 1884, a code of procedure was passed under which it allowed for white men to be convicted of their crimes and sentenced to serve time in jail. Unlike the white man, in many cases, Indians were convicted and hanged.

Sitka was the first and only military outpost in Alaska in 1867. The military commander of the district, General Jefferson C. Davis, established his headquarters in the barracks that had formerly housed Russian troops. He dispatched companies of soldiers from his garrison to Tongass, Wrangell, the Hudson Bay Company post at the mouth of the Stikine River, the international boundary between Canada and the United States, St. Paul, in the Pribilof Islands, Kodiak, and Kenai. For the soldiers it was hard duty. Many of them thought it was a mistake to station troops in this frozen wilderness. In their opinion, it would have been better to bring in a couple of small swift boats.

The solders assigned to Sitka considered it cruel and unjust punishment. Sitka was located on an island and transportation to the mainland was nonexistent. Without boats they were confined to the island, powerless to take aggressive action against the Indian villages in the surrounding area if they felt it was warranted. The thousands of inlets and passages between the islands provided for the Tlingit Indians a safe path of retreat if and when the army pursued them.

The military brass weren't familiar with conditions in territory as they related to the troops in Alaska. While the generals in Washington were working to create a new command they called the Army of the Columbia, Davis learned that since the natives were peaceful, his troops were not really needed to defend the settlements. On more than one occasion, the Tlingit approached the general and announced that they had never sold more than a few acres of land to the Russians and the land belonged to them. A few members of the tribe wanted to go on the warpath and drive the Americans out, but a strong show of force convinced the troublemakers that accommodation with the new government was the best policy to follow.

In Alaska, the military restricted itself to dispensing American-style justice on the Indians without regard to their culture or their dignity. The Indians at Sitka continued to reside outside the palisades of the town. They were permitted to pass through the gates at 9:00 in the morning, but they had to leave by 6:00 in the evening. On one occasion, one of the proudest and most arrogant chiefs of the Colcheka clan had the misfortune to experience military justice.

On New Year's Day, Colcheka was visiting General Davis at his home in Sitka. It has been rumored that the general and the chief enjoyed a few rounds of strong spirits to celebrate the New Year. More than a little drunk, Colcheka crossed the parade ground, not following the path prescribed by the Army. When he ignored a sentry's order to halt, a second sentry kicked him a number of times. Angry beyond words, he wrestled the rifle away from the guard, and knocking him to the ground, he returned to his village in triumph. Davis sent a detachment to the village to arrest and imprison the chief and retrieve the rifle. After a lively skirmish with the Indians, the troops were forced to retreat. A parley was held the next day and Colcheka surrendered. He was placed in the guardhouse for a short time and then released.

Before he sent the detachment into the village, Davis issued an order that no Indians were allowed to leave the village. It was rescinded when Colcheka surrendered, but through an error a few troops didn't get the word. They fired on a canoe with a party of natives who had started out to gather wood. Two men, a Kake and a Chilikat were killed.

The tribal law of the Tlingit was "a life for a life," but there was an alternative to this law. The perpetrator could pay an indemnity to the victim's family or else it had to be paid in blood. The family of the murdered Kake demanded that the army indemnify them a payment of blankets or give them the guilty party. Davis contemptuously refused their demands.

This wasn't the end of the army's troubles with the Indians. The family of the Chilikat waited until they captured a trader in their village and made him pay the blood money in blankets. The Kakes caught two prospectors searching for gold along the shores of the Chatham Strait. The family of the dead Indian took their revenge and murdered the two men. In the eyes of their kinsmen, they had satisfied tribal law by extracting blood atonement for the crime against their relatives.

When word of the Indians' actions reached Sitka, retaliation was not long in coming. Davis called on Captain Meade, the captain of the U.S.S. *Sag-*

inaw, to assist in punishing the guilty parties. The ship sailed for Kake Island, but the Indians fled into the forest. The *Saginaw* opened fire and leveled Old Kake Village, Old Tom's Village and an unnamed village. There was little Justice for the natives in Alaska. A man named Parker killed two Indians in separate incidents. In each case, a military board investigating these cases ruled that the murder of the Indians was not justified. They discharged Parker for lack of jurisdiction over the offense.

Indian troubles continued to plague the Army and the white inhabitants of the territorial outposts. At Wrangell on Christmas Day, 1869, a drunken Stikine Indian named Lowan got into an argument with the post laundress and bit off one of her fingers. A small detachment of soldiers went to the village to arrest the offender. Shots rang out and Lowan was killed. His brother was shot in the shoulder. The Stikines grabbed their antique Hudson Bay muskets to defend their village and drive off the invaders. The post trader, Leon Smith, attempted to pacify the Indians. He was shot to death by a medicine man named Scutdoo. The Army demanded Scutdoo's immediate surrender, but they were met with a defiant refusal. The Tlingit assembled under the leadership of their chiefs and sent their women into the forest and out of the reach of danger.

The cannons in the fort opened fire and canon balls crashed through the walls of the tribal houses. The Indians climbed a hill in back of the town and fired down on the fort's defenders. Heavy cannon fire quickly dislodged them from their lofty perches. All night long the cannons bombarded the village. In the morning, the Stikines yielded and brought Scutdoo to the fort. He was tried by court-martial, and on December 29, 1869, he was hanged in full sight of the assembled natives and the garrison. While the Tlingits were cowed by the power of the Army's cannons, the unhappy memory of those terrible events continued to instill fear in the minds of the inhabitants who remained behind after the troops left the area.

On June 14, 1887, the army commanders in the Pacific Northwest Military District withdrew the garrison from Sitka and shipped them back to the states on the *California*. They needed the troops to pursue Chief Joseph and his Nez Perce and force them back on the reservation. The Army was glad to depart and leave the problems of governing the territory to someone else. Their dismal record during the occupation was mainly the punishment of Indians for quarrels the soldiers initiated by their own acts, and their influence appears to have been devoted to debauching both the natives and the Russians.

Upon the evacuation of the soldiers, the only representatives of the U.S. government were the collector of customs and his deputies. The Treasury's revenue cutters intermittently visited Sitka and the northern posts, and their stays were as short as possible. If the settlements had problems with the Indians, the ships' crews were too small to mount a landing party to go to their assistance.

One week after the troops left Sitka, hundreds of angry Tlingit Indians stormed into town. They tore down the stockade, occupied the empty buildings, and took out doors, windows, and partitions for their own homes. Clan Chief Annahootz told the few remaining whites, "The United States does not want the country. It belongs to us. We will kill the men and make slaves of the women."[6] The chief further stated, "The Russians have stolen the country from the Tlingit and sold it to the Americans for a large amount of money. The Americans are angry that the Russians deceived them about the country's value to the Indians. We are glad to say that after so many years' hard fight we get our country back again.[7] The grievances they harbored for so long and dared not to express while the military was in control had boiled to the surface with a revived animosity.

Annahootz's words alarmed the townspeople, but they were nothing more than competitive Indian bombast. The Indians had no intention of killing them, nor did they want any more bloodshed for their own people. They'd seen the American response to previous attacks on the settlements and they wanted no part of it. There were between three hundred and four hundred whites in Sitka and they were facing upwards to a thousand warriors. The Indians were still distilling their hooch and threatening to attack the settlement. When a newly appointed collector of customs came to Sitka, he became so frightened that he returned to the States on the same steamer he arrived on. He told his superiors that with the Indians making warlike threats, they should abandon the district.

The Keeksitty clan led by Chief Katlean were the most vocal Indians against the whites. In 1878, they killed a white man named Brown and his companion at Hot Springs near the outskirts of Sitka. With the help of Annahootz, the murderers were arrested. The Keeksitty were angered by the arrest of their fellow tribesmen. They fortified themselves with generous portions of hooch and held a council of war. They resolved to rescue the prisoners, sack the town and put it to the torch. On a signal from Katlean, they advanced toward the entrance to the white quarter, where the townspeople had gathered to defend themselves as best they could. Much to Katlean's surprise, outside the town, they were confronted by Annahootz and his Kokwanton warriors. Annahootz had decided to fight for the whites.

Annahootz's warriors blocked their path and refused to allow them to advance any further. The two chiefs had harsh words for each other, but in the end, Annahootz prevailed. The Keeksitty returned to their village, and Katlean went off to other villages to gather recruits for his campaign against the whites. Anahootz and his warriors had saved Sitka from death and destruction. The steamship, U.S.S. *California* arrived in the harbor just as the crisis was winding down. The prisoners were taken aboard and transported to Portland, where they were tried, found guilty, and hanged.

In addition to the prisoners, the women and children of Sitka boarded the *California* and were transported to the States for their own safety. The men of the town sent an appeal to the government pleading for protection from the Indians, but it fell on deaf ears. If the American government wouldn't protect them, then maybe the government of British Columbia would. As a result of the petition to the British Government at Victoria, the H.M.S. *Osprey* under the command of Captain A. Holmes A'Court reached Sitka on March 1, 1869. He anchored before the Indian village and cleared his decks for action. The ship's presence in the harbor put an end to any future demonstrations against the whites. These incidents proved beyond a shadow of a doubt what could happen in the absence of authority and civil government.

The *Osprey* remained at anchor in front of the Indian village when it was joined by the revenue cutter *Wolcott*. Captain A'Court decided that the cutter didn't have a large enough force to protect the people of Sitka from future Indian attacks. When the U.S.S. *Alaska* arrived on April 3, he upped anchor and sailed away to his home port. The *Alaska* was relieved by the *Jamestown* on June 14, 1879. Except for short intervals, for the next twenty-five years, a U.S. Navy warship was stationed at Sitka.

With the arrival of the *Jamestown*, the navy took over the responsibility of governing the territory. Captain A.L. Beardslee, commander of the *Jamestown*, was sent to Alaska without a code of laws to control 360 whites and approximately 6,000 Indians. In Sitka there were 34 native-born Americans, 79 naturalized citizens, and 247 Russians who were naturalized by the treaty of purchase. The population of the town was made up of Irish, Italians, Turks, Jews, Austrians, Germans, English, Russians, and Creoles.

Beardslee had his work cut out for him. He found dissension and anarchy among the whites, and the natives afflicted with superstition, witchcraft, slavery, shamanism, and blood feuds. Almost without exception, the whites were the type of riffraff who sought the frontier to escape the regulations and laws of civilized communities. Beardslee strived to solve the problems plaguing the settlement by organizing a provisional government. A code of laws was drawn up and a magistrate and board of councilmen were elected to fill the offices of the new governing body. The miners at Silver Bay sent an offensive letter to the council voicing their opposition. They refused to participate, alleging that if a government were formed, the warship would leave and they would be unprotected from the Indians.

The provisional government did not have the resources to enforce the laws they passed. To reduce drunkenness of the natives, they tried to stop them from brewing hooch by ordering the merchants to stop selling molasses to them. A Jewish trader refused to abide by the law and continued trading with the Indians. He had broken the law, but the council didn't have the authority to arrest him.

Beardslee was determined to civilize the town and end the drunkenness that he and others believed was the root cause of most of problems plaguing the community. He called the townspeople together to discuss the issues, and then he took immediate and decisive action to solve them. With an armed forced of sailors from the ship, he raided the distilleries and captured and destroyed thirty-eight stills. He compelled the Indians to clean up their village and paint numbers on their houses. He appointed a native police force to keep order among the natives. Beardslee discovered that in a cannery near Sitka, there were forty stills distilling hooch for the natives. He recruited a small force of Indian volunteers, who smashed the stills with axes and clubs and dumped the liquor into the bay. Beardslee had accomplished the impossible. He brought prohibition to the Indians and a modicum of peace and calm to Sitka.

Peace reigned in Sitka, but there were disturbances in many of the other settlements. The cause of most of the trouble was too much hooch. When trouble struck the town of Chilkat, the Indian police were sent to quell the war between the whites and the Indians. In the ensuing battle, a number of Indians were killed and their chief wounded.

At Wrangell, a party of Hootznahoo Indians tried to set up a still at the north end of town. The mission Indians were against strong drink and were not about to follow Jesus's admonition to turn the other cheek. They attempted to break up the operation and a fight ensued between the two groups. At the end of five days, five Indians were dead. The battle might have continued indefinitely, but the director of the mission sent to Sitka for help. A detachment of marines arrived at Wrangell, destroyed the stills, and restored order.

The closing years of the Navy's rule in Alaska were marked with violence. In April 1872, a new commander announced his intentions to withdraw his men from the town and depart from Alaska. The collector of customs protested the proposed action, and the officer left a corporal on guard at Sitka when they sailed for Wrangell. Without a ship to protect them, the townspeople were once again living in fear. As soon as the ship was out of sight over the horizon, a riot ensued. A rock was thrown through the customs house door and a shaman's hair was stolen from where it had been nailed to a wall. Indians and whites took their anger out on each other. In the middle of the brawl, the guard shot an Indian in the leg. The fight continued until the *Corwin* arrived and restored the peace.

4

Missionaries and Miners

In the 1880s, Alaska was for the most part an unexplored wilderness. With a handful of white settlers who may or may not stay in the territory, the United States Congress could not justify the cost of maintaining a military presence or a civilian government. Outside influences and unexpected events would soon make their mark on the land and force the Congress to act and change the destiny of Alaska and the lives of its people forever.

The first great movement forward was the establishment of schools and missions through the efforts of a Protestant missionary. When the Russians departed from Alaska, they left behind seventeen Russian Orthodox chapels and schools. The churches in Russia provided a small amount of financial support, but the burden of maintaining these missions fell to the parishioners. Most of the churches were in the Aleutians or on Kodiak Island and few of the Tlingit villages in southeastern Alaska had a resident priest.

In 1869, a major gold strike near the headwaters of the Cassiar district of northwest British Columbia drew miners and merchants to the area, and Wrangell became a boom town and a service center for the Cassiar. Saloons, houses of prostitution, and gambling halls sprang up overnight. Gambling, drinking, fighting, and carousing quickly came to characterize the town. A few of the Indians who resided in the settlement followed the teachings of Christ. They wrote a letter to a Presbyterian minister and church organizer from Denver, Colorado, Doctor Sheldon Jackson, asking for missionaries to come to their town to help combat the depravity of the population. In 1877, Dr. Jackson and a missionary teacher, Amanda McFarland, traveled to Alaska to establish a church and a school in Wrangell.

Jackson saw a great need for churches and missions, and he dedicated his life and his career to filling that need and finding private and government funds to support them. For the next several years, he followed the same schedule. In the summer months, he brought with him Bibles and building materials, and new missionary teachers to supervise the construction of new mission sites. He spent the winter months in New York and other major Eastern cities, collecting donations and lecturing to education conferences and Indian reform groups. He wrote hundreds of tracts and descriptions of the missions in Alaska. He met with congressmen, senators, and government officials to plead his case for funding. Jackson was a dynamic speaker and a familiar face at almost every Protestant church conference. He urged all the churches, regardless of denomination, to get involved in missionary work in Alaska. There was room for all of them in this vast wilderness.

Not surprisingly, the timing of Jackson's endeavors coincided with the efforts of the Bureau of Indian Affairs and the missionary reformers to civilize the native population. Their idea of civilizing the Indians was acculturation, which meant replacing their culture with the white man's culture. It also meant that the Indians could no longer speak their own languages. They must speak only English. To implement this policy, Jackson instructed his missionary teachers, and the natives who attended the schools, to speak only English.

With the success of the mission at Wrangell, Jackson looked for other communities to expand his acculturation efforts. In 1879, He established a boarding school in Sitka to take in the large number of orphans in the community and teach them new skills. The Sitka Presbyterian Industrial School, known in later years as the Sheldon Jackson School, quickly became the regional headquarters for Jackson's missions and the Bureau of Indian Affairs' acculturation efforts in Alaska. The Presbyterians established a school in Haines for the Chilkats, and for the Hoonahas and the Hydahs on Prince of Wales Island. In 1890, the Methodists founded the Jesse Lee home for Orphans in Unalaska.

According to the terms of their lease, the Alaska Commercial Company built and maintained two schools on the Seal Islands. The Russian Orthodox Church reestablished schools in a number of villages, and the Roman Catholic Church made its presence felt when it established missions in Juneau, Wrangell, and the Yukon Valley. In 1885, funds were appropriated to continue the educational work in the territory: $25,000 was allocated for children to attend school without regard to race and $15,000 for support and education of Indian children at industrial schools in Alaska.[1] This was a paltry sum for a territory with an estimated population of 33,000 inhabitants scattered over 586,000 square miles of territory with almost insurmountable difficulties of travel. Jackson was appointed general agent of education for the territory and was responsible for building schools, procuring books and furniture, and transporting them over thousands of miles of rugged terrain.

The teachers who were recruited to teach in these remote villages faced great hardships in the performance of their duties. Isolated from family, friends and associates, and often times with no one in the village who spoke one word of English, they were confronted by drunkenness, shamanism and witchcraft. In most cases they would spend the winter months in their lonely and remote outpost and never see another white man. On occasion, a whiskey smuggler sailed into the nearby harbor, creating pandemonium among the natives.

The efforts to educate the natives had many successes and some failures. The most successful endeavor was the mission of Dr. William Duncan, a missionary of the Church of England. He established his mission at Old Metlakatla in British Columbia in 1857, while it was still a land of uncivilized primitive savagery. After thirty years of unrelenting work, he petitioned the U.S. government for permission to transfer his settlement to Annette Island. Moving his people to the new location he called New Metlakatla, he built a village that today has become a modern and prosperous city with a diverse population of Tlingit, Haida, Aleut, Yupik, and other native peoples of Alaska. The United States government created the only Indian reservation in Alaska when they granted recognition to the community in 1891.

The task of establishing schools and missions in this wild new country was an attempt to bring the native population out of its primitive and barbarous lifestyle. In a few short decades, the missionaries tried to repair more than a century of slavery, degradation and humiliation the Indians suffered at the hands of the white man. In 1877, Customs Collector I. C. Dennis expressed his opinion of conditions at Wrangell:

> Did they seek the enlightenment of the Indian, and endeavor to elevate him to a higher moral standard? On this point let the Indians themselves testify. Shakes, Toyatt, and Shustaks, chiefs of the Stikine Indians, say this.
>
> For many years we have been desirous of having schools and churches established among us. With the coming of the military among us came a big church "Tyee" who told us that the soldiers were come to protect us, and that he would have schools established and churches built for us. Time passed; no schools were established and no churches built, and instead of the soldiers being any protection to us they sought to debase and demoralize us. Liquor they sold us that crazed the brain and trouble came that ended in Captain Smith being killed and one of our men hung.[2]

The Indian reform groups believed that assimilation was the only viable alternative to extermination of the native population. Jackson's work was an extension of their philosophy and he embraced it with open arms. He and the reform groups were confident that through education, they could wipe out thousands of years of native traditions and culture and turn the Indians into white men in one generation. They mistakenly believed that if one generation was exposed to American values, they would teach those who came after them and the reformers' work would be done. The schools would be the principal agent of acculturation. To achieve that purpose, Jackson's efforts were devoted to establishing Indian schools in as many native villages as the Presbyterian Board of Home Missions could support.

When not in Alaska, Jackson was in Washington, lobbying Congress to allocate funds for his acculturation efforts. While in Washington, he argued that it was the government's responsibility to care for the welfare of the Indians, but few were listening. He sought funding from church groups and resolutions to support his work from state education groups and the National Education Association. In 1884, Congress passed legislation addressing the needs of Alaska, but it may have had more to do with another event that was taking place than with Jackson's efforts to influence them. While Jackson was engaged in establishing his missions, others were following the lure of the gold trail.

The second development that had a major impact on the people of Alaska, both white man and Indian, was the discovery of gold on the Klondike River, a few miles up the Yukon near the Alaska boundary with British Columbia. In 1893, America was suffering through a depression and very much in need of good economic news. The gold rush of 1896 was the shot in the arm that brought the country back to prosperity, and 100,000 would-be prospectors from all over the world rushed to the wilds of Alaska. As this flood of gold-seekers invaded the land, they were followed by a much smaller and smarter contingent who sought their fortunes in a much more practical way. These were the entrepreneurs, the men and women who catered to the miners inflicted with "Klondike Fever." On August 16, 1896, George Washington Carmack and two Indian friends, Skookum Jim and Dawson Charley, pried a gold nugget from the river bed of Rabbit Creek, a tributary of the Klondike River, and set in motion one of the most frenzied gold rushes in history. Over the next two years, prospectors and treasure seekers descended on the gold fields.

Carmack was neither a die-hard prospector nor a keen businessman. The son of a forty-niner in California, George served a brief stint in the Marines, and while on duty in Alaska, he deserted his post when he was refused leave to visit his sick sister. He returned to Alaska in 1885 to engage in trading, fishing, and trapping. In 1887, he married a Tagish First Nations Indian woman named Kate. George was a braggart and the miners had a strong dislike for him. They called him "Squaw Man" for marrying an Indian and for his association with her people, and "Lyin' George" for his exaggerated claims and tall tales.

According to the oral traditions of the Tagish First Nations People, the story of the gold rush began when Skookum Jim and his two nephews, Dawson

4. Missionaries and Miners 61

Charlie and Patsy Koolseen, traveled down the Yukon River from their village in the Southern Yukon. They were searching for Jim's sister Kate and her husband, George Carmack. Years before he discovered gold in the Klondike, Skookum Jim had a dream. His spirit helper, Frog, appeared to him in the form of Wealth Woman. She gave him a golden walking stick and told him he would discover his fortune in the north country.

On a warm summer day in July, Skookum Jim located George and Kate, and the group went fishing on the Klondike River. Carmack stopped to swirl a bit of river sand in his prospector's pan when they were approached by Robert Henderson. He had been mining gold on the Indian River just south of the Klondike, and in keeping with the prospectors' code, he told Carmack that he'd found a little gold on a creek he dubbed Gold Bottom Creek. He suggested George might have better luck on Rabbit Creek. George asked if he could stake a claim on the creek. Glaring at Skookum Jim and Dawson Charlie, Henderson told him that he was welcome, but he didn't want any "damn Indians" staking a claim there.

Like most of the whites in Alaska, Henderson hated Indians, and George and his companions didn't like Henderson either. They didn't like his attitude, and for the next two weeks they ignored his lead. With nothing better to do, they wandered over to check out his claim. The Indians asked him to sell them tobacco, but he insulted them by refusing. Angry and indignant, George and his friends left and set up camp on Rabbit Creek. While washing a dishpan, either Carmack or Skookum Jim found a layer of gold in soft rock near the stream and pried out a thumb-sized nugget weighing about a quarter of an ounce. At the price of gold in 1896, it was worth $4. According to Carmack, they turned over loose pieces of rock and found gold that lay thick between flaky slabs like cheese sandwiches.

Carmack didn't bother to hike the short distance to Henderson's camp to tell him about the strike. Instead, he headed fifty miles downriver to the town of Forty Mile to record claims for himself and his companions. Carmack later recalled that Henderson's obstinacy, and his insults to Jim and Charlie by refusing to sell them tobacco, had cost Henderson a fortune.

On his way to file the claims, he bragged about his good luck to everyone he met. Most of the old timers scoffed at him. "Lying George" had made strikes before that had amounted to little or nothing, so they didn't put much stock in this new bonanza of his. Just in case he might be telling the truth this time, a few of them went upriver to investigate. They verified what George said and within five days the valley was swarming with prospectors. By the end of August, every prospector from miles around had staked a claim along the entire length of Rabbit Creek (later called Bonanza Creek). Many prospectors struck it rich when an even richer vein was discovered on a tributary they named Eldorado.

The news of the strike took about a year to reach civilization. Winter was closing in and the rivers were freezing over. With the heavy snows that covered the land, communication with the outside world was almost impossible. The first reports coming out of the Yukon that rich deposits of placer gold had been struck on the Klondike were vague and didn't give much detail. In February 1897, a few adventurous individuals left the States and headed to Alaska to stake their claims. As word of the strike spread, the trickle of prospectors and miners turned into a flood. Before the gold rush was over, it generated hundreds of millions of dollars in placer gold along the tributaries of the Klondike River.

The news of the strike broke like an erupting volcano when on July 14, 1897, the steamship *Excelsior* docked in San Francisco with more than a half a million dollars of Klondike gold on board. Three days later the steamship *Portland* arrived in Seattle carrying what the newspapers described as "a ton of gold." They may have exaggerated the weight of the gold, but sixty-eight miners walked down the gangway with suitcases, boxes, blankets, and coffee cans brimming with gold.

The newspaper articles fueled a nationwide hysteria, and the stories were picked up by newspapers around the world. By the tens of thousands, men left their jobs and their families to set off an arduous journey to the Klondike. Seattle, Tacoma, and Vancouver were the jumping-off points and men and women poured into the cities seeking transportation north to Alaska. Upon reaching Skagway or Dyea, some went by way of St. Michael at the mouth of the Yukon to meet the steamers that fought the stiff river currents for sixteen hundred miles. Since this route was very expensive and it was almost impossible to purchase a ticket on the Yukon River steamers, most chose to endure the hardships of the Chilkoot and White passes and travel downriver to Dawson.

At Dyea, at the foot of Chilkoot Pass, there was chaos and little else. A trading post and two saloons were the only buildings in this desolate landscape. Four miles away, Skagway consisted of one little log cabin. With the huge influx of gold seekers, everything was about to change. On July 26, 1897, without an office or a building in which to conduct business, the Customs Department declared Dyea a port of entry.

A traffic jam of ships laden with everything a mining camp needed clogged the harbor. There was no wharf and everything had to be deposited on shore. An eighteen-foot tide rose and fell, and crews had to wait until low tide to unload the ships onto a half mile of sloping beach. Freight was dumped into scows, rowboats, rafts and anything else that would float. Horses and

4. Missionaries and Miners

cattle were dropped into the water from slings to swim ashore. When passengers came ashore, they carried the freight up the incline to save it from the returning high tide. A tent city stretched in a row above the high-water line and the newcomers fought to find a place to pitch theirs.

As the prospectors swarmed into Skagway and Dyea, the outposts became typical frontier towns. Every type of wheeled vehicle and every animal was pressed into service to provide transportation for the burgeoning and transient population. Horses, dogs and even cattle had loads strapped to their backs. Stores, blacksmith shops, law offices and restaurants housed in tents seemingly sprang up overnight. As soon as they were built, the businesses moved into wooden shacks along mud-filled streets. On October 15, Skagway got its first newspaper.

Between 1897 and 1898, they were lawless towns. The Northwest Canadian Mounted Police called them "little better than hell on earth." Dance halls and gambling dens roared night and day. Con men plied their trade on the trails and operated crooked roulette wheels and rigged card games. At every campfire along the way they played shell games to relieve the tenderfeet of their hard-earned cash.

Skagway had its own resident bad man, a character named Soapy Smith. He was a sophisticated swindler who saw himself as a benefactor to the poor and needy. He had gracious manners and gave generously to widows and orphans. He often stepped in and stopped mob lynchings, while at the same time he was the ringleader of a gang of thieves who swindled prospectors with cards, dice, and the good old reliable shell game. His telegraph office charged prospectors $5 to send a telegram to their families back home. In reality, there was no telegraph service in or out of Skagway until 1900. Smith also controlled a comprehensive spy network, a private militia he called the Skagway Military Company, the newspaper, and the Deputy U.S. Marshall. Smith was shot dead in a running gun battle with Frank Reid and Jesse Murphy on the wharf in Juneau on July 8, 1898. He managed to return fire. Some witnesses claim they fired at each other simultaneously, and it was Murphy who actually killed him. Reid was wounded in the shootout and died twelve days later.

To reach the gold fields, most of the prospectors followed the route from Dyea and Skagway, over the mountains and through Chilkoot or White Pass. The two passes were separated by a 5,000-foot mountain and a trail had to be cut from Skagway through a heavy forest, past Liarsville, through a river valley, and over a gorge. In the summer, long lines of prospectors zigzagged up the face of the mountain and down to Lake Lindeman and Bennett Lake in Canada. In the winter months, the trail ran up a gulch to the summit and over the ice to the lakes.

The most popular trail was the 550-mile Skagway Trail over White Pass. With its gradual slope, it appeared to be far less demanding than Chilkoot and looked like it should have been suitable for the use of pack animals to haul the prospectors' loads. As soon as they hit the trail, they found it to be nowhere as easy as it looked. In the forest, broken branches hid bottomless pits of muck into which the horses sank and died or were shot to death while miners surged over them and trampled their bodies into the quagmire. No one stopped for man or beast. The canyon became littered with abandoned implements and outfits when their bearers could go no farther. Hundreds got cold feet, turned off the trail and fled back to town. They pawned heirlooms and everything of value they had to pay for passage home on the next ship back to the States.

The steepness of the mountain trails, the cold temperatures of the mountainous terrain, and the weight of the equipment they carried made the climb extremely hazardous, and it could take a day to reach the summit. On the trail, the supplies were broken down into smaller packages and carried in relays. Tlingit and Tagish Indian packers who carried heavy loads for cash were available along the route at a charge of $1 per pound. Avalanches were a constant threat and on April 3, 1898, more than sixty people were killed while traveling over Chilkoot Pass.[3]

Many women made the trek over the passes, but it is difficult to estimate their number. In 1898, eight percent of the population of Kodiak were women, and as high as twelve percent in towns like Dawson. Many women accompanied their husbands, but others traveled alone. The women often proved stronger than their mates in facing the challenges of the trail. Most of them came to the Klondike for many of the same economic reasons as male prospectors. With more men than women in Alaska, young mail-order brides were transported to the territory to marry newly rich miners. Few weddings took place, but some single women traveled to Alaska on their own in the hope of finding a wealthy husband.[4]

Guidebooks of the day recommended what type of practical clothes the women should take to the Klondike. The female dress code of the time dictated that women's wear was formal, emphasizing long skirts and corsets. With the hardships of the trail, they soon discarded them for more appropriate attire. Because of the dangers and remoteness of life in the Klondike, few mothers brought their children with them.[5]

Fewer than one percent of the women actually worked as miners once they reached the Klondike. Many of them were married to the miners, but life in the gold fields was hard and often lonely. They were expected to do the cooking, thaw ice and snow for water, break up frozen food, and collect wild plants for food. In Dawson and other towns, women took in laundry to make money. Others worked as seamstresses or waitresses, jobs that could pay well, but were often beset with periods of unemployment. For some, this type of menial labor was too slow and too hard to make money. They wanted it fast and easy, and working in the saloons, gambling dens, and dance halls or as prostitutes was the way to go. It was a short step from persuading lonely miners to buy them drinks for a percentage of the cost to moving into prostitution, where the profits were more substantial and could be earned more quickly.[6]

Aids for the travelers varied. Some brought dogs, horses, mules or oxen, but others had to carry their equipment on their backs or on sleds pulled by hand. Shortly after the first stampede over the mountains, the Canadian government imposed a rule requiring each prospector entering the Yukon Territory to carry a year's supply of food with them to ensure they didn't starve in the winter. When camping gear, tools, and other essentials were added, a typical prospector's load could weigh as much as 2,000 pounds. Draft animals were in short supply, and even poor quality horses sold for as much as $700.[7]

As the winter progressed, entrepreneurs found solutions to the problems the prospectors faced in getting to the gold fields. They created a 1,500-step staircase in the ice of Chilkoot Pass and charged a fee for its daily use. It became known as the "Golden Steps." By December of 1897, one entrepreneur had built a tramway at the bottom of the mountain to ferry packages up the final parts of the pass. It was powered by a horse walking in a circle pulling a wheel-mounted rope. The horse was soon replaced by a steam engine and the owner charged between 8 and 30 cents a pound. It was replaced with an aerial tramway in the spring of 1898 that was capable of moving nine tons of goods to the summit every hour.

Those who survived the hardships of the first leg of the journey were forced to spend the winter of 1897–98 at the lakes. They still had more than 500 miles upriver to go before they reached Dawson City. In the long, dark months of an Alaskan winter, the gold seekers cut down most of the trees from the surrounding hills, dragged the logs back to the lake shore, and built boats of all types. On May 29, the ice on the river broke up, and a ragtag flotilla of 7,000 barges, rafts and homemade plank boats sailed up the treacherous Yukon River.

The river posed a new problem for the travelers. Until it reached Whitehorse, the prospectors had to contend with dangerous rapids along Miles Canyon through the Whitehorse rapids. Dozens of boats were wrecked and hundreds of people died. The Northwest Canadian Mounted Police introduced safety rules that required them to inspect the boats before they allowed them to proceed. Women and children were forbidden to travel through the rapids and had to walk around. Additional rules stated that any boat carrying passengers required a licensed pilot. To avoid paying the $25 fee to hire a pilot, some prospectors unpacked their boats and let them drift unmanned through the rapids and caught up with them on the other side. One enterprising individual built a horse-powered rail tramway to carry boats and equipment through the canyon, thus removing the need for the prospectors to navigate the rapids.

They arrived in Dawson only to find that they had suffered the hardships of the trail for nothing. These would-be prospectors had risked their lives and now there was no gold for them at the end of the trail. All the claims had been staked two years earlier. Feeling dejected and worse, many of them left Alaska and returned to their homes, but others stayed and found wealth in other enterprises. It has been said that more fortunes were made by entrepreneurs selling goods and services to the miners than was ever taken out of the gold fields.

In many ways, the gold rush had a major impact on the native population and on the environment. As the number of prospectors traveling over the passes increased, they greatly reduced the game the Indians depended on, especially the moose and caribou. Along the rivers of the interior, the steamboats needed wood for their boilers. The riverbanks were stripped of their trees, eliminating cover and driving the animals inland. In the mining districts, the streams were polluted with mercury and huge piles of tailings soon crowded out the vegetation and destroyed game habitats in and around the mines.

In the early days of the gold rush, many natives earned good money ferrying passengers and goods from the ships to the beaches, and they charged exorbitant fees to haul goods up the trails to the summits of the mountains. Steamboat captains hired Indians to cut wood along the riverbanks to provide fuel for their hungry boilers and to act as pilots to guide them through the ever-changing channels of the Yukon River. At each stop along the river, Indian women sold native arts and crafts to steamboat passengers to earn some ready cash.

As conditions in the towns changed, the whites stopped hiring Indians. As soon as they received their pay for services rendered, the Indians would often walk off the job and go into town to purchase the material goods they wanted and had come to depend on. The Indians would only return to work when they needed more of the white man's merchandise. Whites quickly and easily replaced them with their own people, thus creating economic hardships for the Indians. Large numbers of Indians continued to come into town for any job that might be available to them. When they couldn't find work, the men turned to alcohol and some of the women to prostitution. Missionaries attempted to lessen the impact of these vices, but in most cases were unsuccessful. Most whites saw the Indians as lazy drunks, and they became victims of racism, segregation, and discrimination.

The most devastating impact on the native people were the diseases the prospectors brought with them, diseases that were totally unknown to the Indians. Experts estimate that one-fourth of the native population died from an epidemic that swept through western and northern Alaska in 1900. At the same time, influenza and measles raged in other areas of the territory. In June of that year, measles struck the natives on St. Lawrence Island, killing scores of villagers. Doctors and U.S. Army personnel were helpless to stop the scourge. They ministered to the sick and dying, vaccinating those they could and burying the dead.

The stampede for gold that started in 1897 died a slow death. It began in the summer of 1898 when, arriving in Dawson, aspiring prospectors found they were unable to earn a living and many returned to the States. For those who stayed, wages were depressed and unemployment was rampant. The gold rush was old news and the newspapers lost interest in it. The Spanish-American War hogged the headlines. "Ah, go to the Klondike!" became a popular phrase to express disgust with an idea, and unsold Klondike-branded products had to be sold at huge discounts in Seattle.

Another factor in the death of the gold rush was that while Dawson had been a wild frontier town, it had changed from a ramshackle, wealthy boom town to a more sedate and conservative cosmopolitan community. The homes and businesses had modern luxuries including zinc bathtubs, pianos, billiard tables, Brussels carpet in the hotel dining rooms, and menus printed in French. The streets were paved and the inhabitants well-dressed and prosperous. The prospectors were used to a wilder way of life, and Dawson had become too civilized for them. Even Skagway had become a respectable and stable community.

The final nail in the coffin was the discovery of gold elsewhere in Canada and Alaska. During the winter of 1898–99, large deposits of gold were discovered in Nome at the mouth of the Yukon River, prompting a new stampede away from the Klondike. A flood of prospectors from across the region deserted the area and headed for Nome. The Klondike gold rush was over.

5

Alaska, the Last Frontier

The first forty years of American ownership of Alaska have been defined as a period of neglect and abuse by its citizens and the federal government. From the first day of the transfer of the territory from the Russians, a small number of residents were petitioning Congress for some form of civil government. However, Washington saw little reason to concern itself with a district that comprised 900 whites and 31,000 Indians. In 1880, the government hired someone of questionable character, Ivan Petroff, to conduct a census. Even though he could not have covered the entire territory, he reported a total population of 32,996 Indians and 400 whites.

The problem of a small population was compounded by many negative descriptions of the residents by visiting government agents. By 1880, the situation was virtually unchanged. William Morris, a representative of the Treasury Department, visited the territory. He reported, "There are in this country as God-abandoned and God-forsaken desperate and rascally a set of wretches as can be found on earth. Their whole life is made up of fraud, deceit, lying, and selling liquor to the Indians which they manufacture themselves."[1]

Over the years, Alaskans had held a series of political conventions that focused on sending a representative to the United States Congress. Their purpose was to lobby for representation in that august body and later to push for statehood and greater autonomy for Alaska. A nonpartisan group held their first convention in Juneau in 1881, where they elected to send a Democrat, W.D. Ball, to Congress. Although he was not recognized, the action helped to show Alaska's resolve that Washington must either take responsibility or legally pass that responsibility over to the territory to manage its own affairs.

Ball worked with Republican Senator Benjamin Harris of Indiana to craft the Organic Act,[2] which created the District of Alaska and provided for a civil government for the territory. It also provided for the appointment of a skeleton bureaucracy. Although it allowed for a school system, district and circuit courts, and the enforcement of mining laws, it had a number of shortcomings. All officials were appointed by the president, and it did not provide for an elected representative to speak for the people of Alaska. No provision was made for a system of land laws or the collection of taxes.

As Congressional legislation goes, the act was remarkable in its simplicity. However, it wasn't the simplicity of the act that caused problems. The problems were caused by the men who were appointed as officials under the terms of the act. Never before had so colorful a group of characters been given the authority govern a state or a territory. Alcoholism, fraud, incompetence, and mental irregularities were rampant at all levels of the new government. Less than a year after they received their appointments, Governor John Kirkead, Judge Ward McAllister, U.S. Attorney Edward Haskett, and U.S. Marshall Munson C. Hillyer were fired by President Grover Cleveland for a wide range of mistakes they had made including their final mistake. They had raised the ire of Presbyterian Minister Dr. Sheldon Jackson, the first general agent of education for Alaska.

The early years of the twentieth century were a time of great change for Alaska. Americans saw Alaska as the last frontier. The gold rush had painted a distorted picture of hardy prospectors who fought the elements and crossed snow-blasted, windswept mountains to make their fortunes in the gold fields of this vast unexplored territory. The image of the grizzled sourdough panning for gold in raging rivers was imprinted firmly in American minds. Alaska was the land of opportunity, but it was so much more than a land of mountains, glaciers, and snow-covered wilderness. From 1898 to 1938, no less than $1,887,941,309 in furs, minerals, and fish were taken out of Seward's Icebox and shipped to the States. In that same period, government's role in the affairs of Alaska expanded and evolved to meet the changing needs of its people.

Mail service was one of the first of many needs for the miners of the Yukon basin. The old saying that the mail must go through did not apply in Alaska. The immense distances, the inexperience of the mail carriers, and the severity of the weather often delayed the mail from reaching its intended recipient. One carrier's canoe was almost crushed in an ice jam and he nearly lost his life. In the spring when the ice melted, his mail was found 180 miles downriver. Eskimos used reindeer to carry mail in the far northwest. Over a period of time, reliable mail routes were established to carry the mail from Dawson to St. Michael, Valdez to Eagle, and over snow-covered trails from Kotzebue to Point Barrow, the northernmost point in Alaska. Finally, the dog sleds, kayaks, reindeer and other modes of delivering the mail were replaced by airplanes. Shortly after air mail service was established in the States, it was extended to cover the Alaskan mail routes, and in later years to carry passengers to remote villages.

As the territory changed, law and order and government influences in the lives of the people changed with it. Congress passed a number of new laws that included everything from fishing, mining, land ownership, taxes, and penalties for criminal offenses. The federal bureaucracy expanded significantly and became the focus of territorial complaints. Every department of the federal government had jurisdiction over the territory and there was a lack of cooperation and infighting between agencies as they strived to impose their rules and regulations on citizens of Alaska.

Prior to 1900, the Deady Code of Oregon was the law of the land. Named for Mathew Deady, a jurist and politician in the Oregon legislature, it was replaced with a criminal code in 1899 which imposed a tax on liquor, among other things, and a new civil code in 1900. With the enactment of these codes, taxes were imposed on businesses and individuals, the first taxes ever since the purchase of Alaska in 1867.

Until 1900, no one paid taxes on either land or income. Without a source of revenue, improvements to the infrastructure couldn't be undertaken. Millions of dollars were sent out of the territory without yielding one penny to the government for upgrading and building roads, bridges, or other necessary conveniences of civilization.

At the time there was no legislative body in the territory. The governor was appointed by the president and there were three judicial divisions with headquarters in Juneau, Nome, and Valdez. Land laws were antiquated and lagged behind this march of progress. Although the original Homestead Act was enacted in 1862, it was not possible to file on a homestead until an act of Congress extended the provisions of the act to Alaska in 1898. This extension also appropriated funds to establish agricultural stations to determine the territory's farming potential.[3] Like many Americans, Congress assumed that since the west was settled by farmers, Alaska would be too.

As stated in the Act, homesteaders were granted 80 acres of land, and it was up to the applicant to pay for the cost of a survey. Except for short stays off the land for medical reasons, part-time work, or short vacations, they were required to live on the land for a period of five years and cultivate at least one-eighth of their claim. The law also imposed additional requirements on the applicant.

1. Be 21 or older, or the head of a household, or served in the military.
2. Be a U.S. citizen or filed a declaration to become one.
3. Never borne arms against the United States or aided its enemies.
4. Live in a habitable dwelling. A tent does not count.

Single women could homestead if they were a head of household, but the rules were different for the two sexes. If a woman married, she could no longer claim the land in her own name separate from her husband. Together, they could have only one claim, with the majority of it under the husband's name. If a married woman became a widow, she could obtain the homestead of her deceased husband if he had not yet patented it. If a husband became disabled, causing the wife to take over as head of household, she could file in her name if neither one had previously filed.

Farming in Alaska was a poor choice, and those who tried were often defeated by the economics of scale. They quickly discovered the high cost of farm equipment, shelter, labor, utilities, feed for their animals, supplies, transportation, processing and marketing defeated any attempt to get their produce to the Alaskan consumer at a competitive price. This situation would improve drastically in later years as new roads were built and railroads allowed farmers to ship their crops to market, thereby lowering the cost of production.

In June 1900, the mining laws were amended. That same year, the coal land laws were enacted. In 1905, the capital was moved from Sitka to Juneau, and Congress created the Alaska Road Commission to provide for the construction and maintenance of roads. Congress also passed a law governing the care and custody of the insane. This law provided for the maintenance of the insane by sending them to asylums in Oregon.

The new laws allowed for the incorporation of towns, and many of them took advantage of the opportunities it afforded them. It required sixty residents of any community of at least three hundred residents to apply to the district judge to hold an incorporation election. The townspeople could then elect a city council with the power to collect any taxes they deemed necessary for the good of the town, including taxes on real and personal property. These taxes would give them the money to fund school districts, hire police, and provide for sanitation. Incorporation also allowed for a three-member school board with jurisdiction over the town's schools.

During the closing years of the nineteenth century, the boundary between the United States and British Columbia presented a major obstacle for cooperation between the two countries. Shortly after the transfer, Canada claimed the port of Skagway to control access to the Klondike. They stationed a Northwest Canadian Mounted police officer in town to show his authority. Dressed in full uniform, every morning at sunrise, he paraded along the docks and raised the Canadian flag over his office. The citizens of Skagway resented the flag waving in the breeze and cut it down, resulting in a confrontation with the officer. In 1899, the Canadians retaliated by stopping the Americans from hauling whiskey over the trails. The liquor was held at Skagway until cooler minds prevailed.

The treaty of 1825 between Great Britain and Russia laid out a line of demarcation along the southeast coast and described it as follows:

> [The line] shall ascend to the North along the channel called Portland Channel, as far as the point of the Continent where it strikes the 56th degree of North Latitude; from this last mentioned point the line of demarcation shall follow the summit of the mountains situated parallel to the coast, as far as the intersection of the 141st degree of West Longitude (of the same meridian); and finally, from the said point of intersection, the said Meridian Line of the 141st degree, in its prolongation as far as the Frozen Ocean.[4]

The only problem was that there wasn't any well-defined mountain chain that ran parallel to the coast within ten miles of what the treaty described as the extreme limits of the Russian possessions from the coast. White Pass at the head of Lynn Canal in Skagway became the focal point of the dispute. The issue was resolved when on January 24, 1903, the Alaskan Boundary Tribunal signed an agreement fixing the border between the two countries.

The Indians were another issue that Congress was forced to grapple with. The U.S. Army, the Department of the Interior, and other government agencies conducted surveys to determine the status of the native population. Each of these reports concluded that the encroachment of white settlements brought hardship to the Indians through disease, the use of alcohol, and unfair game laws. A Department of the Interior survey concluded that some sort of land allotment act would positively break down traditional Indian culture and speed up the process of acculturation.

Congress responded by passing the Alaska Native Allotment Act. It was modeled after the Dawes Severalty Act of 1887, which dealt with the Plains tribes in the States, and was designed to concentrate them on reservations far away from encroaching settlers. While the primary purpose of the Dawes Act was to force acculturation on the Indians and to break up their lands for distribution to white settlers, the Allotment Act had a different purpose. It afforded individual Alaska natives the opportunity to perfect legal title to lands they used and occupied. Few of the Indians were in a position to take advantage of the Act to acquire ownership of their land, perhaps because they were unfamiliar with and intimidated by government bureaucrats, and because the only federal officers across the territory at that time were school teachers.

The teachers played an important role in native acculturation, and though they were not official government land agents, they could and did advise the natives of their options, encouraging some and not others. The actions of the teachers and a few government officials determined which Indians qualified. They applied rigorous tests of eligibility and the potential impact they would have on the resources of the land. Only acculturated Indians were rewarded, others were not.

Every time Congress passed a new law, it brought a raft of complaints from angry citizens. They were denied representation in Washington, but Congress wasn't listening. Finally, after twenty-five years of petitions, their efforts paid off. On May 7, 1906, Congress gave the District of Alaska the authority to elect a congressional delegate. The first representative, Democrat Frank H. Waskey, served for four months and was replaced by an Independent, Thomas Cale. While their representative still had no vote in Washington, the Alaskans saw it as a step forward in their pursuit of self-rule.

One of the most important and influential politicians in the territory in his day was James Wickersham. Born in 1857, he studied law and was admitted to the bar. In 1883, he and his wife, Deborah, migrated to Tacoma, Washington, where he took up the practice of law. After serving as city attorney and probate judge, he was elected to the Washington State legislature. To reward him for his party loyalty, in 1900, President McKinley appointed Wickersham to the court in the new Third District of Alaska.

The Third District covered some 300,000 square miles and had no roads, no public buildings, and almost no U.S. currency. The district court and its officials were the only federal government in the interior of the territory. In addition to traveling the entire circuit, Wickersham was expected pay his own way and procure land and materials to construct his own courthouse and jails. It was fortunate that his duties included the collection of mercantile and saloon license fees because Congress failed to provide any funding for the construction and operation of the court. Wickersham resigned his judgeship in 1906 and in 1908 was elected Alaska's delegate to Congress. He was reelected four times and had a hand in almost every piece of legislation dealing with Alaska that Congress passed. He was a major force in shaping the destiny of Alaska in the early years of the twentieth century.

Congress continued to pass laws that regulated every aspect of daily life. For years, the citizens of Alaska had pushed for self-government, but there were a number of issues that had to be resolved first. In 1906, J.P. Morgan and Simon Guggenhiem formed the "Alaska Syndicate" to rape the territory of its mineral resources. In a short time, they controlled the Kennecott copper mine, steamship and railroad companies, oil interest, and salmon packing. Opposed to any further movement toward home rule, they employed lobbyists to influence Congress. Wickersham grew increasingly concerned over the exploitation of Alaska for personal and corporate interest, and he took it upon himself to fight for the people of his beloved territory. He used the Ballenger-Pinchot scandal to overcome the power and influence of the corporations.

The scandal was a major news story that involved favoritism, kickbacks and coal-mining in the administration of William Howard Taft, the 27th president of the United States. Ballenger was Secretary of the Interior and Pinchot was Curator of Forests within the department. Pinchot discovered that on the promise of substantial kickbacks, his boss had let out a series of no-bid contracts to companies intent on mining coal on federally protected land. Pinchot went to Taft and informed him of Ballenger's activities. Taft replied that what his secretary was doing was legitimate and that the contracts would stand.

Collier's magazine published an article accusing Ballenger of shady dealings in Alaska coal country. The article charged that the secretary improperly used his office to help the Guggenheim conglomerate and other powerful interest to illegally gain access to the Alaskan coal fields. Pinchot began to openly criticize Taft and Ballenger, claiming they were violating the fundamental principles of conservation and democracy. Livid with anger, Taft fired Pinchot, inspiring another round of scandalous headlines. Taft was forced to send a message to Congress insisting they listen to Wickersham and act on passage of the Second Organic Act. The act was passed on April 16, 1912. In 1916, as a delegate to Congress, Wickersham proposed the first bill for Alaskan statehood. The bill failed partly due to lack of interest among Alaskans for gaining statehood.

The Second Organic Act created the Territory of Alaska and gave to its people the first measure of self-government. After forty-five years of petitions and efforts by Wickersham and others, Alaska was granted a legislative assembly. The law spelled out the powers given to territorial governments, along with a long list of prohibitions. Local governments were not permitted to control matters pertaining to fish and game, borrow money, create counties, or deal with the management or disposal of land. Power to deal with natural resources, land and money would remain with the federal government, which was exactly what the fish and mining companies wanted. Such matters as divorce, gambling, liquor sales, and town incorporation were reserved for Congress. Any action by the legislature could be overridden by the Congress or vetoed by the governor. The legislature had limited power to tax its citizens and was nothing more than a paper tiger.

The Act specified that members were to be elected in even-numbered years and to sit in session for sixty days in March and April in odd-numbered years. Eight members of the Senate and two from each district were elected to four-year terms, and sixteen members of the House of Representatives, two each from four election districts, were elected at every election.

5. Alaska, the Last Frontier

The people of Alaska were angry with the Congress for the limitations that had been placed on them. In his opening remarks before the first session of the territorial legislature, Representative Charles Ingersoll of Ketchikan addressed the issue:

> Looking for substance, we find the shadow. Asking for bread, we get a stone. History repeats itself. When our fathers met to form the constitution of the United States, they felt the same distrust of the rank and file of the people that Congress has manifested in passing the Territorial Act. Between the lines there runs that careful trimming of the sails, the effort to avoid sunken reefs, that same distrust of permitting the common people to have a voice in the government.[5]

The following day, Wickersham addressed the legislature and responded to Ingersoll's remarks. He was stung by the criticism and he questioned his opponent's motives:

> Perhaps Ingersoll is in the pocket of the absentee fishing companies who naturally object to any efforts to protect fishermen and prevent exploitation of fishing resources. It is as good a bill as the people of any territory have had. It gave Alaska home rule without the expenditure of a nickel.[6]

For all of the complaints about its limitations and lack of power, the legislature passed 84 bills. They gave women the right to vote and instituted a $4 head tax on all men between 21 and 50 who were not volunteer firemen. The amended mining laws and passed laws to regulate the banks, made school attendance compulsory, and allowed local governments to create and enforce rules for health and sanitation. Legislators approved an eight-hour day for hard rock miners, but not for placer miners or women. They approved plans for an Alaska Pioneers' Home designed to help poor prospectors. In their final action of the session, they made two requests of Congress: build a railroad to make Alaska more accessible, and ban the use of fishing traps.

Prohibition came to Alaska in 1915. The legislature asked their constituents if they wanted to ban the manufacture and sale of liquor in the territory. Alaskans were generally of the same opinion as their counterparts in the States. The United States Congress was moving toward passing the 18th Amendment, which mandated prohibition, and Alaska was moving in the same direction. Alaska Governor John Strong believed the citizens of the territory would vote for it. In 1916, the vote passed by a more than two-to-one margin. The only places that didn't vote to go dry were Eagle, St. Michael, and the nearly abandoned town of Chena near Fairbanks.

Governor Strong was convinced that granting women the right to vote in 1913 had been critical in the campaign against alcohol. Wickersham said the anti-liquor sentiment was due to the dissatisfaction with the way saloons were being run, and they were regarded as a menace to many people. The results of the vote were sent to the Congress, which still held the power to make laws about liquor for Alaska. It honored the wishes of the people, and the ban became law at the start of 1918.

The building of the railroads from White Pass and the Yukon to the completion of the Alaska Railroad wrought major changes to the entire system of transportation in the Yukon Valley. Where the river system was locked in ice from October to May, boats were replaced by trains, motorized vehicles, and airplanes. A trail that took a month by dog sled could now be traversed in a matter of hours.

These changes in transportation were hastened by the outbreak of World War I and the need to draw the miners from the gold fields to the battlefields of Europe. More Alaskans went to the front in proportion to the population than from any state in the Union. Men from remote villages answered the call or were drafted into the army.

As the war raged in Europe, the War Fund and the Red Cross needed money and the natives were generous in their response. From the villages of southeastern Alaska they sent $12,320 for war relief, $9,700 for war bonds and $280 for saving stamps. The Eskimos at Point Barrow donated hundreds of pounds of eiderdown for comfort pillows for the soldiers. The natives of White Mountain gave everything they had: $100 they had saved toward the purchase of a sawmill for their village.[7]

The influenza epidemic of 1917 took its toll on Alaska. Without medical assistance, medicines, or proper accommodations in remote villages to care for the sick and dying, entire communities perished from the disease. Some 1,500 people died on Seward Peninsula, and at Unalaska and Bristol Bay, 258 orphans were all that survived of a population of 1,000 residents. By the time the outbreak was over, more than 2,000 people died from its touch.[8]

6

Prelude to War

War came to Alaska in 1942, and this corner of the conflict has often been called the forgotten war. In the context of global war it was relatively small: 300,000 Americans, Canadians, and Russians faced battle-hardened troops of the Japanese Imperial Army and drove them out of the Aleutians. This was the only campaign of an international war to be fought on American soil since the War of 1812.

Military planners considered Alaska the "Achilles heel" of our national defense. Historian C.L. Andrews stated, "One of the pressing reasons for Russia's 'gift' of Alaska to the United States was that to retain the land with its sparse population was an expense in time of peace and a menace in time of war, for both men and ships would be required for its protection."

Concerned with Japan's expanding empire and its growing military dominance in Asia, the U.S. Government felt a strong need to increase its military presence in Alaska. American strategists realized that the shortest and most direct route between Japan and the West Coast of the United States followed the Great Circle Route near Alaska's shoreline.

Testifying before the U.S. House of Representatives and its Committee on Military Affairs in 1935, General Billy Mitchell urged Congress to buy airplanes and equipment with which to survey and defend the extended reaches of U.S. territories. In his last public appearance before he died, Mitchell pleaded with Congress to recognize the strategic importance of Alaska. He said, "Japan is our dangerous enemy in the Pacific. They won't attack Panama. They will come right here to Alaska. Alaska is the most central place in the world for aircraft, and that is true either of Europe, Asia, or North America. I believe that, in the future, whoever holds Alaska will hold the world.... I think it is the most strategic place in the world."[1]

The legislators ignored Mitchell's warnings. America was in the middle of the Great Depression, and Congress had more immediate issues to contend with. As far as they were concerned, Alaska was a sparsely populated, largely unknown territory, and it was too far away to worry about.

In 1937, Alaska's Congressional representative, Anthony Diamond, echoed Mitchell's warnings when he told Congress:

> Alaska today could be taken almost overnight by a hostile force. It is today without any form of defense. At least $450 million have been spent in the defensive installations [at Pearl Harbor and Hickam Field in Hawaii] and yet the inescapable conclusion to be drawn from the most casual inspection of the globe ... is that, so far as the main body of the United States is concerned, the defense of Alaska is of much greater consequence than those all but impregnable defensive works [in Hawaii].... What's the use of locking one door and leaving another wide open?[2]

Congress was slow to act. Three years later, nothing had changed. Territorial Governor Ernest Gruening expressed his frustration when he said, "A handful of enemy parachutists could capture Alaska overnight."

Gruening knew how ill-prepared Alaska was to defend itself. He had inspected the territory's defenses and visited Checkout Barracks on the Canadian border. It hadn't changed much in the forty years since it had been built to guard the gold trail to the Klondike. It housed four hundred soldiers with World War I rifles, and military discipline was lax. The only artillery piece in Alaska was an old Russian cannon filled with flowers. Remembering his visit to Checkout Barracks, in 1969, Gruening said:

> Checkout Barracks had about as much relevance to modern warfare as one of the frontier Indian-fighting posts from the days of Custer and Sitting Bull. It had no road or air connection with the outside world. Its only transportation was provided by a 51-year-old harbor tug. When we went up the Lynn Canal, the terminal fjord of the inside passage, we encountered a 30 knot headwind that stopped us cold and stranded us for three days. We had to be rescued by the Coast Guard. If war had come, we'd have to sue for peace and ask for a wind check.[3]

As Japan's belligerence grew, Congress provided funding for a military buildup. In 1939 and 1940, the U.S. military established forts and airfields in Anchorage and Fairbanks. They constructed naval air stations, destroyer bases, and submarine pens in Sitka, Kodiak, and Dutch Harbor. In eighteen months, Alaska's military population expanded dramatically from 1,000 soldiers to 35,000 troops. The civilian population also grew as contractors and a robust economy near these new military posts provided employment for thousands of construction workers.

Joseph Driscoll, a reporter for the *New York Herald Tribune*, spent most of 1942 touring these new bases and forts and interviewing everyone from generals and admirals in charge of operations, to privates and ordinary seamen, to territorial officials, to Aleuts, Eskimos, Indians, and the white man in the street. In his book, *War Discovers Alaska*, he wrote:

> I lunched with the Army; I dined with the Navy; and I had nightcaps with the Governor of the territory. I saw and heard more things than it would be wise to print. Much information was given to me in confidence which I must respect.
>
> What I can tell you is that Alaska is ready, ready to defend herself, ready to carry the war across the Bering Sea and down to Tokyo itself. But there is a catch, a joker, to Alaska's preparedness to victory. Alaska's degree of readiness is conditioned by what we in the States, in Albany and Keokuk and Topeka and Washington, D.C., think about Alaska and what role we assign to her in what is more truly a world war than the fracas of 1914–1918.
>
> If Alaska is to be forgotten once more, to be left to "mingled skill and chance," with the accent on chance, well then, Alaska is doomed to humiliation and disaster. But if we recognize Alaska for what it is, the first fighting front in the Americas, a bridge to Asia and the most convenient jumping-off place for Tokyo, we will fly all the planes we can spare into Alaska and we will blast Japan in the shortest possible time.[4]

To support these installations, and to transport much-needed supplies and equipment, the Army built a primitive road known as the Alcan Highway (Alaska Highway) through the Canadian and Alaskan wilderness from Northern Alberta to the Richardson Highway at Delta, Alaska. At the same time, they constructed a road (present-day Glen Highway) to link Anchorage to the Alcan. Alaska was at last ready to go to war.

7

War Comes to Alaska

In the struggle for naval supremacy in the Pacific theater of war, the Aleutian Islands were strategically valuable to both the United States and the Empire of Japan. On a map of the world, the Aleutian Chain provided a natural path for the Japanese army to attack Alaska, Canada, and the west coast of the United States. It also provided stepping stones for the United States to launch attacks on the Kurile Islands and the Japanese mainland. Neither side considered the forbidding weather and wretched terrain of this natural route.

In addition to creating a diversion to trap the U.S. fleet at Midway, the invasion and occupation of the Aleutians by enemy forces appeared to have other purposes. In secret intelligence memorandum No. 8, issued by the Headquarters of the Western Defense Command and Fourth Amy in San Francisco,[1] Colonel John Weckerling wrote:

> This report is a summary of all combat intelligence information as it pertains to the enemy operations on ATTU, chiefly during the period from 20 October 1942 to 31 May 1943, the date on which our forces completed the occupation of the island. This report is based on the following sources. Prisoner of war interrogation reports; translation of captured enemy documents; reports, studies and sketches prepared by the A.C. of S. A2 Eleventh Air Force; and Observer's reports.
>
> It is estimated that the enemy seized ATTU and KISKA for the purpose of: a. observation in the Aleutians area; b. disruption of lend lease supply system between RUSSIA and the UNITED STATES and c. establishment of bases for further offensive operations in the Aleutian-Alaska area. The enemy apparently abandoned ATTU from about 20 September 1942 to 20 October 1942 leading to the conclusion that there was a complete change of plans regarding the ultimate purpose of the ATTU base.
>
> That the enemy never exhibited any particular determination to improve the ATTU and Kiska bases and was very dilatory in the construction of proper facilities for the basing of land-based aircraft, coupled with the lack of enemy naval strength in the Aleutian area, leaves to the assumption that the enemy is

not giving the Aleutians theatre a very high priority. The conclusion can also be drawn that he lacked the necessary equipment, material, planes, and naval forces required to adequately exploit his holdings in the Aleutians.

JOHN WECKERLING
Colonel, G.S.C.
A.C. of S., G-2

Following the attack on Pearl Harbor, Admiral Yamamoto was convinced that with their limited resources, Japan could not hope to defeat the United States in a war that might drag on for years. Having spent considerable time in the States, he knew Japan couldn't match the productivity and industrial might of America to manufacture enough ships, planes, armament, and munitions to win the war.

Yamamoto knew there was only one option for victory available to the Japanese if the Empire was to prevail. If he could destroy American naval power in the Pacific and the four American carriers that had missing from Pearl Harbor during the attack, Japan would gain naval superiority. His government could then negotiate a peace treaty that would prohibit political and military interference by the United States in the affairs of the expanded Japanese Empire and its sphere of economic influence over its captive subjects.

The Japanese High Command disagreed with Yamamoto's assessment of the situation. Emboldened by their successes in the South Pacific, they argued that the invasion of Australia should proceed as planned. Yamamoto argued that the destruction of the American Navy was paramount. The issue was decided for them when on April 18, 1942, General Doolittle's Raiders took the enemy by surprise and dropped their bombs on Tokyo.

Perplexed by the attacks that they thought could never happen, staff officers studied their maps in an effort to determine where those planes came from. Some officers argued that the planes must have come from carriers, while others believed that since they were land-based twin engine bombers that were too large to be launched from carriers, they must have come from secret bases in the Aleutians or mainland Alaska. It wasn't until the end of the war that the Japanese learned the truth.

By the spring of 1942, the Japanese army occupied the Philippines, Malaysia, and the Dutch East Indies. Australia and New Zealand were virtually defenseless. The main Allied supply lines extended across the Pacific from America to Australia and the imperial staff wanted to isolate them. On March 12, 1942, Japanese Prime Minister Hideki Tojo issued the following statement:

> Australia and New Zealand are now threatened by the might of the Imperial forces and both of them should know that any resistance is futile. If the

Australian government does not modify her present attitude, their continent will suffer the same fate as the Dutch East Indies.²

Japan's military planners were divided over the need to invade Australia or to engage and destroy the American fleet. With the possibility that Doolittle's planes may have actually come from carriers, the imperial staff agreed that before they could extend their defensive perimeter outward from Rabaul in New Britain, Yamamoto must first neutralize the American aircraft carriers. To isolate Australia and draw the American fleet into battle, the imperial staff approved plans for a three pronged operation:

1. Occupy Tulagi in the southern Solomon Islands in order to establish a naval air base to control the northern part of the Coral Sea. Follow this with a landing at Port Moresby in southeast New Guinea so as to bring Northern Australia within range of Japanese aircraft.
2. Carry out an overwhelming attack on Midway and occupy strategic points in the Aleutian Islands to trigger a decisive naval battle.
3. Once these two operations are complete, overrun the Fiji and Samoan Islands in order to cut off the lifeline from the United States to Australia.³

Yamamoto immediately put "Operation MO" (Japanese code designation for Port Moresby) into action. Commanded by Vice Admiral Shigeyoshi Inoue, the operation included two seaborne invasion forces, one to land troops at Port Moresby on the southern tip of New Guinea, and the second one to put troops ashore on the island of Tulagi in the southern Solomons. They were supported by a task force consisting of fifteen destroyers, nine cruisers, two fleet carriers, *Shokaku* and *Zuikaku,* and one light carrier, *Shoho*, assigned to provide air cover for the invasion fleet.

American intelligence had already broken the Japanese naval codes and were fully aware of the movements of the enemy's combined fleet. In April 1942, the code breakers sent a message to the commander of the Pacific Fleet, Admiral Chester Nimitz, advising him of the presence of the enemy task force. To counter the threat, Nimitz deployed Rear Admiral Frank J. Fletcher's Task Force 17 with the carriers *Lexington* and *Yorktown,* and a joint Australian-American cruiser force to the Coral Sea to search out and destroy the enemy invasion fleet advancing on Port Moresby.

On May 3, Japanese forces successfully invaded and occupied Tulagi. In a surprise raid the next morning, planes from the *Yorktown* sank or damaged a number of ships covering the invasion. Now that they were aware of the presence of American carriers in the area, the Japanese fleet entered the Coral Sea with the intention of destroying Allied naval forces.

The first confrontation between the two opposing forces occurred on May 7 when Fletcher attacked the invasion force and sank the light carrier

Shoho. In a southerly position some distance away from the American fleet, Japanese dive bombers sank the U.S. oiler *Neosho* and the destroyer USS *Simms*. The following day, the Americans launched a massive air assault on the Japanese and inflicted heavy damage to the fleet carrier *Shokaku*. In turn, Japanese bombs and torpedoes sank the *Lexington* and severely damaged the *Yorktown*. With both sides suffering heavy losses in aircraft and ships sunk or damaged, the two fleets withdrew from the area. Because the Japanese carriers could no longer provide air cover, Vice Admiral Inoue canceled the invasion of Port Moresby.

The Battle of the Coral Sea may have been a tactical victory for the Japanese in the number of ships sunk, but it was a strategic victory for the Allies. They had thwarted the enemy's plans to invade Port Moresby and cut the supply lines from America to Australia. More importantly, the Japanese were denied the use of their carriers *Shokaku* and *Zuikaku* in the upcoming Battle of Midway.

Yamamoto's next targets were the Aleutians and Midway and the destruction of American naval power in the Pacific. In his view, the capture of Midway would give the Japanese a base of operations in the Central Pacific to expand their empire and provide a forward outpost to warn of future threats from the American navy.

Yamamoto's plan called for the deployment of multiple task forces to Alaska to strike a decisive blow at Dutch Harbor while imperial troops occupied Adak, Kiska, and Attu. This would protect their northern flank and enable them to build a staging area for bomber attacks on Canada, Russia, and the American mainland. The invasion of the Aleutians would then be followed by the successful invasion and occupation of Midway.

Yamamoto believed that as soon as his planes dropped their first bombs on the facilities at Dutch Harbor, the American fleet would steam north from Pearl Harbor to Alaska. His carriers and battleships would be lying in wait several miles west of Midway to ambush the unsuspecting Americans. On May 5, 1942, the Imperial General Headquarters issued Navy Order Number 18 directing Yamamoto to carry out the occupation of Midway Island and key points in the western Aleutians in cooperation with the Army.

American code breakers knew the enemy planned to attack Midway and the Aleutians sometime in May or June, 1942. With his men and equipment spread over thousands of miles of ocean, Admiral Chester Nimitz, commander in chief of the Pacific Fleet, faced serious logistic problems. Supplying war materials to Allied forces in Europe took first priority over combat forces in the Pacific.

The defenses of Midway and the Aleutians were totally inadequate to stave off a determined enemy. Approximately 5 miles in diameter, Midway is a pair of small flat islands enclosed in a nearly circular coral reef. Limited manpower and equipment, and the topography of the islands, combined to make Midway all but impossible to defend. While Alaska was important, as far as the War Department was concerned it came last in defense priorities after Hawaii and the Panama Canal.

Alaska defense commander General Simon B. Buckner, Jr., disagreed. In its present state, Alaska was hopelessly unprepared for war. His command was limited to a few remote airfields guarded by a small number of outdated bombers and fighters. His navy consisted of a small fleet of World War I destroyers and unseaworthy wooden boats. If he was to defend Alaska from the Japanese, he would need additional manpower and equipment for his Army garrisons.

In Hawaii, the Joint Chiefs of Staff met in an emergency session to discuss the enemy's plans and decide on a course of action. Officers who'd served in Alaska preferred to let the enemy have the Aleutians. The horrendous winter storms that battered these islands would quickly take their toll on the enemy. It would be extremely difficult to maintain and supply a coherent fighting force with enough manpower and equipment to defend their bases of operation. Given the remoteness of the Aleutian Islands, and the enemy's intentions to expand their empire in the Pacific, they believed that Midway was strategically more important than a string of barren, windswept islands in the Bering Sea.

German U-boats had sunk so many convoys in the North Atlantic that military planners believed the next best route for shipping lend-lease equipment to Russian ports in Siberia was through the narrow straits of Umnak Pass. In their opinion, the ships would be protected from enemy attacks by the guns of Dutch Harbor. They argued that that if the Allies abandoned the Aleutians and allowed Dutch Harbor to fall to the enemy, it would become a staging area for the enemy to invade mainland Alaska and cut the sea lanes to Siberia.

The Joint Chiefs listened to both sides of the argument and concluded that the lend-lease route to Russia was too important to America's defense to be abandoned. In anticipation of orders from Washington, Nimitz took matters into his own hands. On May 21, 1942, he dispatched five cruisers and four destroyers under the command of Admiral Robert A. Theobald to Alaska to intercept the enemy. He directed Theobald to be governed by "the principle of calculated risk," which some of Theobald's staff took to mean that in an encounter with the enemy, the task force was to sacrifice itself if it would stop the Japanese from occupying Dutch Harbor: "You will be governed by the principle of calculated risk, which you shall interpret to mean avoidance of exposure of your force to attack by superior enemy forces without good prospect of inflicting greater damage on the enemy."[4]

On May 25, Theobald received a dispatch from CINCPAC informing him that a task force had sailed from Japan and an attack on the Aleutians may be imminent.

25 May 1942
FROM: CINCPAC
TO: COMNORPACFOR
THE JAPANESE HAVE COMPLETED PLANS FOR AN AMPHIBOUS OPERATION TO SECURE AN ADVANCED BASE IN THE ALEUTIAN ISLANDS ... FOLLOWING ESTIMATED JAPANESE TASK FORCE HAS LEFT JAPAN WITH PROBABLE OBJECTIVE ALEUTIAN ISLANDS AND/OR ALASKA 2 AIRCRAFT CARRIERS, 2–3 SEAPLANE TENDERS, 3 HEAVY CRUISERS, 2 LIGHT CRUISERS, 12 DESTROYERS, 8 SUBMARINES, HEAVY BOMBERS, (PROBABLY FLYING BOAT TYPE) AND TRANSPORTS AND CARGO VESSELS ... ON MAY 25 THE ABOVE FORCES WILL ARRIVE IN NORTHERN JAPAN, FUEL, AND PROCEED TO THE ALEUTIANS.[5]

On May 15, 10 days before CINCPAC sent the dispatch, the task force sailed from Ominato, Japan, to Dutch Harbor. The Japanese planned to launch a surprise attack, but a PBY scout plane spotted the fleet and radioed their position to U.S. Naval Headquarters in Kodiak. Since Dutch Harbor didn't have any runways, army engineers built secret emergency airstrips at nearby Cold Bay Harbor and Umnak Island.

Expecting to pull off the same kind of surprise they had achieved at Pearl Harbor, on June 3, the Japanese launched a massive airstrike against Dutch Harbor. They were surprised to discover that the Americans were waiting for them and subsequent attacks were beaten back. With the element of surprise gone, and with assaults from American fighter planes, heavy flak, and arctic storms, the enemy withdrew and sailed west.

No one knew where the enemy would strike next. Foggy weather and poor radio communications made it impossible for Theobald's ships to find the elusive fleet. While they were searching for the task force in the Bering Sea near the Pribilof Islands, the Imperial Northern Force landed 2,500 soldiers on Kiska and Attu.

In the early morning hours of June 7, 1942, the first platoon of the Special Landing Force went ashore at Kiska, followed by 1,250 Japanese soldiers. A steady rain muffled their movements. They moved through the canyons with lightning speed and advanced on an American radio shack.

Navy Aerographer's Mate Charles House was in charge of the ten-man weather team stationed on Kiska. He thought he was having a nightmare when Walter Winfrey screamed in pain.

"Quit yelling and go back to sleep," House shouted sleepily.

"So what am I doing with a bullet in my leg?" Winfrey yelled.[6]

Japanese 13-mm machine guns slugs rained down on the cabin and splintered the walls. Diving for cover, the sailors wormed their way across the floor to the door. Hoping to find concealment in the heavy fog, eight of the sailors crawled into the brush on their bellies. House and J.L. Turner stayed behind to burn vital code books and smash their radio transmitter. While bullets riddled the radio shack and tore the walls to ribbons, the two men slipped outside and hid in the brush.

Their little dog, Explosion, ran outside, yapping at the enemy. Ensign William C. Jones had brought him to Kiska from Dutch Harbor to keep the sailors company. No one knows how Explosion survived the war, but more than likely he was adopted and cared for by Japanese soldiers.

"The Japanese were firing as we took off," House said. We could see their tracers coming in like baseballs. We kept running and falling. I fell to the ground and heard a loud thumping noise. I thought it was the footsteps of the Japanese. It was my heart beating."[7]

The Americans became separated in the rain and fog. Winfrey and another man were captured immediately. In a makeshift operating room in a hastily erected tent on the beach, a surgeon removed the bullet from Winfrey's leg. A short time later, Japanese patrols captured all but one of the fugitives. They had found the Americans' buried emergency cache and staked it out to wait for the sailors to give themselves up.

House was the last holdout. With 110 square miles of rugged mountains and caves, he had plenty of places to hide. He found a cave on the far side of the island and made a bed of grass and a blanket he carried from his quarters.

"It was very cozy," House said. "A nice spot with a creek."[8]

Evading Japanese patrols and avoiding bombs from American planes, he kept himself alive with a diet of tundra grass and worms, and shellfish he found along the beach. On occasion, House saw American B-17s circling overhead and making bomb runs on the enemy. Attacked by cold, hunger, and the wild Aleutian weather, sapped of his strength, on the 49th day of his ordeal, this twenty-nine-year-old American decided to surrender.

"I didn't like the idea, but my health was ruined," said House. "I held out as long as I could."[9]

House tied part of his underwear to a stick of driftwood and walked slowly through the fog into the Japanese camp. Waving his white flag, he approached a Japanese antiaircraft gun crew. They took him into custody and gave him biscuits and tea. Their mood changed when a B-17 flew over the gun emplacement. They fired at the plane, but they missed.

"Then the officer in charge was in a nasty mood," House said. "Jabbing me with bayonets, they started walking me down to their old camp."[10]

A long brown beard covered his sunken cheeks and his clothes were in rags. He weighed less than a hundred pounds and resembled a walking skeleton. As His strength returned, House was put to work filling sandbags and digging sod for camouflage. During one major air raid, the Japanese permitted House to crawl into a tunnel with them.

"You are a lucky man," a Japanese officer said later. One of the American bombs had made a direct hit on House's bunk in the camp powerhouse.

According to House, on September 29, he was placed aboard the *Nagata Maru* and told he was going to Japan. He stated that 39 Aleuts from Chichagof Village on Attu, including the chief of the village, Mike Hodikoff, were also on board the ship. House's memory of the date of his departure from Kiska, the name of the ship, and who sailed with him appears to be incorrect. Witnesses and Japanese records indicate that House and the Aleuts sailed from Kiska on the *Osada Maru* on or about September 19.[11]

Not long after his arrival in Japan, House was forced to work in a shipyard near Yokohama. He contracted diphtheria, and unable to perform his assigned task, he was thrown in a corner and left to die. His life was saved when a Japanese doctor and an official from the Swiss Red Cross came through the camp. They decided House should receive medical treatment at the camp hospital. He was nursed back to health and survived the war. At the end of the war, House and his nine shipmates from Kiska were released and returned home. House retired from the Navy with the rank of lieutenant commander in 1966.

8

Blood on the Sand

The occupation of Attu was an important step in Admiral Yamamoto's plan to destroy American naval power in the Pacific and prevent the United States from using the bases in the Aleutians to attack the Japanese mainland. While Yamamoto's staff was drawing up plans for the attacks on Midway and the Aleutians, on May 5, 1942, the Imperial High Command issued its own plans which explained how the occupation of Attu was to be carried out. The plan called for the occupying army to remove the native residents of Attu to the Japanese homeland and the troops to withdraw from the island to their base in the Kuriles. They would return to the Aleutians in the spring to reoccupy the islands.

The Japanese military had studied the Aleutians for years, but their intelligence was inaccurate. It was based on information from fishermen who had visited every harbor in Alaska and every island in the Aleutian chain. That they visited these isolated islands is evidenced by the remains of their campfires and other debris.

One of the many tools the Japanese military strategists may have employed to gather information was the goodwill flight to America in 1939. It is now believed that it was used not to promote international fellowship, but to survey the Aleutian chain and bombing routes to Alaska and the United States.

The Nippon round-the-world flight was sponsored by the *Maionichi* newspaper in Osaka, Japan. At the ceremony where the plane was named, the president of the newspaper, Nobutaro Okumura, introduced the crew and its goodwill ambassador, Takeo Ohara, to His Imperial Highness, Prince Morimasa Nashimoto. Ohara was the official Japanese envoy and goodwill ambassador and the only passenger on this round-the-world flight.

On one occasion, a Japanese naval mission steamed into Attu Harbor and went ashore to inspect the island. Once ashore, they encountered a solitary

8. Blood on the Sand

Aerial view of Chichagof Village, Attu, the westernmost island in the Aleutian chain, circa 1920. On orders from their headquarters, the Japanese army burned the village to the ground when they evacuated the villagers and their troops and equipment to Kiska on August 25, 1942 (673rd Air Base Wing History Office Joint Base Elmendorf-Richardson, Alaska).

white trader who welcomed them with traditional American hospitality. They told the trader that they had come there to welcome the goodwill flight, which was due to fly over at any time.

They set up their tents on the beach and for the next two months they tramped all over the island, exploring and taking soundings of the adjacent waters. They made a complete survey of the island, noting its topography and weather conditions.

At the end of two months, they broke camp, packed up their tents and equipment, and prepared to leave the island. After informing the trader that the goodwill flight wasn't coming, they presented him with gifts, shook his hand in a fond farewell, and sailed for home. They had accomplished their mission, which had nothing to do with goodwill or international fellowship.

By invitation of the United States government, in 1936, a Japanese scientific mission landed at Bristol Bay. The bay is situated slightly north of Dutch Harbor and east of the Pribilof Islands and was considered one of the most lucrative salmon fishing grounds in the world. The fact that in one month its canneries could pack forty-eight million pounds of Alaskan salmon made it a prime target for Japan with its millions of hungry mouths to feed. Even though the Japanese did have a few scientists in their landing party at Bristol Bay, most of them were naval officers. For days, they had the run of the place, to see and hear and gather information.

In the next four years, these pseudo-scientists petitioned the U.S. government to allow them to inspect ports and industries all the way down the Alaskan coast to Juneau, Sitka, Petersburg, and Ketchikan. United States representatives of the International Fishing Commission became suspicious of these activities and protested to government officials in Washington. As a result of these protests, the U.S. government no longer extended invitations or cooperation, thereby putting the brakes on further Japanese espionage.

Reconnaissance reports from submarines and aircraft in the area were often incorrect. One such report indicated that Kiska was occupied by 10 Aleuts raising foxes, and 200 to 300 U.S. troops. Forty natives resided on Attu. After the invasion, the Japanese learned there were no military forces on Attu.

In the initial planning stages of the invasion, the planners believed that due to harsh climatic conditions, the winters in the Aleutians were too severe to permit their troops to remain throughout the year. They concluded that in the event of a temporary withdrawal, it would be inadvisable to leave the islanders on Attu. They'd be an invaluable source of intelligence for the Americans and they feared that the Attuans might commence a guerrilla war against the Japanese army when they returned in the spring.

Within hours of landing on Kiska, Rear Admiral Sentara Omori sailed into Holtz Bay. The ships swept the bay for mines and when the all clear was given, Omori dispatched a reconnaissance party onto the beaches. They expected to encounter a heavy concentration of American soldiers, but opposition from the enemy was nonexistent. Omori landed 2,000 troops on the beach and they traveled three miles over rough mountains to the village of Chichagof.

Omori's orders were to cross the island and occupy the village. Due to faulty intelligence and a lack of maps of the interior of the island, Omori's troops became lost in the heavy fog. Some of them almost starved before they found their way to the village. In describing these events in *ArushanShuhekI SenkI* (*Attack on the Aleutians*), Mikado Fukazawa wrote:

> The troops split into two parties, a forward scouting party and the main force. Both groups were to move into Chichagof. However, the forward scout party became lost due to poor maps, and marched to a hill overlooking Massacre Bay. The mistake was immediately realized and the party returned to Chichagof, arriving at the west peak, overlooking the village at about 7:30 the same morning. The main force had already reached the village.[1]

Chichagof Village, Attu, Aleutian Islands, 1934 (U.S. Navy).

The Japanese saw themselves as liberators of an oppressed people. Their records paint a picture of an invading army that cared for the welfare of the natives. Witnesses who were present during the occupation and subsequent internment in Japan often tell a far different story. In many instances, the invaders left out any mention of the brutality they imposed on their captives. Japanese records often contradict the truth and are at odds with eyewitness accounts. Different versions are presented here for comparison.

The Attuans had just attended a church service and were returning to their homes when they glanced up at the mountains. They were horrified to see armed men in unfamiliar uniforms, shrieking in loud voices, shooting their guns, and charging down the snow-covered slopes. Soldiers slipped and fell on the icy terrain and some of their comrades were killed or wounded by random bullets. The villagers were intimidated and consumed with sheer terror. They gathered up their frightened families and barricaded themselves in their homes while the gunfire and yelling continued.

Attu native Olean Prokopeuff has strong memories of the attack:

> The year 1942, on a Sunday morning, the Japanese Armed Forces came and captured us. They came from the interior of our island after day-break. That morning, a Japanese airplane flew around the village three times. The teacher [Etta Jones] was informed of this by the villagers. Instead of informing the authorities, the teacher told the villagers that there were lots of American patrol

planes patrolling this area. After the teacher told them that, the villagers felt secure.

After they came down from the hills, it was said that our village was surrounded.

After that, the villagers went up to the observation hill and saw the Japanese fleet anchored in the bay on the other side. As they were attacking in force, one of our ladies was shot in the leg. As they were firing their weapons in all directions during their assault, their forces also hit their own men and it is believed that a few of their own men had been killed.[2]

The Imperial Army entered the village and the inhabitants were panic-stricken. They were confused and some of them hid in their homes or ran into the hills. When they realized the gunfire wasn't aimed at them, they came out of their houses with their hands over their heads. Even the natives who ran into the hills came back into the village. A woman identified as Annie Hodikoff was hit in the thigh by gunfire. After the attack, she received medical attention

Aleuts at Killsnoo, 1942. (Left to right) Andrew Snigaroff, Nick Prokopeuff, Constantine Golley, and William Dirks (Sonny). Photograph by Don Prokopeuff (APIA P225, courtesy Aleutian/Pribilof Islands Association).

for her wound. She succumbed to her injury on board ship while being transported to Japan.

Olean's account of these events differed from the Japanese account:

> After we arrived at the school, when a fire was made outside, I was afraid that the school house was going to be set afire with all of us in there. Since we weren't being set on fire, we were asked if we were all present. We stated that three of our young men were out. They waited for the young men to come back to the village, but there was no sign of them. The young men did not return from hiding until some of the village men went out and escorted them back to the village. Only then did they return.[3]

There were 42 natives and two Americans, Foster Jones and his wife Etta, living in the village. Married on April 21, 1923, the Joneses taught classes at a number of Indian schools in Alaska and had arrived in Chichagof in August 1941. Foster was a large man of 63 years at the time of the attack and was assigned to Attu as a communications and weather technician. In addition to sending routine weather reports to the mainland, he was responsible for keeping watch along the coast for enemy activity. Etta was described as a chubby, middle-aged woman who worked as a nurse for many years on the Alaskan mainland.

Once the shooting started, Foster opened the door and stepped out of the shack. He was surprised to see the troops coming over the mountain. He rushed back inside and immediately sent an emergency message to his headquarters.

In his article Attsu To ("Attu Island"), Tomoya Tsuria described his impressions of the attack:

> The village was sighted (by the invasion force of the Imperial Army) from a distance of 1000 meters. After the attack on the village had commenced, a large "American" appeared from the communication post. He took 5 or 6 steps from the beach, and then turned toward us. It was then that he first realized that the village was being attacked from the mountains and not the beach. He quickly ran back into the building. The troop commander noticed that he was an old man.
> "Open Fire. Fire warning shots."
> The troops opened fire with light and heavy machine guns, but only to intimidate the occupants of the village, not to wound or kill.
> "Attack." The order to advance reverberated across the tundra, and a group of soldiers hurried to the building containing the communication equipment. Another corps, which had already surrounded the village, began to close in.
> The "American" came out of the communication station, holding his hands above his head. The soldiers realized that he was not on combat duty. The corps commander ran up to the old man, and held his military sword to the old man's chest as he handed the man an ultimatum printed in English. The old man ran his eyes over the ultimatum. After having read it, he mumbled something unintelligible, lowered his hands and then saluted.

The natives began to come out of their houses, hands held high in the air. "There is a woman inside," said the man, Foster Jones, who we later learned was a weather observer and communications technician. We opened the door to one of the rooms of the communication station, and inside a plump old lady rose to her feet. She was trembling, her hands flying about her bosom. Both "Americans" were unarmed.

The troop commander ordered the couple to put on overcoats and go outside. They were given permission to smoke.

All the natives were also made to gather in front of the communications post. "The Japanese Army does not kill prisoners, you have nothing to worry about," said the commander, in perfect English. The Aleuts appeared to understand what the commander said, and were talking among themselves.[4]

Foster, Etta, and the villagers were marched under guard to the schoolhouse and interrogated for hours. The Americans took the initiative to help the natives adjust to the realities of their new situation. The Joneses listened carefully to the interpreter and promised to obey all orders of the Imperial Army of Japan. Mothers held their children in their arms and tried to calm their fears, but to no avail. Babies and young children cried in fear of the unknown. When a child became too loud, the parents gently scolded them.

The interpreter reported to his superiors that the American military was

Island steamer entering Chichagof Harbor, Attu (673rd Air Base Wing History Office Joint Base Elmendorf-Richardson, Alaska).

planning to evacuate all residents of the Aleutians to the Alaskan mainland, station troops throughout the islands, and use the islands for military purposes. He further reported that there was already an order for all residents of Attu to evacuate the island by the end of August. Because of this order, the yearly supply ship sent from the mainland for which the islanders had to pay hadn't arrived. The ship was canceled to impress upon the Attuans that if they didn't follow the order to evacuate, they would have to deal with the lack of further replenishment of supplies.

The prisoners also told the interpreter that precision communications equipment, aviation fuel, and fuel and oil for ships had been offloaded from an American ship in April. A few weeks previously, a second freighter sailed into the harbor but was forced to turn back when high winds and heavy seas prevented the crew from unloading its cargo. It was scheduled to return in June with wireless communications equipment and fuel. American naval personnel were expected to arrive in August once the inhabitants left the island.

With interrogations completed, the inhabitants were sequestered together in a house located between the church and the schoolhouse. The soldiers searched the entire village, collecting weapons and items they thought might be used against them. They were taking no chances on a possible native uprising.

The Army established their headquarters in the Joneses' home, the only home on Attu with electricity. They confined the natives to their homes, but the Joneses' were taken to a *barabara* (a subterranean pit house constructed of sod over a wooden frame) that was no longer in use. Foster and Etta were reluctant to enter because it was so dirty inside and they demanded that the enemy allow them to stay in their own home. The soldiers ignored their demand and forced them to enter the structure. Their interpreter kicked them, severely beat them with the butt end of his rifle, and struck them across their backs. This was the only demonstration of resistance against the invaders during the occupation.

Sentries were posted throughout the village. A special guard was stationed in front of the pit house where Foster and Etta were confined to ensure that they could not gain access to weapons or communicate with the outside world.

The islanders were frightened by the presence of armed soldiers. While searching the village, the soldiers confiscated all of the outboard motors from the natives. As a result, the men were unable to go out on the bay to fish. They complained to the commander and he ordered his men to return the motors to their owners. Each time a villager caught fish, the soldiers stole them.

The corps commander, Colonel Yamazaki, ordered a single strand of barbed wire strung around the perimeter of the village. It extended from the schoolhouse on the west side of the village, to the homes on the east side, to the south side of the village to the edge of the bay. Fearful that their freedom had been curtailed, the residents soon learned that the purpose of the wire was not to confine them to the village. According to Colonel Yamazaki, it was to separate the troops from the islanders and forestall any additional crimes by Japanese soldiers. In reality, the natives were placed under house arrest, guarded constantly, and occasionally allowed outside for fishing.

The Japanese insisted that relations between the residents and the Army were amicable and relaxed, but in reality, the islanders hated the invaders. With the exception of the regulation that required the villagers to obtain permission to put their boats in the water to fish, the Aleuts were given the freedom to move about the island with few restrictions. As time passed, a mutual feeling of trust developed between the Army and the natives. The residents accompanied the soldiers and civilian news cameramen on excursions around the island.

Some Attuans wanted to fight the "Japs," and assembled guns and bullets in secret. Others cautioned against it. They feared that the enemy might send more troops into the village and retaliate. A village elder reminded them that the village was surrounded and that they were outnumbered. He convinced them that it was better to think of their God than to do battle with the enemy.

The residents didn't openly resist, but they reacted to their captivity with clandestine activities. They made fun of their captors by referring to the "Rising Sun" of their flag as the "Japanese meatball." Alex Prossoff purposely gave the enemy misinformation when he directed them to a cache of military supplies hidden on a deserted beach. He knew that a storm would come along and destroy the supplies, which is exactly what happened. The soldiers threatened to kill him if he ever deceived them again.

The soldiers continued to unload supplies from the ships in Chichagof Bay, and to construct defensive positions around the village. The Japanese expected the Americans to launch a counterattack, but it never came. They were unaware that the message Foster sent out when the first shots were fired wasn't received by the U.S. military. To protect the ships, they ordered them to up anchor and sail to Holtz Bay on the other side of the island.

Foster Jones was the only person killed in the invasion. There are at least three versions of his death. In his book, *The Thousand Mile War*, Brian Garfield wrote: "When Omori's troops rushed into Chichagof village, Jones made a dash for his secret hideout in the hills. He only made it as far as the edge of the village. The Japanese shot him down."[5]

Official Japanese files, witnesses, and Etta Jones contradict Garfield's account. Jones believed her husband was shot in the head during his interrogation. A number of villagers said Jones committed suicide, and official Japanese documents bear this out. Mikado Fukazawa, who was present at the time, tells his story:

> I don't know how long it was that I slept, but when I awoke, it was the morning of our second day on Attu. As I threw off the blanket to get up, the medical officer Ihozumi came in.
> "It has started out to be a very bad day," he said.
> "What happened?" I asked.
> "It's those Americans, a double suicide."
> The Joneses had tried to commit double suicide early this morning by cutting the blood vessels in their wrists. They were discovered by the natives who had heard their moans of pain. The natives immediately informed the medical officer, who went to the aid of the old couple.
> "They have bled profusely, but maybe they can be saved," said the doctor.
> I thought of the plump old couple who had taken the initiative in helping the natives adjust to their new situation, and had promised through our interpreter to obey all orders of the Imperial Army.
> "Let us do all we can to save them." Obeying the orders of the troop commander, we did everything within our powers to nurse the old couple back to health, but that evening, June 9, 1942, the husband died at the age of 65 on a little island at the tip of the Aleutian chain. His wife was saved, and thanked the medical officer profusely. "Thank you for your kindness. When you first came to help us, my husband said that he was beyond help, and asked that I put him out of his misery."
> The medical officer explained all of these events to me. Afterward, the body of Jones was buried with proper ceremony in the graveyard of the church at the foot of the hill. He was buried by the troops.[6]

How Foster Jones died is still open to conjecture. Other than the statements of the Japanese and Aleut witnesses, there is no proof that Etta and Foster slit their wrists to avoid captivity. One of the villagers, Mike Loaning, was ordered to bury Foster's body next to the church without a coffin. He was convinced the American was shot and killed by his captors.

In 1946, the U.S. Army ordered the exhumation of Foster's body. An examination of the remains revealed a small bullet hole in the right front temple of his skull. The slightly chipped edges and the angle of the bullet indicated that Foster was seated when the shot was fired. He was reburied in Little Falls Cemetery beside the American soldiers who died in the battle of Attu. In 1949, the remains were exhumed and interred at the Post Cemetery at Fort Richardson in Anchorage. Etta chose Fort Richardson as his final resting place and he was buried with full military honors.

Etta Jones was sent off Attu about a week after the Japanese landed. She survived her imprisonment in Yokohama and at war's end was repatriated to the U.S. mainland. Etta passed away in Bradenton, Florida, at the age of 86.

9

Prisoners in the Land of the Rising Sun

By 9:00 a.m. on June 8, the Third Special Landing Combat Group and units of the 301st Independent Infantry Battalion of the Japanese Northern Army had completed their invasion and occupation of Attu. Throughout July and August, the garrison installed antiaircraft batteries at Chichagof and Saranac Bay in preparation for the anticipated landing of American troops.

On August 25, the Japanese High Command ordered the invasion force and the villagers to evacuate the island and transfer troops and equipment to Kiska. They soon learned that it was possible for their troops to remain on the island throughout the winter, but they still considered it advisable to evacuate.

The decision was based on a combination of intelligence reports, the possibility of guerrilla action against the Japanese in the event of an American counter invasion, and the weather. Their sources reported an American naval force moving westward along the chain that planned to launch massive attacks on the Japanese on the westernmost islands. Convinced of its strategic importance, and that the first attacks would be directed at Kiska, Imperial Military Headquarters decided to transfer their men and equipment from Attu to Kiska. They knew that when the winter storms struck, it would be impossible to transport the garrison to Kiska and the entire population of the village and their personal goods to mainland Japan.

The evacuation commenced with the arrival of two ships, the *Osada-Maru* and the *Yoko-Maru*. The first contingent of 97 soldiers and their equipment were loaded aboard the *Osada-Maru* and sailed for Kiska. The remainder of the troops and equipment, along with the Aleuts and their possessions, were loaded on board the *Yoko-Maru*. Their captors insisted that the Aleuts take household goods, boats, outboard motors, ovens, stoves and anything else that could be stowed in the holds of the ship.

9. Prisoners in the Land of the Rising Sun

The Japanese wanted to ensure that nothing was left on Attu for an American invasion force. All prefabricated barracks were dismantled and put aboard ship. Equipment too heavy or bulky to move or no longer necessary, along with construction materials and extra rations, were burned. Japanese records indicate that the entire village, including the church, was reduced to rubble and ash.

Once again, other sources dispute the Japanese version of events. At the Alaska at War Symposium held in Anchorage in 1993, the Director of the Aleut Church Restitution Project of the Aleutian/Pribilof Islands Association, Barbara Sweetland Smith, reported:

> The fate of the churches and their furnishings during World War II depended a good deal on the degree of warning the people had about evacuation and on the military commanders in charge thereafter. The first to feel the panic of war were the Attuans. Their island was invaded on June 7 by the Japanese and they were taken prisoner. When the 41 Attuans left the island in September for Japan, their church was intact and they thoroughly expected to return. They even concealed their church treasury in Japan throughout their imprisonment, with the intention of putting it to use to make repairs to the church building. Their hopes were

Attuans line up on their second day of captivity in June 1942 to await transport to an internment camp in Japan. Chief Mike Hodikoff is in the front row, third from left (National Archives).

tragically in vain. The church, the only building standing in Attu village, was obliterated by a U.S. B-24 on October 15, 1942.[1]

At Kiska, 41 Aleuts were transferred to the *Osada-Maru*. Sometime in late September, the ship departed the island for Oar, the main port in Japan servicing the military in the north Pacific. Forty natives survived the voyage, but Annie Goldof who was wounded in the invasion and later died of her wounds, was buried at sea. The natives disembarked from the ship and were taken to a vacant railroad employee dormitory at Wakatake-Cho about a mile from the pier.

The villagers were now prisoners in a strange land far from home. Olean Prokopeuff's story paints a vivid picture of her captivity:

> We all stayed inside our homes. The guards stayed by our homes with bayonets. They were standing around guarding us like that for three days. Once daybreak came, some flares were shot into the air. We went under our beds because of being scared, not knowing what was happening. After three days we were taken aboard a ship and we were on our way.
>
> My house was opened and burned. We were taken out to the ship when it was getting dark. After spending the night on board the ship with much whistling and running and going on, and because of our ignorance of exactly what was happening, we were very anxious. Later on we were told that an American submarine was detected and that was the cause for all the commotion. A shortcut was said to be taken to where we were going. (I was not aware of what a shortcut meant.) After traveling for some time, we were told that we were passing a navy yard. All during the voyage, we were kept in a hold which was very unpleasant smelling, and it was also dark. We never once saw daylight until we reached Japan.[2]

A week after the Japanese landed on Attu, Etta Jones was separated from the Aleuts and transported to Yokohama. Upon arriving in Japan, she was imprisoned with seventeen Australian nurses and a female plantation owner captured at Papua New Guinea. They were installed in the Bund Hotel on Bund Street in Yokohama. After a few weeks, they were moved to Kanagawa Internment Camp #2 (formally known as the Yokohama Yacht Club), located at Shin-Yamashito-Chow in the Naka-cu Prefecture of Yokohama.

The women endured abuse from the guards, but they weren't subjected to the same kind of treatment meted out to POWs in the prison camps. Their captors forced them to make envelopes and little cloth bags, for which they were paid six yen a month. Six yen was one seventh of the salary a new graduate from a girl's school earned.

The yacht club was a large, square, concrete building that fronted the Yokohama Yacht Harbor. It was surrounded by a high fence and an iron gate that was originally built to keep undesirables out. Ironically, it was now being used to keep prisoners in. The women were given a certain amount of freedom and allowed to walk along the sea wall. Food was scarce, so the women resorted to fishing with makeshift poles and lines to supplement their meager diets.

The war situation worsened for Japan. The area around the harbor became a major target for American bombs. After two years of captivity, the prisoners were moved to an isolated compound at Totuska-ku. They were housed in a one-story wooden building on a twenty-acre plot of land surrounded by trees. The building was a former isolation ward for contagious diseases such as typhoid, dysentery, and cholera. The women were allowed to grow vegetables in a small garden plot. As long as they were in groups, they were permitted to take walks around the camp.

Some of the farmers living in the vicinity of the camp offered the prisoners potatoes and vegetables in exchange for clothing the women made from wool supplied by their captors. The authorities soon put a stop to the farmers' generosity. They told the local people, "These ladies believe that someday Japan will lose the war and the Americans will come to help them. Therefore, do not offer them anything and do not hurt them in any way."[3]

A female cook took care of the prisoners' needs. Her twelve-year-old son, Kenji Yamakawa, and his siblings lived in a small hut inside the camp. In an interview in 1995, Kenji described his memories of the nurses[4]:

> The foreign ladies lived in seven former bedrooms of the patients, each of which was around 13 meters, and there was a police guard and Mr. Yoshida, an interpreter in the two Japanese-style rooms by the front door. The ladies were growing vegetables and flowers in the garden. All of them were sweet and kind, but he was once scolded by Miss Parker as he naughtily took a vegetable. A few policemen took turns, and they were gentle people.
> In Totsuka, the nurses were not forced to do any work but had to pump water at the well as well as carry wood and stumps home for fuel. They were not used to the vegetable growing either, and *Obasan* instructed them.

Testimony that the women were subjected to violence, atrocities, and harassment by their captors contradicts Yamakawa's account. They were slapped in the face for not bowing deeply enough and kicked by the soldiers for minor infractions of the harsh rules the enemy imposed on them. The guards took great delight in chasing the nurses and urinating on them.

At all hours and late into the night while the women were trying to sleep, the guards stormed into their room and screamed at them to line up and stand at attention. Then they would retreat to their own quarters a short distance away only to return later to make certain the women were standing at attention. These frequent intrusions continued until the guards tired of their games and retired for the night. The women could then collapse onto their straw mats and go to sleep.

Often during the day when the women were busy knitting little bags for religious items or folding and gluing envelopes, the guards burst in and ordered them to line up and stand at attention. They strutted up and down the line, glaring menacingly at the prisoners. They screamed at the nurses and brandished their swords at them, knocking some of them to the floor.

During the lineups, the guards ordered the women to bow. When the prisoners didn't bow low enough to suit them, the guards slapped them viciously across the face. Most of the women were taller than the guards. When the guards walked up and down the line, they screamed at the nurses, and had to stand on tiptoes to slap their victim's face. Another time, one of the guards who barely came up to the prisoner's shoulders placed a stool in front of his target of intended violence to bring him eye level with her. He screamed at her, called her names, and viciously slapped her.

The Japanese government never ratified the Geneva Convention of 1929. They weren't bound by its accords and had no legal obligation to treat their POWs or noncombatants humanely. The accords stated that prisoners of war must at all times be treated humanely, and be protected from acts of violence or intimidation, insults and public curiosity. Captors were required to provide daily food rations in sufficient quantity, quality, and variety to keep the prisoners in good health and to prevent weight loss or nutritional deficiencies. Prisoners were to be involved in the preparation of their meals. Clothing, underwear, and footwear were to be supplied in sufficient quantities and suitable for the region where POWs were held. POWs should be permitted to send letters and receive parcels containing food, clothing, medical supplies, books and religious articles.

One of the greatest atrocities among many committed by the Japanese was to starve their prisoners to provide additional food rations to their military. The health of thousands of prisoners worsened and many of them weakened and died.

The Japanese government violated international wartime law when they purposely failed to notify the Agency for POWs and Non-combatants in Geneva, Switzerland, of the internment of the Australian nurses and Etta Jones. They kept the nurses' existence secret and rejected inquiries from the Australian government and the international Red Cross. On December 9, 1941, the International Red Cross in Geneva proposed to the Japanese government that they open a POW Information Bureau concerning the treatment of prisoners based on the accords of the Geneva Convention of 1929.

The Japanese accepted the proposal and established the POW Information Bureau within the Army Ministry. They had a duty to provide a list of civilian internees and POWs, but it wasn't until July 1945 that they provided the names to the Red Cross. Had they been informed of the names and location of the nurses earlier, the women wouldn't have suffered as much at the hands of the Japanese. They wouldn't have been denied visits by representatives of the IRC and they would have received aid money, relief supplies, and letters and packages from home.

On July 1, 1945, a representative of the IRC visited the women. This was the first visit from the Red Cross since Christmas Eve, 1942. He informed them that no one outside the camp knew where they were or that they had been imprisoned for almost four years. He told them that the war in Europe had been over for two months and that the Allies were victorious over Germany. The representative promised to give the names of the prisoners and their location to the Swiss government.

One month later, the Americans dropped the atomic bomb on Hiroshima and on Nagasaki. On August 9, 1945, Japan surrendered, but the women remained in prison. A few days later, the Army Air Corps dropped a drum of supply goods for the POWs in the isolation ward building at Izumi-Cho. With a noise that sounded like an explosion, the drum crashed through the roof of the Nakawada Primary School. It hit the ground, broke open, and scattered the contents. Members of the Japanese Civil Defense Force rushed to the scene, collected the supplies and delivered them to the nurses. Starvation changed to abundance, and the internees ate the food so quickly they became ill.

Freedom for the nurses came on August 30, when American occupation forces liberated the camp. The Red Cross provided each woman with a dress and a pair of shoes, and two days later they boarded a bus for the ride to Atsugi Air Base and the flight home. When they arrived in Manila, they were informed that Etta Jones, who was now 64 years old, was the first American woman to be rescued. The nurses were the first Australian women to be freed.

Every newspaper in Australia carried the story of the rescue:

AUSTRALIAN WOMEN RELEASED FROM JAP PRISON CAMP
General MacArthur's motor convoy roaring through Totsuka en route to Yokohama on Thursday was the first indication that 18 Australian women, consisting of nurses, missionaries, and ordinary civilians, who were taken at Rabaul and New Britain, heard of the allied landings in Japan. The women were held in Kumado for 3½ years and were not permitted to contact the Red Cross or write home. The inmates included Miss Lorna Whyte, of Hay, Miss Jean McCleland of Dalby and Captain Kay Parker of Sydney [*Canberra Times*, September 3, 1945].5

18 AUSTRALIAN WOMEN FREED IN YOKOHAMA
U.S. troops on Saturday liberated 18 Australian women from a prison camp near Yokohama. They included Lorna Whyte of Hay, NSW; Jean McLallan of Dalby; and Captain Kay White, of Sydney.

The prisoners came from all states and were nurses, missionaries, and civilians. Seven were captured in Rabaul in 1942, the others in Kavieng. They were held at Totsuka near Atsugi, and had not been permitted to make contact with the Red Cross or write home for three and a half years.

The women have boarded planes for Australia.

"After internment they were first housed in the Bund Hotel, later in Yokohama Yacht Club, and for the last year in a house," Lorna Whyte said.

"This gave us a wonderful view of air raids that used to terrorize the guards," says Lorna Whyte. "They were greatly impressed when we would stand up and yell, 'Drop some more. Drop some more.' We hoped the bombers would come over more and more."

Describing their treatment, she said, "One girl was thrown down on the floor and kicked to pieces. Even the cook was allowed to crack us. But mostly we were not treated too roughly. They were all so small that it is a pleasure to see men you can look up to again."

"One guard got mad at me, took off his gloves, stretched up on his toes, and slapped me. He had to reach so high it was hard not to laugh."

"Worst experience was short rations. We used to take turns stealing food left on the guards' plates. A month ago about all we had to eat was boiled carrot and greens, but in the last fortnight, my word, how the food has improved [*The Argus*, Melbourne, September 3, 1945].[6]

Some time after their return to Australia, one of the nurses, Eileen Callaghan, who was suffering from a serious case of tuberculosis, passed away in a South Australian hospital. One of her last acts before she died was to send a cheerful letter to fellow prisoner Alice Bowman saying she was glad she would die in Australia.

10

Aleuts in Japan

The Aleuts disembarked from the *Osada-Maru* and were transported through town to the second floor of a two-story building near the post office in Wakatake-Cho. The civilians who lived in the vicinity of the building weren't given any advance notice of the arrival of their new neighbors. It wasn't until daybreak that they were even aware of their presence. The two policemen assigned to monitor their activities lived in a small room on the first floor. The personal belongings of the Aleuts that they brought with them on the ship were stashed at the rear of the building.

Without guards or the military to accompany them, the prisoners were permitted to walk freely around the neighborhood. Their children frequented the local sweet shop and the adults bought food at the butcher shops and fish markets. The merchants were reimbursed by the government for the purchases.

There were several instances of violence committed against the internees from 1943 to 1944. Before the Aleuts were moved into larger quarters, one policeman in particular mistreated them. He stole their rations and severely beat Angelina Hodikof for not performing work in her living quarters. He beat her so badly that her wounds did not heal until 1946, one year after she returned to the United States.

Olean Prokopueff experienced the horrors of the internment firsthand:

> When we reached Japan, the Captain collided with the dock, and when this happened, we were thrown from our seated position right on the deck. Then we thought to ourselves, "Ayayaa! Did our ship get shot?" This was a scary experience.
> Finally, we gathered on top of the dock. Then we were sprayed. Later on we were picked up by a vehicle and taken to a black house. Since we fed ourselves with our own food from home during the trip, the only different food that was given to us was some warm rice. It was the only warm rice we ate.
> When asked if we were hungry, we told them yes. A meal was cooked for us that day. They brought our food on a tray. Chopsticks, which we did not know how to use, were given to us to use. There was a policeman present there with his

partner. So as soon as they started talking with each other and not paying attention to us, we would quickly eat with our hands. When the policeman turned towards us, we would pretend like nothing happened at all. We were also served with an unusual looking cooked bird with its feathers still on it. We felt suspicious and so we did not eat it.

After we were fed, we were put to bed. Our mattresses were laid on the floor. Pillows were also given to us. And they were very hard, but we did not complain. The blankets that were given to us were almost as thick as the mattresses, but we used them anyway.

Every morning we mopped. The house that we were staying at had a kitchen downstairs. We had a stove that we had taken from Attu which we used there.

We had soup that looked like grass and some dried rice. When we ran out of grass soup, we started making rice soup. Prior to this, we ate the food that we brought along from Attu, like dried fish, the salted fish, and so on, but when we ran out of food, we were given vegetables like carrots, potatoes, and so on. After eating the boiled potatoes, we would have very bad stomach aches, and they were very painful.

It happened one day that we were told that some officials were coming there to our place for a visit. A Japanese cook was brought there for us. They told us not to go away and the Japanese cook put wood into the oven. He lit it, and as a result of that, the smoke filled the room. I can't remember whether or not cooking took place that day.

We were once again grouped and questions were asked of us. They asked if we were eating good food. We did not give them a reply. They once again asked us if we wanted to talk. We refused to talk. Then after that we were given food once more.

As things were, our men were put to work. Shortly after that, they started admitting our people to the hospital. The people were getting sick one after the other until I was almost the only one left at home to cook. While I was doing that, they took my husband to the hospital. After they took my husband, my children were starving. So when I went to fetch some water, I would pick up orange peelings off the ground. Then I would cook them on top of the heater. Then I fed them to my children, and only then would they stop crying for a while.

Shortly thereafter, they admitted my children to the hospital. They asked me to come to the hospital. So I went there and "Ayayaa!" The people who were admitted to the hospital were very sick. That day a few went home. Being unable to hear what was happening, I begged to be returned to work. So they started me working on clay.

The land where we were was very hot. We worked with picks and shovels shoveling away at the clay. Then the clay was dried and crushed. The clay was also being worked on in the factories during the winter.

While working on the clay, a particle of it went in my right eye. I was afraid that I was going to lose my eyesight, but l have managed to arrive here [on Atka] without having to wear glasses. Later on, those who were sent home from the hospital took ill again. They were taken once more to the hospital. We were allowed to visit the hospital for check-ups. Whenever they did that, I would ask my people what they were doing to them. They replied, "We are being inoculated." "Ayayaa!" We did not know what was being done to them.

But then the people were dying. Lots of people died there. My daughter and son were among those who were in the hospital. They would say, "Mother, come here and scratch me." So I would go over to him/her and not knowing exactly where they wanted me to scratch, I would scratch and then move away from them. The reason why they were unable to specify where they wanted to be scratched was because they could not move.[1]

Unlike the POWs, who were forced to work in the mines, shipyards and factories, the Japanese didn't use the Aleuts for slave labor. Those who were able and willing to work were permitted to do it on a voluntary basis. They volunteered to dig clay at a nearby bentonite mine for which they were paid one and a half yen a day. Only four to six Aleuts went to the pits during their first year of internment. They ceased working in the mine in 1944, when they moved to larger quarters in Shimizu-Cho. Reasons for no longer digging clay may have been their deteriorating health, and that the mine was now further away from their previous residence. This voluntary labor performed by the Aleuts stands in sharp contrast to forced labor imposed on Chinese and Korean prisoners who were marched to and from the piers and shipyards every day.

The Japanese yen earned by the Aleuts during their internment amounted to about $700 U.S. (1945 exchange rate) and was sent with them when they returned to the States. When they arrived in Seattle, government officials confiscated the money for safekeeping. To this day it has never been returned to the rightful owners.

Dr. Fujino lived near the Aleuts and was responsible for their medical treatment during their stay at Wakatake-Cho. He made house calls, and patients who were too sick to be cared for were sent to the National Tuberculosis Center. It's impossible to know what kinds of medical treatment Dr. Fujino prescribed for his patients. His medical records were destroyed before the arrival of the occupation forces in September 1945.

In the fall of 1944 the Aleuts moved to a large wooden building in Shimizu-Cho. It was originally used as a religious office and living quarters for Shinto priests at the Shimizu-Cho Meiji shrine. Police Officer Takeshiro Shikanai and his wife, Toki, lived in the front part of the house and took responsibility for the Aleuts in April 1944. The Attuans were relegated to the rear three quarters of the building.

The house had electricity and fresh water. In the winter each room was heated by a coal stove provided by the government. They were not the same stoves the Aleuts brought with them. The stoves from Attu combined heating and cooking and were stored in a warehouse along with other household goods.

Aleuts from Chichagof Village on Attu were interned in this ramshackle house in the Japanese prefecture of Shimiza-Cho from 1944 until their release in 1945. Half of the prisoners died as a result of a lack of heat, an inadequate diet, and an outbreak of tuberculosis (National Archives).

The last time the Alluans saw their property, it was loaded into the hold of the *Osada-Maru*.

Commissioned in 1943, Officer Shikanai was assigned to the Foreign Affairs Division of the Otaru City Police Department. This department was responsible for all foreigners and aliens living outside of prisons and POW camps in Japan. The Aleuts trusted and respected the Shikanais, and apparently the feeling was mutual. The Shikanais did their best under the prevailing conditions of war to help the prisoners adjust to their environment. Even though it was against the law, they often gave the internees extra food and shielded them from certain military regulations.

Prisoners who took sick were transported to the National Tuberculosis Center in Minamoto-cho for treatment. Prisoners who became seriously ill were admitted to the hospital. Men and women were placed in separate wards, and there were always 10 to 15 Attuans in intensive care at any given time. The doctor who examined them when they first arrived in Japan, Dr. Satoru Noguchi,[2] claimed that 20 of the 41 Attuans, including children, were suffering from advanced cases of tuberculosis and poliomyelitis.

Dr. Noguchi surmised that the long ship voyage to Japan and the reluctance of the Aleuts to eat raw fruits and vegetables served to worsen their medical conditions and may have contributed to their high mortality rate. In his opinion, because the Aleuts' diet during their internment was lacking in protein and calories, it contributed to their medical problems. On Attu, the internees had access to an abundance of fish and sea mammals, but in Japan, rice, fish, and meat were strictly rationed. Even though they didn't starve, there was never enough food to satisfy their hunger.

Rice, fish, and meat were rationed as a result of the war. Many Japanese believed the Aleuts ate as well or better than they did and that the prisoners received special rations. Rice was the staple food, but the Aleuts were not familiar with how to cook it. They tended to undercook it or burn it. Consequently, they suffered severe stomach problems until they learned to cook it properly.

The Attuans preferred to preserve their food in a mixture of lard and salt. One of their favorite foods was herring marinated in lard. The Japanese preferred a combination of rice and vegetables. Food marinated in salt and lard was simply unpalatable to them and they refused to eat it.

The Aleuts had their own opinion about what may have contributed to their declining health. They were distressed that twice a week, the Japanese forced them to go to the local bath house. They felt that the practice of bathing on a regular basis was detrimental to their health. They believed that two persons had died as a direct result of bathing. Despite their protest, they were forced to bathe twice a week.

Noguchi also claimed that with the exception of two cases of poliomyelitis and diphtheria, the only medical treatment the prisoners required was for tuberculosis. According to Noguchi, other than the death of an unidentified woman due to dyspnea, a respiratory failure brought on by poliomyelitis, all of the Aleuts recovered. Given the fact that sixteen of the internees and four of the five babies born at Otaru died, and only 20 the original 41 residents of Chichagof survived their internment, Dr. Noguchi was obviously wrong.

There are many contradictions and disparities in the Japanese accounts of the internment. According to the Japanese, Fred Hodikoff contracted diphtheria and was quarantined in another hospital. They claim he subsequently recovered and was among the 22 Aleuts who returned to the United States. The Aleuts released a list that shows that Hodikoff died during his imprisonment. His remains were brought back to Alaska with the returnees.

Aleuts who died in the hospital were ministered to by others of their group. According to Fuyo Kusaka, a nurse well acquainted with the Attuans in the sanatorium, they preferred that they handle their own dead. First the body was cleansed and dressed in a gown-like garment before being placed in the coffin. Flowers, when available, were also placed inside the coffin. A service similar to Catholic funeral rites (probably Russian Orthodox) was led by one of the group. The coffin was then taken to a crematorium for final disposal of the remains. The remains of 20 persons who died in Japan were returned with the 20 survivors and a newborn baby in September 1945. Throughout the whole operation, the Japanese staff was not permitted to touch or handle the deceased.[3]

Olean Prokopeuff was at her husband's side when he died. Her account differs slightly from Kusaka's account.

> When my husband was close to death, he sent for me. I went to the hospital and he gave me some cigarettes which he had stashed away. Then I stayed awake with him most of the night. Then he told me if I were sleepy to go to sleep. So I went to sleep, and during my slumber, he died.
>
> When I was awakened, I got up and I noticed that in our religious custom when a person dies, he is not dressed, but I watched them dress him. After he was dressed, he was taken out. I did not know what they did to him. It was not until my Leonty died that I went to where they must have taken him. Leonty was put in an oven, and I was told to light some flowers, so I did. Then I went to the other room. After that they pulled him out and I did not like what I saw. I approached a Japanese priest and asked him if it was a sin to do that. He told me that the reason why they did that was because they did not have any burying space. They said that they hardly had any space for burying people.[4]

In preparation for the invasion, in July and August 1945, the American military bombed Otaru and other cities in Japan. The hospital wasn't hit, but the doctors suspected that the Aleuts were signaling the bombers with flashlights. They searched the prisoners and the sick bays, but failed to find flashlights or other signaling devices. They were afraid that smoke from the cooking fires might alert the bombers as to their location, so all fires had to be extinguished between dusk and dawn. Patients at the sanatorium who were able to walk were taken to the woods behind the hospital.

On August 15, the warring parties met on the deck of the battleship *Missouri* and Japan surrendered. Following the armistice on September 3, the first contingent of occupation forces arrived in Otaru. A representative from the International Red Cross met with the internees. He sent his report to the authorities, and soon food, cigarettes, candy, cosmetics, and other items were dropped by parachute to the hospital and the Shimizu-Cho house. As much as they needed them, the residents of Otaru were under strict orders not to touch any of the packages when they hit the ground. The police collected the packages that fell too far from their intended targets and gave them to the intended recipients.

10. Aleuts in Japan

The war was over and the Aleuts wanted to go home. On September 17, 1945, a large bus arrived at the Shimizu-Cho house. The internees began the 45-mile ride to Chitose Airport. Officer Shikanai and his immediate superior, Police Sergeant Toshiikatsu Endo, were delegated by the Japanese government to accompany the former prisoners now freed from their captors, but they remained behind when the internees departed.

The Attuans were scheduled to fly to Atsugi Air Base near Tokyo, but their flight was delayed for three days due to bad weather. As soon as the plane landed and they deplaned, they were directed to a vacant hangar where they were instructed to remove their clothing, sprayed with insecticide, and given new clothes. They were told that they were allowed one piece of baggage per person. All other items had to be left behind.

The flight carrying the Attuans home left Atsugi Air Base at 8:00 a.m. on September 21, 1945. After four years in captivity, they were going home. Their route took them to Guam, the Philippines, and Hawaii. On November 20, they landed in San Francisco, then on to Seattle by U.S. Navy ship. Why it took so long for these brave people to return home has never been explained.

Olean Prokopeuff remembered the trip home quite differently:

> The people continued to die. All that was left was just a few of us. Time passed until we heard an airplane. We went out and we stepped out to look. We saw drums coming down in parachutes, and evidently, the plane was an American plane and the drums contained food. So we stayed up and ate all night.
>
> After the food was dropped, the Americans came. We could see cars running around and they made a lot of smoke. These cars had to be cranked to get them started so one got tired of cranking a car before it could be started. They also had some cars that didn't make any noise at all when running.
>
> Then we were taken inside the house. We were asked if we wanted to go home. We all said, "Yes!" They were Americans and they told us the war was over, and we were going to be taken home. The next day, we were taken to the airport. We stayed there for three nights. Our flight must have been late or something. I never did find out.
>
> We finally departed that place and we landed on a number of islands. I don't even know the names of the islands.
>
> We saw where the Americans dropped their atomic bombs. It looked like a bundle of kindling wood. The place appeared demolished when viewed from the airplane. When we were in Japan, we used to be evacuated to the interior whenever the Americans dropped their bombs.
>
> Then we flew once more. I still can't remember the names of the three islands [over which we flew]. I think we were still flying, and I remembered Okinawa, because we were there for two and a half weeks. Then once again we were airborne heading for the mainland. When we arrived on the mainland, it was miserably hot there.
>
> We caught a boat from Manila bound for San Francisco. During our trip, we

encountered a storm, and we were told that we were in Alaskan waters. We were hoping that they could let us off at Unalaska, but instead the boat continued on to San Francisco. From San Francisco we took a train to Seattle. From Seattle, we boarded a ship, *Branch*, and later arrived at Adak. When we were in Seattle, we were there for some time and it was getting close to Christmas. We did not really want to go home, but we were brought here. At that time, they dropped off many soldiers on Adak. We were brought here from Adak in a small tug. I had gotten used to the big ship that brought us from Seattle, and I did not feel very safe on that small tug.

When the tug arrived at Atka, a truck picked us up and we were taken to the school. At the school, we were assigned to where we were going to live. I was placed in Cedor's house.

A year passed, and then the houses were built for us. Army Quonset huts was made for us to live in and we stayed in the huts for another year. Then our houses were finished so we moved in. Since then, they have been our houses for a long time. Today, whenever there is a storm, I don't trust my poor house.[5]

Sickness and starvation were responsible for the deaths of many of the captives. Only 24 of the original 42 Aleuts lived through their ordeal. One newborn baby survived, but four other babies died of starvation in Japan. On their return to Alaska, 16 former prisoners were repatriated to the village of Atka with the approval of the residents of the village. The remaining natives were resettled in other locations.

Attu was their ancestral home. They'd lived there for more than 3,000 years. The Japanese had torn the people from their homes and the only life they ever knew. The war ended, but they were not allowed to return to their beloved island. To this day the U.S. military has refused to allow the people to go home due to Attu's strategic importance, unexploded ordnance, and the war debris that litters the Aleutian Islands.

The people were given a choice that was more like an ultimatum: live at Atka or resettle somewhere else, but not on Attu. The survivors chose Atka. Because there were only a few of them left to take care of themselves, and because their relatives had been from Atka and other villages, they agreed to become members of the village. Because of the long distances between the islands in the Aleutian chain and cultural differences between the inhabitants of each village, it wasn't easy for them to live with a group of strangers at first. As time passed, they overcame their cultural differences and learned to live comfortably with their new neighbors. As of May 2011, only two Attuans were alive to tell the story.

11

War and Evacuation

By spring of 1942, the war in the Pacific had spread eastward toward Alaska. Army Intelligence reported that a Japanese offensive could be expected at any time. As Japanese victories in the Pacific continued and their ships approached the Aleutians, discussions between the military and the Department of the Interior concerning the evacuation of the Aleuts from the islands and the Pribilofs began.

The Interior Department was responsible for policies affecting the Aleuts and their protection, and it was divided into three divisions: the Office of Indian Affairs (OIA), the Fish and Wildlife Service (FWS), and the Division of Territories and Island Possessions. The OIA was limited to providing education to the natives in the island chain. They established primary schools throughout the Aleutians, and through its Alaska Indian service, provided teachers for the larger villages. The FWS managed the profitable fur seal harvest in the Pribilofs. Since the Aleuts provided the only source of labor for this enterprise, the FWS maintained control over the Pribilof natives and assumed responsibility for their education and general welfare.

Immediately following the attack on Pearl Harbor, General Buckner ordered the evacuation of military dependents from Alaska. On January 16, the Navy Department sent the following message to Paul Gordon of the Division of Territories expressing their concern for the civilians living near the military installations at Dutch Harbor: "It is felt that the evacuation of all white women and children from Unalaska would be in the best interest of the present military situation."[1] The military recommended that in the event of an evacuation, Aleut women and children be removed to other villages. The Division of Territories relayed the recommendation to Governor Gruening. They concurred with the Army that the activities of the Army and Navy connected with evacuation be coordinated with the activities of the governor's office.

In Gruening's absence, on March 13, 1942, Acting Territorial Governor

E.L. Bartlett called a meeting to discuss evacuation planning for Alaska in the event of an enemy attack. The military was absent from the meeting, but representatives of various civilian agencies, including a junior OIA officer from Juneau, were in attendance. The group agreed on the following policy:

> No attempt should be made, even in the case of actual enemy attack, to evacuate Eskimos or other primitive natives from Alaska. It is felt that these people could never adjust themselves to life outside of their present environment, whereas they could "take to the hills" in case of danger and be practically self-sufficient for a considerable period.[2]

After further discussion, the group decided that the Aleut women and children of Unalaska, but not the men, near the military installations of Dutch Harbor, should be moved to other villages less exposed to military and social dangers. Conferring with a representative of the OIA, the Aleuts at Unalaska informed the agency that if it were necessary to evacuate their homes, they preferred to be moved to other native villages such as False Pass, King Cove, Akutan, Sand Point, and Belkofsky.

The attendees were cognizant of the necessity for further planning and the need to coordinate evacuation efforts between the military and civilian agencies. They came to the following conclusions:

> There is a need for basic thinking and definite decisions on matters of broad policy relating to evacuation, beyond what has been evidenced to date.
> A joint declaration of some kind might be prepared by participating agencies stating evacuation problems and recommending lines of procedure. This should be addressed to the Army and Navy commands in Alaska and the Governor.[3]

The meeting concluded with the recommendation that given the urgency of the situation, another meeting should be held in the near future.

Governor Gruening was opposed to the evacuation of the Aleuts from their villages on the grounds that bombardment of non-military areas was highly unlikely. He felt that the dislocation from a forced evacuation would do greater damage and involve greater risk to the ultimate welfare of the people than a probable risk if they remained in their home villages.

Some high-ranking members of the OIA and the Department of the Interior were apprehensive about removing the natives from their homes. They had many of the same reservations that Gruening did. On April 10, Commissioner John Collier of the OIA sent a memorandum to Secretary of the Interior Harold Ickes, calling attention to the OIA's responsibility for establishing plans for the Aleuts residing in the Aleutian Island. In his memo, he pointed out that the Navy had said it would not protect the villages west of Dutch Harbor, and that the Aleuts from the westernmost inhabited islands of Attu and Atka showed no inclination to move:

11. War and Evacuation

> Our representative at Juneau, Superintendent Hirst, is in favor of evacuation. Governor Gruening is opposed to it on the grounds [that] the dislocation resulting from a forced evacuation would be a greater damage and involves greater risk if they remain where they are. Admiral Freeman ... has sent us a wire in response to our request for advice which places the responsibility upon us. His wire seems to say that evacuation is desirable, but not mandatory. He does say that the Natives are "wholly unprotected from enemy raiders."[4]

As the government official with the responsibility to decide if the Aleuts should be evacuated and relocated, Collier concluded his letter with his feelings on the matter: "I am inclined to leave the Natives where they are, unless, the Navy insists that they be moved out."[5]

The dissension between civilian agencies and the military resulted in serious delays in implementing a plan for the evacuation. The OIA wanted to permit the natives to remain in their villages, but Claude Hirst dissented. The Navy wanted the OIA to make the final decision, and the OIA wanted to leave it up to the Navy. Secretary Ickes approved the OIA's position with the stipulation that the Aleuts would be evacuated, but only if they wished to be.

The counselor from the Alaska Office of President Roosevelt's National Resources Planning Board, James Rettie, was watching the interagency bickering from the sidelines. Concerned with the lack of coordination between civilian agencies and the military, he contacted the director of the Bureau of the Budget, Harold Smith, with a long list of complaints about Alaska's unpreparedness for war.

> I feel it is my personal duty ... to express to you again my grave concern about the present state of affairs in the territory.
> We shall be worse than fools if we do not anticipate an attack in force against Alaska within the next two months. If nothing is done to remedy the administrative paralysis and lack of clearly defined responsibility now prevailing in Alaska and the inadequate preparations to evacuate civilians, the confusion and loss of life which will follow an attack may easily be worse than it was in Hawaii. The record of inaction, delays, inter-agency squabbles and bickering and lack of proper liaison with the armed forces will be terribly ugly. There will also be the vital question of the need for a unified military command. An outraged public opinion in the United States will rightly insist upon a hard-boiled investigation which might easily shake this administration to its very foundations.
> I therefore plead for the utmost speed and resolution in the issuance of whatever Executive Order the military authorities can and will effectively use to achieve proper coordination between military and civilian activities.[6]

Smith forwarded the letter to Secretary of War Harry Stimson, who in turn sent it on the president. On June 11, 1942, Roosevelt signed Executive Order 9181[7] to establish the Alaska War Council. The order named the territorial governor as chairman. The commissioners were drawn from various civilian agencies. It stated that the Council was responsible for maintaining a close liaison with the military commanders and for conforming civilian policy to military objectives relative to the safety and security of the civilian population of Alaska. It required the governor to keep the president informed with regard to major steps proposed or adopted to carry out protection of Alaska's civilians.

Gruening met with the commander of the Alaska Defense Forces, General Buckner, to discuss the evacuation. On June 14, Gruening sent a letter to Ickes characterizing the general's position on the proposed evacuation:

> I recently discussed the matter with Major General S.B. Buckner, Jr., Commander of Alaska Defense Forces. He gave me his opinion that it would be a great mistake to evacuate these natives. He said, in effect, that evacuating them was pretty close to destroying them; that they now live under conditions suitable to them; and that if they were removed they would be subject to the deterioration of contact with the white man, would likely fall prey to drink and disease, and probably would never get back to their historic habitat.[8]

Gruening didn't want to see the Aleuts evacuated. In a letter to Ickes, he recommended that the evacuation not proceed without first soliciting the views of the natives. He wanted the interviews conducted by a qualified representative of the Office of Indian Affairs.

Before Gruening's plan could be enacted, the situation in the Aleutians changed with the Japanese occupation of Attu. The actions of the enemy prompted Ickes to respond to Gruening in a rather terse manner:

> Although I agree heartily with your proposal [to solicit the views of the Aleuts involved], recent events have changed the situation. Attu is now occupied by the enemy, and the Navy is in the process of evacuating the natives of Atka and of the Pribilof Islands. Arrangements are in progress for settling the evacuees during whatever period may be necessary in Southeastern Alaska.[9]

On June 20, the Alaska War Council held its first meeting. Gruening was convinced that the Japanese invasion of mainland Alaska was imminent. Acting as chairman, he sent a letter to Ickes urging immediate unification of the military command in Alaska:

> In pursuance of your executive order of June eleventh, the Alaska War Council holding its first meeting urges immediate unification of the command in Alaska as has been done elsewhere. Enemy has already invaded the Aleutians in force entrenching himself and moving his new bases of operations toward mainland invasion of which is imminent thus operations for major offensive against enemy and unified command, indispensable prerequisite as situation clearly calls for.[10]

The evacuation of the Aleuts from the Aleutian Chain and the Pribilofs was chaotic. As a result of bureaucratic indecision and delays, there was no coordinated government policy for developing evacuation plans. A clear policy to define the division of responsibilities between civilian agencies and the military was nonexistent. The results were disastrous for the Aleuts. They paid a terrible price for the failure and indifference of the governmental agencies whose job was to protect them.

12

Atka

Atka is 600 miles east of Attu and 360 miles from Kiska. For years before the attack on Pearl Harbor, the Japanese conducted reconnaissance of the Aleutians. They visited Atka many times and on occasion explored the island. There were no U.S. military bases, landing strips, naval facilities, garrisons, arsenals, or artillery emplacements on the island. Japanese military planners didn't consider it important enough to include this information in their plans. They were interested in Dutch Harbor, Adak, Kiska, and Attu.

Atka's geographical position should have kept the island and its people out of the war, but it was the halfway point between the occupation forces on Kiska and the American military forces at Dutch Harbor. It had a large protected harbor (Nazan Bay), and upon learning that Japanese troops occupied Kiska, the Navy decided to use the bay to land and service seaplanes. Landing on the bay, the planes were tied to buoys, refueled, rearmed, and repaired by crews from seaplane tenders anchored nearby. The tenders provided hot meals and sleeping quarters for the exhausted aircrews, and fuel, bombs, and ammunition for the seaplanes. As soon as the tenders depleted their cargo, they returned to Dutch Harbor to replenish their stores.

The Navy sent two destroyers, USS *Gillis* and USS *Hulbert*, to Atka to tend the twenty-four seaplanes moored in Nazan Bay and to support the bombing campaign against the entrenched enemy on Kiska. Patrol Wing Four was ordered to exert maximum effort to attack the enemy around the clock with bombs and torpedoes. The attacks continued night and day until the *Gillis* issued every bomb and bullet in its inventory. The *Gillis* was then replaced by the *Hulbert*.

The residents of Atka did their part to support the war effort. They fed and housed some of the air crews and donated pencils from the school to plug holes in the pontoons of the seaplanes riddled by antiaircraft fire as they flew over Kiska.

12. Atka

All of the planes suffered serious battle damage and many of them were unfit for further combat until they were repaired. Of the three planes damaged beyond repair, two of them were sent to the bottom, and one was beached and burned to prevent its use by the enemy. One air crew member was killed and two were wounded.

The bombing raids on Kiska commenced on June 11 and continued for eighteen hours. Everyone expected the Japanese to retaliate. American pilots flying 120 miles west of Atka reported a large concentration of enemy ships and increased shore activity on Kiska. Admirals Nimitz and Theobald were convinced these ships were the remnants of Japan's Combined Fleet that the U.S. had defeated at the Battle of Midway. They believed an attack on Atka was imminent.

To offer the inhabitants some measure of safety from enemy attack, the Navy declared the village off-limits and ordered the Aleuts to seek safety in their summer camps. One officer was struck by the scene. "They were evacuated while eating breakfast," he noticed, "and the eggs were still on the table—coffee in the cups. A lot of personal clothing and stuff was still hanging in closets," and "the village was declared off-limits for all but medical personnel."[1]

The natives were sent to fishing camps, where summer fishing was already in progress. Afraid the Japanese planes would soon drop bombs on Atka, the Navy ordered the Aleuts to camouflage their tents.

Some time after the war, one of the villagers, Larry Dirks, Sr., related his recollections of the evacuation. His story was written in the Western Aleut dialect in the early 1970s[2]:

> During the time of war, I was at my hunting grounds hunting and fishing. I did not know that the war was going on until I had returned back from my camp to my village, Atka. Even then I assured myself that our islands were and might still be too far from the war zone. But, my feelings of being safe were forgotten soon because I learned that the Japanese had come to our islands. A year since I had heard that this war had started these our enemy, the Japanese had landed on Attu and Kiska.
>
> Without our knowing it, the Japanese had been flying throughout these islands searching and studying in our area. Only later, they the Japanese, after having secured their stronghold on Kiska and Attu, had come into our area. This was a surprise to me. When they were seen flying in our area, the school teacher who was here at Atka made the radio contact with Attu. After this call, we heard Unalaska trying to reach Attu but no contact was made. At that time it was not known that Attu had been taken but it was thought that they may have received this call. We did not know at that time that the Japanese had already taken Attu. That is why we think they could not have answered our calls.
>
> When that winter was at its end, we learned that our people would have to be evacuated. This we were told. We waited but no boat came. The weather was

good but we thought that no attempt was being made at that time to take us away.

We kind of thought that the boat that was coming to take us away was coming near because the airplanes kept coming in and out. When they do land in the bay they would take on some fuel and take off again. Then others would also come. They were shot up. Some men on these planes were dead and some were wounded. Having seen this, our people were getting more scared. Even I was getting more scared. Since these planes were seaplanes, they landed in the water and came ashore to the beaches.

Everybody was excited. Many of our people were at their camps. If the weather is bad you just get yourself isolated at your camp. Many of our people were at their camps like this. Only those who were at the village when the boat came to take us away, were boarded and taken to Dutch Harbor. We could see this boat anchored out in the ocean. Also the airplanes were still around at this time. But in our camps we had no way to get to the boat. I suppose we might have tried.

The Japanese planes came over Atka by surprise having come in through the islands then into the bay. After flying in low, they circled around and left. And when evening came and we were thinking of going to sleep, the young people from our camps [be]came very restless, wanting to go to the boat they said. They said they thought that we wouldn't be bothered. Me, I said I would stay at my camp. After they said what they wanted to say, they left. Since I was here and that we were hoped to get provisions, here I stayed. At this time also, we really did not know if our people were on the ship.

On June 12, the children in one of the camps heard the unmistakable sound of an approaching airplane. Believing it to be an American plane on its way to bomb the Japanese, they ran to the top of a hill to wave to the pilot. The plane was a Japanese scout. As soon as the children realized it was the enemy, they scampered down the hill and hid. Other Aleuts were on their way from camp to the village to retrieve supplies and personal belongings left behind when they were ordered to evacuate. Sailors armed with guns and bayonet-tipped rifles refused to allow them to enter the village and ordered them to hide. They informed them that more Japanese planes might soon be dropping bombs on the village.

The *Gillis* and the *Hulbert* were busy preparing the seaplanes for a bombing raid the next morning. At approximately 8:00 p.m. the commander of the *Gillis* received orders from the commander of Patrol Wing Four to burn the village to the ground, evacuate the residents from the island, and relocate them to a safe place. Apparently, the orders came directly from General Buckner.

When the detail from the *Gillis* came ashore, the only residents they found were C. Ralph Magee, and his wife Ruby, the two Indian Affairs employees assigned to the community. Ruby was the school teacher and her husband was a maintenance man for the village. In their personal narrative of their experiences on Atka, the Magees reported that after eighteen hours of bombing raids launched from Nazan Bay, and the sighting of a Japanese patrol plane, the Atkans had been instructed to "move out of their fish camps about three miles from the village, [as we were] thinking they might be safer in their tents."[3]

The Magees were given twenty minutes to pack their belongings and ordered to board the ship. Once they were safely out of the way, the sailors sprayed gasoline on the buildings, including the church, and put the village to the torch. Only four houses were left unscathed.

The villagers were three miles away and unable to salvage anything from their homes. Later that evening, as the crew of the *Hulbert* watched the fires, they saw a number of villagers venture into the burning village. The ship's captain ordered boats ashore to evacuate the natives. Sixty-two Atkans were taken aboard the *Hulbert* for temporary relocation to Nikolski on Umnak Island.

Larry Dirks tried to salvage much-needed provisions from the village before it burned to the ground:

> Our village was to have been on fire. We were then, was able to see the fire. The church and school house were showing more brighter flames. The coal which was to be in storage place was burning very brightly. The store house also along with my ranch house area. We knew we needed provisions so we went to the burning village. I went with one other male person from our camp seeing that the flames were getting more brighter. At night this we saw and came towards by the way of the bigger island and into Atka Bay. The fire was burning vigorously. Even the store had burned up. Seeing that we could not do anything, we went back out again. But before we left, we stopped at other houses and found that there was nobody left at the village. After checking every place, we left by our skiff back out to the camping grounds again. We went by the island of Katherine headed outside the pass when we spotted a burning campfire on the beach, so we headed towards it. When we got to that camp, we found Peter and his family at that camp. When we all left the camp, since Tube and two of his daughters asked to come with me. We left with them. We were then leaving Atka Village area.[4]

An entry in the log of the *Gillis* presents evidence that the Japanese did respond to the bombing raids on their forces in Kiska:

> On the night of 13 June advice was received from LINPAC that the Japanese commander in Kiska had directed his aircraft to bomb Nazan Bay. By this time Nazan Bay had been completely evacuated and our forces were safely away. On the 14th, PBY's returning from scouting trips to Kiska reported that about twenty natives were seen on the beach looking up at the planes as they passed over and apparently in distress as their homes had been destroyed. With due precautions not to be taken in by an enemy ruse two PBY's on the following day landed at Atka and brought out the nineteen remaining natives found there. These natives informed the pilots that on the morning of the 14th, five 4-engine bombers had flown across the village and dropped two large and small bombs.[5]

The evacuation and the Navy's scorched-earth policy could have been implemented more carefully if planning had been coordinated between the Navy and the OIA. The Aleuts were prepared to evacuate their village before a Japanese attack. Proper planning would have given them time to take their belongings before the village was burned to the ground. As the Magees described it in their journal:

> [Right after Pearl Harbor] we went to tell the villagers that they ought to pack up and be prepared to leave at any time, for we thought that surely the Coast Guard or someone else would come to evacuate us. However, it was not until six months later that we were taken off the island.... [Also] a letter came from the Juneau Alaska Native Service Office in April of 1942 requesting us to talk over with the people the possibility of having to move to some other part of the territory to be safe from any possible aggression by the Japanese.... We were to be ready to go at a moment's notice, so all packed up a few belongings to take with us.[6]

In their personal narrative, the Magees wrote their thoughts on the people of Atka and the conditions in the village prior to the evacuation and destruction of their homes:

> We had sufficient medical supplies for the people. We never heard of their using any native treatments. We really did not find these people very different from other Americans. They were not primitive at all the way isolated Eskimo villages were twenty or more years ago. They had their own midwives. About once a year a Coast Guard doctor would call in, and a dentist would pull teeth.
>
> We had from twenty to twenty-five children in school before and during the war. We used the schoolhouse for the monthly community meetings. The school activities were always open to the people. Often four or five parents would come to observe the school work. The Christmas entertainment was always the highlight of the year. We invited the village "choir" to bring the traditional Russian star to that program to sing their carols.
>
> In teaching the children about life as it is carried on in the United States, I think we didn't have to make any special build-up for them to understand. They had the radio for years, and magazines gave them an understanding of how others lived. They could all read English. Their little homes were quite livable, with running water piped in from a mountain stream. A few of the children were sent to Mount Edgecombe School in Sitka after the war and two or three of the girls went to the States for further training.[7]

In the evacuation, the people lost everything they owned. Their lives were enriched by education, religious activity, and adequate medical care, but now it was taken from them. Arriving in Killisnoo with nothing more than the clothes on their backs, the people faced years of unrelenting hardship, deprivation, and death.

13

The Pribilofs

With the evacuation of Atka now complete, the Navy turned its attention to the Pribilofs. Located two hundred miles north of Dutch Harbor in the Bering Sea, and six hundred miles northeast of Kiska, the islands include St. Paul and St. George, the only inhabited islands in the group. The military value of these islands was questionable at best. Maps of the islands were misleading in that they presented a false picture for military planners. The Pribilofs appeared to guard Unalaska Island to the south and Bristol Bay and Nunivak Island to the northwest. They looked like giant stepping stones to St. Mathew, St. Lawrence, and Nome.

The reality was that the Pribilofs had no military value. They lacked good harbors and their riptides and heavy waves were hazardous to shipping. The shorelines were steep and dangerous and there were no docks anywhere along their rugged coastline. The topography was not conducive to the construction of landing strips and airbases.

Administered as a federal preserve by the U.S. Fish and Wildlife Service, the islands are the principle breeding grounds for the North Pacific fur seal. In 1942, St. Paul and St. Matthew were among the largest Aleut communities in Alaska. The annual seal harvest was an extremely profitable venture for the United States government. It generated millions of dollars in revenues when the furs were sold on the open market. It was dirty, strenuous work and the FWS employed the natives to harvest the seals.

At the end of May, Admiral Freeman told the FWS to implement a scorched-earth policy if the Japanese attacked the Pribilofs. In a letter from Superintendent Edward Johnston to Ward Bower, chief of the Division of Alaska Fisheries of the FWS, Johnston instructed him to follow the admiral's order in the event of an attack[1]:

Air Mail

Seattle, Washington
May 28, 1942

Mr. Ward T. Bower, Chief,
   Division of Alaska Fisheries,
     Fish and Wildlife Service,
       Washington, D.C.

Dear Mr. Bower:

In my letter of March 18, 1942 addressed to the Director and marked "attention Mr. Paul H. Thompson," I stated that the Commandant of the 13th U.S. Naval District had asked that we follow a "scorched earth" policy on the Pribilof Islands in case of an enemy attack. All supplies of value including seal skins to be destroyed.

As to the destruction of the seal skins, we know of no practical way to destroy any skins that may be in the washing tanks. Those on hand in barrels could be rolled over the cliff back of the village on St. Paul and to the east of the village on St. George. We believe the fall is great enough to break the barrels, and skins that are not carried away by the sea will soon be destroyed by sand fleas.

Gasoline, diesel, seal oil and kerosene can be destroyed by burning or draining the tanks. Food stuffs will be destroyed, but we are not certain of the extent to which this should apply to general stores.

If the Washington Office has any directions along these lines please advise.

We understand that the take of sealskins is not to be limited to 50,000, but that as many additional seals are to be taken as possible up to the total take of last season. Killing will continue until skins become too "stagy" for commercial use.

Very truly yours,
Edward C. Johnston
Superintendent.

    The talk of war and the belief that the Japanese would soon invade the islands created a sense of nervousness among the residents. As a keynote speaker at the Alaska at War Symposium at the University of Alaska in 1993, Flore Lekanof, Sr., shared his memories of the evacuation and relocation[2]:

I was drafted into the U.S. government workforce in May 1942, after the elementary school was closed for the summer. As long as I lived on St. George Island, I would never return to the classroom for schooling. This was the normal practice of the U.S. federal government on the Pribilof Islands since the purchase of Alaska in 1867 from the Russian Government.

It was while a handful of U.S. work force was repairing the landing dock that a messenger brought word of the Dutch Harbor bombing. It was about lunchtime. We were told to stop working and go to our homes. People all over the village were scared to death. On that foggy day, some of us heard airplanes flying over the island. The fog was so thick we could not see whether they were American or Japanese planes. I heard my grandmother say it was time for the creator (God) to come back.

A few days later, my family and others attended the local Russian Orthodox Church, where my father was a reader. After church on that beautiful Sunday afternoon, we had our usual Sunday brunch of coffee and bread. While we were gathered around the kitchen table, shocking news was delivered to our home. At once we were to prepare to board a ship. The village was to be evacuated. Every person was to leave on the ship.

Where we were to be taken, we did not know. We were instructed for each person to take the clothing they wore and a sack of personal clothing and effects to the ship. Domestic animals such as cows and pigs were disposed of by shooting. After much commotion, we were on the U.S. Army transport ship *Delarof*. The St. Paul people were already on the ship.

Although there were pleasantries exchanged by the St. Paul and St. George people as they met, one could see anxiety.

In later years, my Uncle Gabriel Stepetin told me that my maternal grandmother on St. Paul Island went into her bedroom to take her own life. She did not want to leave her home. My uncle was able to stop her, but she died in Funter Bay that winter.

Much illness, physical and mental, was experienced by the Aleut people at Funter Bay, where we were taken. St. Paul people were put on one side of the bay at an old dilapidated cannery site, while the St. George people were put two miles across the bay at an old gold mining camp. Ten percent of the Pribilof people died at the camp during the two years of encampment. Most of these were the elderly and the very young. Many of the deaths were caused by unhealthy living conditions and by pneumonia, tuberculosis, measles, and general depression. I lost both my grandmothers and a sister at Funter Bay. My father suffered from pneumonia and I contracted tuberculosis of the lungs and spent three and a half years in a sanitarium where I nearly died.

On St. Paul, a village committee composed of Aleut leaders and Carl Hoverson, the FWS storekeeper in charge, met on June 4, 1942, to discuss war matters and rumors of a Japanese invasion. They adopted a wartime policy and drew up a set of rules they hoped would ease the tension of the inhabitants. The notice was posted on a workshop door. The most dangerous contingencies in the notice were capitalized: WHEN AIRPLANES ARE SEEN COMING and IF ENEMY BOATS COME.[3]

The notice warned the villagers that it would be difficult to differentiate between American and Japanese planes. At the sight of any approaching aircraft they were directed to seek the safety of their homes or other buildings and avoid standing near windows that might shatter, spewing broken glass fragments and causing serious injuries. The people were told not to "run wildly outside or stand and look at the plane because you may be shot down with machine gun bullets."

Other rules stated, "If you are out in the open lie down flat on the ground in a ditch behind a rock, under a truck or tractor, or anything else that will give you protection. When you are out in the open it is best to wear clothes which are not too bright colored."

If the enemy appeared by boat, residents with firearms were directed not to start shooting at the enemy, or take matters into their own hands. Those who were in charge would decide what action was to be taken and if there was to be any fighting, they would tell them when and where to do it.

Children were ordered to stay close to home at all times and if they should wander very far from the village, they must be accompanied by an adult. A curfew was put into place that required all children to be off the streets and at home by 9 o'clock in the evening. New officers were added to the police force and blackouts were enforced. Movies and dances were banned and an all-night watch force was organized to make the residents feel safe at night.

Members of the committee and the watch force were each in charge of a row of houses where they lived. Residents were ordered to obey all of the instructions of committee members or the police. In anticipation of the danger of fire from falling bombs, all fire extinguishers and firefighting equipment was checked and made ready to quench any fire, no matter how small. An air raid shelter was being erected for the hospital staff and the patients. The committee suggested, "Any of you who feel your safety would be increased can build a shelter for yourselves. It is simply a ditch a few feet deep covered with heavy timbers and sandbags." The last item on the notice reminded the Aleuts to "keep a cool head." To reassure the people, the committee said, "We have your welfare at heart and will endeavor to keep step with whatever develops."

The evacuation of St. Paul was as chaotic as the evacuation of Atka. A converted mine sweeper, USS *Oriole*, arrived on June 14, with orders to evacuate the island. Army transport U.S.A.T. *Delarof* arrived the next day. Aboard the *Oriole*, a nine-man volunteer unit organized by General Buckner and led by Sergeant Lyman Ellsworth waited to go ashore. Their orders were to warn Dutch Harbor if the Japanese appeared and to blow up St. Paul to keep the enemy from getting it. Before they departed from Fort Richardson, Buckner told them, "If you get into trouble we won't be able to give you any help."[4]

On the evening of June 14, officers from a Navy patrol boat came ashore to notify the residents that their village would be evacuated in the immediate future. They were directed to pack their belongings and be prepared to leave the island. The evacuees were told that they were allowed one suitcase. With the assistance of crews from both ships, the loading commenced on June 15.

After the cargo and their personal belongings were stowed aboard ship, 294 Aleuts and fifteen non–Aleut FWS employees departed for St. George on June 16. Before they left the island, the natives turned their cattle loose. Many of their personal belongings as well as government property were left behind.

In an article for the Associated Press, Jeannette J. Lee recounted Mary Bourdukofsky's account of the evacuation:

13. The Pribilofs

Mary Bourdukofsky was at home after church on rugged St. Paul Island one Sunday in the summer of 1942, when her agitated husband rushed breathless through the door from his weekly baseball game.

The game had been canceled without warning, he told her. The Federal Government was forcing them to leave their home on the Pribilof Islands in the Bering Sea for a wartime internment camp in Southeast Alaska, 1,500 miles away.

He came running in and said, "They've stopped the ballgame. They've come to evacuate us people," Bourdukfosky said.[5]

The evacuation was not a pretty scene. "Excitement and confusion stepped up," Ellsworth conceded. One sailor grabbed a "beautiful set of chinaware," an heirloom, from an elderly Aleut woman and "heaved the carton over the side into the water." A look of mingled horror and misery came over the woman's face; a faint moan could be heard coming through her sunken lips. Ellsworth "felt sorry for her."[6]

A short time later, the Signal Corps sent four soldiers to the islands to set up two radio stations to warn of an enemy attack. They remained on a round-the-clock watch from June to September. As part of the military buildup in preparation for an offensive against the Japanese, the Army sent a small military detachment to the islands with orders to construct an airstrip. They were billeted in the empty homes the natives were forced to abandon.

In St. George, the villagers were ready for the *Delarof* to evacuate them. They were notified on the night of June 14 to pack their belongings and to be ready to leave when the ship arrived. FWS agent Daniel C.R. Benson had the responsibility to prepare the village for destruction to make certain that nothing was left intact for the Japanese:

> I was first instructed to prepare the village for destruction first that night by placing a pail of gasoline in each house and building and a charge of dynamite for each other installation such as storage tanks, light plants, trucks, radio transmitters, receivers, antenna masts, etc. The packing of everybody was to be very simple—absolutely nothing but one suitcase per person and a roll of blankets.[7]

Once Benson completed his preparations, he had a ton of dynamite left. He threw it over a cliff and ran for his life before it exploded. He was one of the last residents of St. George to leave the island.

The *Delarof* dropped anchor at 5:30 a.m. on June 16 and by 10 a.m. was underway with 183 Aleuts and seven white FWS employees. Before they departed the island, the natives killed their cattle and chickens rather than leave them for the enemy. For two days before their voyage, the natives dined exclusively on chicken.

14

The Voyage of the Delarof

The hardships the Aleuts suffered during relocation and internment in southeastern Alaska began with the voyage of the *Delarof.* The ship has been described as a huge, ugly, grimy gray combination freight and passenger vessel with guns mounted on its decks. Escorted by the Coast Guard cutter *Onandaga*, the ship zigzagged through the water to avoid enemy submarines that might be lurking below the surface of the ocean.

Upon the ship's arrival at Dutch Harbor on June 17, the Army ordered most of the medical supplies and equipment from St. Paul to be offloaded and transferred to the Fort Mears Army Hospital. In a letter to F.G. Morton of the Seattle FWS office, Ward T. Bower, chief of Alaska Fisheries for FWS, attempted to reconstruct the events that led to the transfer of the Aleuts' medical equipment before they sailed from Dutch Harbor:

> Dr. Barenberg packed eight sealskin barrels with medical supplies and equipment, and packed also the X-ray machine. This is assumed to mean that the remainder of the equipment and supplies was left on St. Paul Island instead of being taken to Funter.
> At Dutch Harbor on June 25, 1942, these eight barrels and one opened package of X-ray film were turned over by Capt. Fred H. Aves, Medical Corps Transport Surgeon of the *USAT Delarof,* for use at Fort Mears Hospital, where a receipt in duplicate was signed by Captain Guy O. Mundem, Medical Supply Officer. The X-ray machine remained in our possession, and I assume it is now at Funter.
> In his letter of July 9, 1942, Mr. Johnston indicated that he did not know of the transfer of the eight barrels of medical supplies and equipment and the package of X-ray film to the Army at Dutch Harbor until the return of Dr. Barenberg to Seattle. Dr. Barenberg said he did not know who authorized the transfer. We do not find anything to show that the Army requested him to turn over the supplies and equipment for use at Fort Mears, and thus apparently Dr. Barenberg did so upon his own responsibility.[1]

Aleuts from St. George and St. Paul sail aboard the USAT *Delarof* in August 1942 to their new home in the burned out cannery and an abandoned gold mine in southeastern Alaska. They would not see their home again for three and a half years (National Archives 80-G-206–199).

Transferring the medical supplies and equipment to the hospital denied essential medical care to the Aleuts during their internment.

The large number of evacuees on the ship, and the Aleuts from Atka already on the island, were causing food shortages in Unalaska. It was imperative that a decision on a permanent relocation site be made quickly. The ship was built to carry 376 passengers, but it now carried 560 men, women, and children. On June 18, it sailed for an unknown destination.

Conditions on the *Delarof* were extremely unhealthy for the evacuees. Space was limited and the sick and the healthy were forced to share the same living spaces. Fredrika Martin, a nurse and wife of an FWS doctor, was an eyewitness to a particularly tragic event during the early days of the voyage from Dutch Harbor:

> Since once aboard the ship the doctor felt completely free of responsibility for his islanders and had no personal interest in any of these patients of his. He could not be coaxed into the disagreeable crowded hold even before all the Aleuts and many non–Aleuts came down, after our stay over at Dutch Harbor, with "ships cold," a serious grippe infection. He did not come to assist even at the

birth of a St. George baby or its subsequent death of bronchial pneumonia because of our inability (D.S.R.B. and mine) to separate mother and child from the other grippe sufferers, and the mother herself was ill. I think I recall this doctor attending the midnight or after funeral of the poor little mite, such a tiny weighted parcel being let down into the deep waters of the Gulf of Alaska against a shoreline of dramatic peaks and blazing sunset sky.[2]

This three-day-old infant was the daughter of Innokenty and Haretina R. Kochutin, former residents of St. Paul. The baby was the first of many casualties of the evacuation and internment of the Aleuts during World War II.

In a deposition hearing in 1978, for possible reparations from the government, 71-year-old Haretina R. Kochutin was asked, "By what means were you removed [from St. Paul] and under what conditions?" In a brief reply, she responded by writing down her answer: Transport ship: Delarof; in the hold of the ship, with a mattress to sleep on and one bathroom for everyone. The men were in another part of the ship, no baths for two weeks, the very sick were not separated and we had to live with them.[3]

Neither the Captain of the *Delarof* nor anyone else on the ship knew what their final destination was. No one had any idea what to do with the evacuees. The military had evacuated the Aleuts, but it was now up to the Department of the Interior to figure out what to do with them. Even as the ship got under way, officials in the Department were searching frantically for a place to settle the natives for an indefinite period of time. The lack of a coherent policy was now demonstrated. They had discussed plans for evacuation, but they were never able to reach a consensus. Prearranged plans of action and contingency plans were non-existent. Civilian authorities were now forced to make hasty decisions.

As the evacuation of the Pribilofs commenced, high-ranking military officers and OIA Superintendent Hirst were meeting to select relocation sites. They decided that Killisnoo Bay in southeastern Alaska was a potential location for resettlement. Edward C. Johnston, superintendent of the Seal Division of the FWS, assumed responsibility for settling the natives in the camps.

On that same day, Johnston sent a telegram to Alaska Fisheries Chief Ward Bower, requesting information on the availability of CCC (Civilian Conservation Corps) camp facilities at Lyman, Washington, or space on the Tulalip Indian Reservation at Marysville, Washington. Johnston changed his mind when he learned that the CCC camp was already occupied and the reservation required that buildings be constructed to house the evacuees. He concluded that he must have a location for the Pribilovians within a week.

On June 15, 1942, Indian Field Service Agent Donald Hagerty informed Commissioner William Zimmerman that the military authorities had requested immediate and definite instructions from the Indian Office as to where the refugees could be landed and taken care of. He further stated that Superintendent Hirst was working directly with the commander of the Navy's Alaska Sector, Captain Parker, and that Hirst would notify the military where the Aleuts should be relocated.

The OIA in Washington, D.C., decided that it was in their best interest to keep the evacuees in Alaska. On June 16, Zimmerman contacted Hagerty to inform him that the Aleuts from the same villages should be kept together to preserve their community cohesion. He asked local FWS and OIA officials to select relocation sites, and he suggested using fish canneries that were abandoned or vacant at the end of the fishing season.

Apparently, Hagerty was the principal official of the OIA who made the final decision on specific sites. On June 17, he informed Zimmerman that an agreement had been reached with the P.E. Harris Company for the use of its cannery at Funter Bay. The contract stipulated that the company would not assume liability for any injury on its property. He concluded similar agreements with A.J. Hatlund of Portland, Oregon, for a lease on their abandoned cannery at Killisnoo, and with the Admiralty Alaska Gold Mining Company for its abandoned gold mine located across Funter Bay from the Harris Company cannery. These locations became the mandatory living quarters for most of the Aleuts for the duration of the war.

Atka, St. Paul, and St. George weren't the only villages evacuated in response to the Japanese occupation of Attu and Kiska. The Aleut villages of Nikolski on Umnak Island, Makushin, Biorka, Chernofski, and Kashega on Unalaska Island, and Akutan on Akutan Island were also evacuated. Admiral Freeman believed these villages were in danger. On June 29, he issued an order directing the evacuation of all natives from the Aleutian Islands. One week later, two ships arrived at Nikolski. Seventy Aleuts, the OIA teacher Barbara Whitfield and her husband Samuel, and the non–Aleut foreman of the Aleutian Livestock Company were evacuated from the island.

Many of the Aleuts residing in Unalaska Village believed they might be the next Japanese invasion target. The presence of a large military force gave some of them a false sense of security, but others weren't so certain, and they left the island at the first opportunity. Philemon Tutiakoff expressed the feelings of the people:

> We had been notified prior to the bombing [of Dutch Harbor] that we may be evacuated. Naturally, listening to the radio, people were alarmed. They became afraid. The most affluent Aleuts and civilians bought their way by Alaska Steamship to places of safety. The Unalaska Aleuts felt that with the presence of the military and the preparations we could see them taking, [we] thought and hoped that the U.S. military would protect us in case of what we all thought was a direct assault on the town of Unalaska.[4]

Evacuees from St. Paul and St. George, Pribilof Islands, aboard the USAT *Delarof*, August 1942 (673rd Air Base Wing History Office Joint Base Elmendorf-Richardson, Alaska).

The Aleuts were forced to leave behind most of their personal belongings. This included clothing, family albums, musical instruments, priceless religious icons, unique craftwork, boats, and essential hunting and fishing gear. Left unpacked and secured by locked doors and boarded-up windows, they were destroyed by thieves or deterioration from the harsh Aleutian winters. It was 3½ years before natives saw home again.

When the S.S. *Alaska* docked at Unalaska to evacuate the villagers, the commanding officer of the Dutch Harbor Naval station, Captain William N. Updegraf, issued an order that all natives, or persons with as much as one-eighth native blood, were compelled to evacuate the island. They were only to take what they could carry. Updegraf's order treated whites and non-whites differently from each other. A white man named Charles Hope was the postmaster. He remained in Unalaska while his Aleut wife and daughter were required to evacuate.

Harriet Hope was five years old when Unalaska got its orders to go. She remembers being dressed in her Sunday school coat and gloves and her mother

14. The Voyage of the Delarof

holding her up at the rail of the ship. She remembers watching her house get smaller and smaller and her father, a white postmaster left behind to help with the war effort, jumping up and down, waving his arms over his head to say goodbye. It would be three and a half years before she saw her home again and it would never be the same.[5]

The rationale for removing the natives from Unalaska while not evacuating non–Aleuts residing in the Dutch Harbor-Unalaska area has never been fully explained. One explanation that has been put forth is that the Navy was concerned with a severe labor shortage, so they prevented defense and construction workers from leaving the village. Even though the workers were not employed by the government, the Navy refused to allow them to leave.

There are not many documents available on the evacuation of these villages. Most of the information comes from eyewitness accounts. According to the natives, they were transported to southeastern Alaska on the Alaskan Steamship Company vessel, the S.S. *Columbia*. The evacuees remained at the Wrangell Institute for several weeks until the OIA eventually relocated them to a CCC camp at Ward Lake near Ketchikan.

15

Strangers in a Strange Land

After a 1,500-mile voyage from Dutch Harbor, on June 24, 1942, the *Delarof* dropped anchor at Funter Bay on Admiralty Island. For the 560 Aleuts packed aboard ship, the beauty of the island, with its towering green Sitka spruce spilling down the mountains to sandy beaches, western hemlocks reaching halfway up snowcapped peaks, and colorful wildflowers covering the land, soon proved to be deceptive. They had no idea that the overcrowding they had endured on the ship would soon be surpassed by the horrendous living conditions of the camps.

The Pribilovions and their personal belongings were transferred ashore to an abandoned cannery in two canvas-covered baidars (fashioned after skin boats sewn together from sea lion hides and driftwood) and motor launches from the transport. The temperature was about 80 degrees, and coming from the cold, damp climate of their islands, they perspired freely in the hot sun as they assisted the ship's crew to pile mattresses, blankets and supplies into the launches.

The evacuees were not happy with their new home. A national correspondent for the *New York Herald-Tribune*, Joseph Driscoll, was the only reporter on hand when the Aleuts disembarked from the ship. He was in Juneau when Governor Gruening invited him to join the official party aboard the FSW ship, the *Brant*. Late in the afternoon, they arrived at their destination in time to witness the disembarkation of the Aleuts from the Pribilofs. Driscoll was fascinated by what he called the strangest cargo any ship had ever brought to American shores. As the only reporter on hand, he had an excellent opportunity to interview the evacuees.

"I don't like this hot country," was the grumbling verdict of one old native.[1]

"Too many trees, no room to walk around," was the snap judgment of the newcomers, used to their own treeless rocks on which nothing but moss and wild grass grew.[2]

15. Strangers in a Strange Land

Evacuees from St. George and St. Paul watch from the decks of the USAT *Delarof* as their homes disappear into the distance, August 1942 (673rd Air Base Wing Joint Base Elmendorf-Richardson, Alaska).

Driscoll liked the Aleuts but like most whites in Alaska at that time, he believed he was superior to them. His description of the evacuees tends to bear this out[3]:

> The Aleuts are bilingual, speaking with equal ease either English, colored by American slang, or their aboriginal tongue mixed with a dash of Russian.
> Physically, the Aleuts are not the tall, silent, unsmiling Indian of whom James Fenimore Cooper wrote. Instead they are wiry, they chatter incessantly and they grin and laugh on the slightest provocation. They are cousins to the Eskimo and there is an oriental strain in them. On the whole they are fairly intelligent. They are stronger than they look, but are subject to tuberculosis and the white man's burden, venereal disease, a gift from the American and Russian traders and whalers who formally frequented the islands. Many of the faces are pock-marked.

From past experience with the natives, Driscoll knew that the Aleuts were afflicted with a weakness for candy and alcohol: "The natives are not good drinkers. Drinking sends them to the dogs and gutters." If they step out of line, "their white guardians discipline them by cutting down on their allowance of sugar and candy until they reform."[4] He thought that these were not their only disabilities: "They lean too heavily and too often upon the government, to let Uncle Sam do things for them that they and their ancestors used to do for themselves and were better off for the doing."[5]

Despite what he thought about the evacuees, Driscoll believed they were good, loyal Americans:

> Chatting with the Aleuts, you discover they are as 100 percent American as anybody from Georgia or Arkansas. They are interesting people with broad taste, ranging from baseball and sealing to Bing Crosby and blue foxes. They were well worth rescuing. Their mere existence is proof that the human race can and will survive under the most adverse conditions.
>
> "We are American citizens," the Aleuts told us with quiet pride. Part of the great American Republic since 1867, when we bought Russian America, this was the Aleuts' first trip to our shores. They discovered us and we discovered them. No doubt they thought us odd too.[6]

There are no trees on the Pribilofs or anywhere else in the Aleutians. This sophisticated news reporter from New York City condescendingly asked a "dirty-faced" Aleut boy if he knew what a tree was. The answer came as no surprise to Driscoll.[7]

> "Do you know what a tree is?" I inquired of a grinning, dirty-faced boy.
> "Sure," he answered instantly, "a tree is a stick with grass on it."
> "Did you ever see a tree before?" I continued.
> "Sure," he said, "at Christmas time we always had trees. Christmas trees our teachers bought for us."
> "Christmas trees?" I repeated. "Where did you get Christmas trees?"
> "From Sears Roebuck," was the answer that left no doubt those mail-order houses must be numbered among the missionaries of American civilization.

After the natives were transferred to the camp at Funter Bay, the *Delarof* steamed farther south down the strait to a deserted herring saltery at Killisnoo. At three o'clock in the morning, the refugees from Atka were ferried to their new home in an ugly red fishing scow. Rather than disembark at Funter Bay or return to the mainland and desert their people, Ralph and Ruby Magee chose to remain with them. They were scheduled to transfer to a native school at Port Graham, but they begged to stay, watch over their wards, and help them get settled in their new surroundings. Their request was granted.

Driscoll had poignant memories of the events of that morning:

> As the native children were carried down the transport's gangplank and lined up in the fish-stinking scow, Mrs. Magee led them in a vocal salute to America. First they sang with gusto *Alaska, My Alaska* to the tune of *My Maryland*. Next, they sang *Cheer for Old Atka* to the tune of *Roll Out the Barrel*. They wound up with *God Bless America* to the tune of Irving Berlin. Somehow it was rather touching to hear the little aborigines singing their heads off before breakfast to prove that

they were just as patriotic, just as Rotarian, as the rest of us. The least we could do was to clap hands and toss them some coppers, for which we were politely and shyly thanked. I must say these little yellow-skinned barbarians were much better mannered than many children back home.[8]

In comparing the evacuees from Atka to the natives of the Pribilofs, Driscoll favored the Atka natives. The Atkans scratched for a meager living out in the middle of the ocean, but the people of the Pribilofs were pampered. Government officials called them "steam heated Indians." Once the annual seal harvest was over for the year, each of the individuals who participated in the hunt was given a bonus of $750 for six weeks of work. Their benefits included housing, food, clothing and all of the necessities from the government commissaries, and they could fish and hunt or remain idle for 46 weeks. The people of Atka called thatched huts or caves home, but the residents of St. George and St. Paul lived in relative comfort in concrete homes equipped with washing machines, phonographs and radios. At community cinemas, they enjoyed some of the latest movies from the States.

Dan Benson and his wife Catherine had resided in the islands for twenty years when the war broke out. Dan was the agent and caretaker for the St. George natives. Though they raised three sons in this harsh environment, the Bensons considered the natives of the Pribilofs their adopted children.

"You have to do everything for them, even think for them," Catherine Benson said.

With Uncle Sam providing free food, clothing and housing, the natives tended to be extravagant and throw away goods less fortunate aborigines would envy. "We have to caution them that everything cost money, even though they don't have to pay," said Mrs. Benson. "We remind them that their teachers don't get things free. They are surprised when told that Americans have to pay at stores. And they ask: Aren't all Americans rich?"[9]

The OIA was running out of time. They'd failed to plan for this emergency and were scrambling to find a place for the evacuees. They selected Wrangell Institute on Shoemaker Bay, about two miles from the center of Wrangell. This small incorporated city on the northern tip of the Island had a strong Tlingit Indian culture, and half of the residents were indigenous natives. After 1867, the city was a U.S. Army outpost for few years, but the base had long since been abandoned. Shrimp canneries, a cold storage plant, and a faltering lumber mill were all that were left to support the city's three churches and the staff of a one-doctor hospital.

On July 13, 1942, one hundred and sixty Aleuts arrived at Wrangell Island aboard the S.S. *Columbia* and were immediately transported to the institute. Built in 1932, this Alaskan Indian Service coeducational vocational boarding

Wrangell Institute, Shoemaker Bay, 1942. Aleuts were brought to the institute prior to their relocation to the camp at Burnett Inlet (courtesy Aleutian/Pribilof Islands Association).

school had separate wings for boys and girls and housed over 100 students. With summer vacation in full swing, it was a convenient location for the evacuees, but it was only a temporary stopgap measure to buy time until other sites were found.

Because there wasn't room inside the building for all 160 Aleuts, the U.S. Army erected tents with wooden floors on the grounds of the institute. The overcrowding was made worse with the arrival of an additional 137 Aleuts from Unalaska aboard the S.S. *Alaska* on August 1. They too were housed in tents.

For two weeks they camped out on the school grounds while waiting to learn where they would be resettled. They received three meals a day, mostly dog salmon, tea, and bread. No one died from eating the food, but in many cases it wasn't fit to eat. Men and women of all ages were assigned to work in the institute's kitchen, laundry and bakery. One group of Indians built a barge to transport lumber and supplies to their future home at Ward Lake.

Some of the evacuees were destitute and had only the clothes on their backs when they were forced to evacuate their homes. This influx of refugees created serious logistical problems for the government officials responsible for their care. They were faced with the monumental task of obtaining mattresses, bedding, dishes, and other necessary items the Aleuts needed.

15. Strangers in a Strange Land

Wrangell Institute, Shoemaker Bay, 1942. Tents were erected to relieve overcrowding and to provide temporary shelter to the internees who couldn't get in (courtesy Aleutian/Pribilof Islands Association).

Military and civilian doctors examined the Aleuts and gave them shots for typhoid and smallpox, but failed to treat them for tuberculosis, pneumonia, or viruses. Adults and children were infected with head lice. Their hair was cut short and their scalps doused with kerosene to exterminate the parasites.

16

Burnett Inlet

The first group to leave the institute were the recently arrived Aleuts from Unalaska. They were at Wrangell for almost two weeks when the OIA decided to move them 45 miles away to Burnett Inlet on the western side of Etlolin Island. On August 12, an advance party of 16 Aleuts and OIA Assistant Superintendent Fred R. Geeslin boarded a barge loaded with building supplies. Surrounded by lumber and supplies, the Indians and Geeslin were confined to an open space in the middle of the barge. Covering themselves with a tarpaulin for protection against the unpredictable Alaska weather, they were forced to drop anchor and spend an uncomfortable night on the water.

The job of the advance team was to repair the buildings at a long-abandoned cannery. They got little sleep that night. The next morning, 16 tired Aleuts went ashore and started to work. Geeslin returned to the institute to pick up the remaining 122 natives from Unalaska. Late in the afternoon of August 14, he returned to Burnett Inlet and the Aleuts went ashore.

At first sight, the evacuees were shocked beyond words. As bad as conditions at the institute were, this was far worse. They were greeted by an isolated, burned-out cannery. The only buildings left standing were the homes of the former cannery workers, eleven decrepit cottages and a bunkhouse. New cottages would have to be built, but until they were ready for occupancy, the Aleuts were forced to sleep on the floor for a lack of beds. None of the existing buildings had electricity or plumbing and there was no church, school, hospital or store. Fortunately, some of the refugees were skilled carpenters.

In testimony before the National Coalition for Redress/Repatriation in November 1980, Philemon M. Tutiakoff stated that when the Aleuts arrived at the camp the conditions were unacceptable:

> The most galling and demeaning feature that many of us recall explicitly is that those in charge regarded us as incapable ... of any form of decision making. At no time throughout this entire process were we given the right to make choices of any kind.
>
> Initially, the overcrowded conditions were an abomination. There were twenty-eight of us forced to live in one designated 15 × 20 foot house. There existed no church, no school, no medical facility, no store, no community water or sewage system, no recreation or community facility, no skiffs or dories, no fishing gear and no hunting rifles. We had to abandon our heirlooms and pets even before the evacuation.[1]

Tutiakoff further stated, "Medical care was limited to the service of midwives, augmented by one doctor who removed tonsils and adenoids and gave cursory examinations."

Each person was forced to fend for himself, but in a show of community support, they helped each other. Without a doctor or nurse to provide for their medical needs, some of the women took it upon themselves to care for cuts, bruises, injuries and sickness. Soon after they arrived in camp, everyone got boils and some people were covered with them. A visiting doctor examined them and decided the boils were the result of the people adjusting to their new environment.

Martha Newell was part Aleut and, because she did not wish to accompany her husband when he left for the lower 48, she was evacuated with the other Aleuts from Unalaska. In March 1943, she wrote her husband Kenneth, encouraging him to write to their friend, Congressional Delegate Anthony Diamond.

> We're all anxious to go home. I can't think of staying another winter, and most of the folks feel the same as there is no work and we are paying for our food. In the first place, we shouldn't as we didn't ask to come. The Japs in the states are not, and are probably treated better than we are. I wonder if Mr. Diamond could do something, at least get us near home in the Aleutians. The False Pass and King Cove people are still there, and don't expect to be moved and at other places near there, they are home.[2]

Diamond forwarded Newell's letter to Hirst and Geeslin. Their reply left no doubt in anyone's mind what they thought of Mrs. Newell's complaints. They considered her a nuisance:

> The complaint of Mrs. Newell is the first to our knowledge, with the exception that the Burnett inlet people made a complaint while I was at Ketchikan in August before we could get transportation of the needed building materials to them. However George T. Barrett, Principal Wrangell Institute and myself made special trips there to further explain to them that we had surveyed all southeastern Alaska in attempts to find the best available quarters for them

and that one of the groups would have to be stationed there. To date we have reason to believe that all possible has been done to accommodate them, and that there is no reason for complaint.

Naturally these people hear of the Pribilofs going back and think they should go back also. Especially as they have property at Unalaska, with which this office is also assisting them with the rental collections where leased. We have also arranged with Parley H. Pratt, Unalaska, Alaska to assist in the protection of the Native property there. The defense authorities there are also assisting as you will note from the following wire dated March 24: "NATIVE HOUSES HAVE ALL BEEN BOARDED UP AND ALL ARE GUARDED BY A MILITARY POLICE PATROL FORCE BOTH MR. ROBINSON U.S. MARSHALL AND MR. COREA JUSTICE DEPT AGREE THAT ALL REASONABLE PROTECTIONS ARE BEING FURNISHED BY ARMY AUTHORITIES—COLLADAY CG"

Even though these evacuees may be receiving less than Japs in concentration camps, as stated by Mrs. Newell, I am sure that the large majority of them are satisfied under the present conditions, and they have expressed that they wish to be self-supporting as they were at their original homes where there are wage earners in their families. We are not asking for payment for the supplies issued to them where there are no wage earners. Under the present condition with the great shortage of labor I see no reason why Mr. Newell should not pay for the supplies issued to his wife. However we will investigate her case further and if she is estranged from her husband, we will furnish supplies to her as long as she remains at Burnett Inlet and cannot obtain employment.[3]

Edythe Long, the school teacher at Burnett Lake, showed little compassion for Mrs. Newell. She brushed off the complaints as quickly as Hirst and Geeslin did:

Mrs. Newell has a firm conviction that the more complaints she registers and the more dissatisfaction and discontent she can arouse amongst the evacuees, the sooner the authorities will be obliged to move her back to Unalaska. Her entire being is centered on that one purpose—-to go back home this spring, and it seems she will go to any lengths even of gross misrepresentation to attain this end. She refuses to face the fact that Unalaska is in a war zone and that no women or children can be returned there at present regardless of anyone's views or wishes. She not only complains for herself, but goes from house to house spreading discontent. Several people have expressed disgust at her unreasonable talk and refuse to listen to her.[4]

Martha Newell finally got her wish to return to her home to Unalaska. She died at Burnett Inlet, but she was buried on her beloved island.

Conditions at the camp had reached a crisis point and created an emergency for the OIA. Less than ten days after their arrival, the evacuees had had enough. They wanted to leave this place immediately. The Aleuts remaining at Wrangell were dissatisfied and insisted that if they were sent to the inlet, they wouldn't stay. Their leader, William Zaharoff, sent a telegram to OIA

Superintendent Hirst, protesting the conditions his people were forced to endure. He bemoaned the fact that the water was low and not fit to drink. Illness struck the camp, there was no fish or game anywhere, and the houses weren't fit to live in. His people wanted a better place.

In a telegram to Hirst, Assistant Superintendent Geeslin and Director of Education George Barrett confirmed the situation. The teachers they sent to the inlet advised against proceeding with construction of living quarters. Hirst refused to move the people to another location and responded to their concerns by outlining his plans for the camp. The teachers who complained about their assignment would be replaced by Edythe and Elmer Long. A nurse and an Indian Service doctor from Juneau would be sent to the inlet to assess conditions at the camp. The decision to relocate the Aleuts to another location would be dependent on the advice of the medical team.

One week later, Barrett informed Hirst that the doctor was leaving, but the nurse would remain to provide medical care for the natives. The Longs were doing an excellent job. As far as he was concerned, everything was okay and the natives were satisfied with the improvements. The doctor assured Hirst that the water supply was being improved and except for shots for whooping cough, all immunizations had been completed. Despite their protest to be removed to a new location, the Aleuts remained at Burnett Inlet for the duration of the war.

17

Ward Lake

Once the evacuees from Unalaska were resettled at Burnett Inlet, the only Aleuts remaining at the institute were the 200 refugees from Akutan, Biorka, Kashega, Makushin, and Nikolski. With the exception of 25 natives who temporarily remained behind, the rest were shipped to an abandoned CCC camp at Ward Lake. Geeslin and the others followed a few days later on a lumber-laden barge towed by the OIA boat, *Penguin*.

Geeslin had a difficult time arranging transportation for his charges. He attempted to pay for steerage on a Canadian cruise ship, but the captain refused to take them. He appealed to the Army, but they also refused. Coast Guard Captain Fred Zeusler intervened and arranged the necessary transportation. The tents on the grounds of the institute were dismantled and loaded aboard the barge. The floors were to be used to construct new cabins at Ward Lake.

Ward Lake is located about eight miles from Ketchikan. With a population of 5,000 in 1940, Ketchikan was Alaska's second largest city and an important seaport and the gateway to the last frontier. Unlike other centers of population in southeastern Alaska, Ketchikan had 24 miles of highway for its 450 motorized vehicles. This proximity of the camp to the city caused major problems for residents and Aleuts alike.

The lake was a fifty-seven-acre public recreation area administered by the Forest Service for the Department of Agriculture. This scenic wilderness was a favorite spot for Ketchikan's residents to swim, fish, and picnic, and was the location of a CCC camp. With the attack on Pearl Harbor, the CCC was disbanded and the camp abandoned. The 10th Army Air Force Rescue Boat Squadron moved in and used the camp as training facility. With the OIA's decision to use the camp as a relocation site for the Aleuts, the squadron was transferred to the Army Air Field at Annette Island. Ironically, the evacuees did not live on the lake or nearby Ward Cove. The camp was hidden in a dense forest, but the Indians didn't even have a view of the lake.

17. Ward Lake

Two hundred Aleuts were dropped off at the camp at 2:00 in the morning and told, "Find your house." The camp consisted of nine small cabins, four communal buildings, a mess hall, a school, and a church. Each cabin had a small kitchen and a bedroom with two bunk beds. Until new quarters were built, the Aleuts were reduced to sleeping on the floor in their bedrolls and blankets or staying in tents.

The cabins had no running water or electricity, and transportation into Ketchikan wasn't available to the Aleuts. The first impression of Dorofey Chercasen was that he was being put in prison and he felt a deep separation from the home he was forced to leave behind.

Each household was issued a wood-burning stove. Buckets filled from an outside hydrant were carried into the cabins, heated on the stove and taken to the community laundry. The laundry was a large tin basin with four cold-water faucets and there were only two shower stalls for the entire camp. The village outhouse was a long open trough without seats. Despite the constant flow of water through the trough, it was thick with flies and insects and the stench was unbearable.

Food preparation was a major challenge until Geeslin and Leonard Allen, principal of the Ketchikan Indian Service School, established a more efficient system. The restaurant-style kitchen range in the mess hall was in deplorable condition. It took two days of scrubbing and cleaning before it could be used to cook their first hot meal. According to Geeslin, the evacuees experienced strong feelings of oppression and suffocation.

The most serious problem for the residents of Ward Lake was the lack of adequate medical care. Except for an occasional visit by a doctor from the Indian Service, no doctor was available when someone became sick or hurt. When medical personnel made their infrequent visits to the camp, those with tuberculosis were sent to the Indian Service hospital in Tacoma, Washington, for treatment. Before the Aleuts arrived at the camp, the Alaska Territorial Medical Director suggested that it should be utilized as a detention facility for persons who failed to obtain treatment for venereal disease.

The teacher for the Indian Service School, Pauline Whitfield, and her husband Sam were placed in charge of the camp. They didn't understand the problems the OIA created for the people when they took them from their homes and brought them to this place. They felt that the majority of the evacuees were doing a fairly good job of adjusting to their surroundings.

In truth, the Aleuts had a difficult time adjusting to the conditions of the camp. The ground was wet all the time and they had to live in tents with leaky roofs until the cabins were built. Their clothes, bedding, and mattresses were always soaked from the constant rain and the camp itself resembled a swamp.

When the sun did shine, its rays were blocked by huge trees that offered little shelter from the elements.

Their sense of isolation deepened when the Aleuts realized that neither the OIA nor any other government agency would provide transportation into town. They could call for a taxi, but the only telephone in the camp was at the school. The Indian School Service teacher refused to allow them to use it.

The residents had two choices. They could walk the eight miles into town or they could pay a local taxi owner, Eugene Wacker, 35 cents to take them. To accommodate the large number of riders who wanted to go to town, he purchased a small bus. Now, they were able to ride into town and shop for necessities. It gave them the freedom to work at jobs away from the camp during the day, and return to their families at night.

The men found employment at canneries and sawmills in Ketchikan, commercial fishing boats in Sitka, or in construction at the Army base at Metlakatla. During the summers of 1943 and 1944, some of them went to work on the Aleutian Livestock Company sheep ranch near Nikolski. As soon as the men found outside employment, the OIA no longer supplied them with food and other necessities.

The Aleuts owed a large debt of gratitude to Wacker for his many kindnesses to them. He bailed them out of jail and helped many of them to find employment. Whenever he heard of a job opening, he came into camp and told the people about it. For those who wanted the job, he drove them into town, after which he drove them home at night. Wacker did this for the three years the Aleuts lived at Ward Lake.

The experiences of the residents of Ward Lake were vastly different, and in many ways more tragic than those living at Killisnoo and Funter Bay. The residents of those camps were subjected to a serious lack of modern conveniences, but the Ward Lake natives suffered from the culture shock of exposure to a small but modern town.

Gilda Shelikhoff had vivid memories of Ward Lake. In an article she wrote in 1996, she told the story of Anna Hoblet, one of the many evacuees at Ward Lake:

> Anna was 18 years old in July of 1942 when the people from Akutan were evacuated, 41 of them in all, along with people from Nikolski, Kasgega, Biorka, and Mukushin on board the S.S. *Columbia*, an Alaska Steamship Company vessel. They were taken to Wrangell Institute. There the entire group of 160 refugees remained, living in tents and old houses, until their final destination, a Civilian Conservation Corps camp at Ward Cove near Ketchikan, was established several weeks later.

The Aleut people of Akutan, along with Nikolski and the three small villages of Unalaska Island, had a much different experience at Ward Cove. In many ways, it was much more tragic than those of the other internment camps. Whereas the other camps were plagued by an almost complete lack of twentieth-century benefits, such as clean and warm houses to live in, a clean water source for drinking and other uses, adequate food, and indoor bathroom facilities, the Aleuts near Ketchikan were subjected to some of the worst aspects of modern civilization. The majority of them had never been far from their isolated island homes. Having been evacuated from villages of no larger than a few dozen friends and family, the Aleuts faced a population of about 5,000 people, native and white, living in the Ketchikan area. During that time period, Ketchikan, like many other towns in Alaska, catered to the loggers and fishermen. The Aleuts being friendly people welcomed them into the camp, and soon became victims of bootleggers and white exploiters. With the exception of tuberculosis the Aleuts were in good health when they arrived in the Ketchikan area. The sad result was that Ward Cove Aleut refugees were struck with epidemics of venereal disease, alcohol abuse, and poor conditions. Although the Aleuts were free of venereal disease when they left Wrangell for Ward Cove, the camp within months was ravaged by gonorrhea. The death rate at Ward Cove was perhaps the highest among all the Aleut internment camps.

She described the conditions at Ward Cove as very unsanitary. There was no good water source, many people got sick and many people broke out with terrible sores. The children didn't have anything to play with and were often seen playing with used condoms. It was during this time she got Hepatitis B, probably due to unsanitary conditions that they were forced to live under. There was no penicillin so they mixed sulfa with some purple stuff to try to treat the venereal disease that was spreading through the camp.

While she was working at Juneau, she got raped. The people at the hospital wanted her to take the guy to court, but she felt that she would not be able to handle the additional pain this would cause. She and her family were going through enough pain and suffering as it was. After this incident, she went back to Ketchikan where she spent most of her time there living with a [local] guy who wanted to marry her. She wanted to come back home so she refused to marry him.[1]

Geeslin remained at Ward Lake for several weeks. He understood the evacuees' propensity for alcohol and placed a ban on liquor. On one occasion, he impounded a taxi and arrested the driver for smuggling liquor into the camp. In response to the impoundment and arrest, the cab driver took the matter to court and instituted a lawsuit against Geeslin. To enforce the ban, Geeslin requested Captain Fred A. Zeusler to arrange for surveillance of the camp and to provide a guard at the entrance if it should become necessary. Zeusler enthusiastically honored Geeslin's request. He saw it as a way to reduce the expanding vice in the environs of Ketchikan.

The benefit of living a few miles from Ketchikan should have made life easier for the camp's residents, but unfortunately, it made their lives more complicated. In 1943, Ketchikan was in an uproar. The townsfolk accused the Aleuts of causing major health hazards for its citizens. After claiming that the evacuees were spreading "virulent sex diseases," Harry G. McCain, the chairman of the city council's Committee on Police, Health, and Sanitation, quarantined the camp. On May 19, 1943, McCain wrote a letter to Governor Gruening: "[W]e have recently been forced to quarantine their camp in order to ... catch up to their venereal disease situation.... These people are also badly honeycombed with tuberculosis, from which disease a considerable number have died since they were placed at Ward Cove.² McCain wanted to rid the city of this "dangerous menace," and he wanted Governor Gruening to remove them from Ward Lake. He charged that they were infecting public places and causing an epidemic in the city. He told the governor that the latrines emptied directly into Ward Cove Lake, one of the most beautiful recreation areas in Alaska. They killed off the wildlife and they hurt local businesses because they were "unsanitary, diseased, and obnoxious." He suggested that the governor should find a way to care for the welfare of the Aleuts without menacing established communities of people:

> There are a large number of service men in and near Ketchikan and neither they nor the civilians should be infected with their diseased conditions.... The proprietor of the Totem Lunch inquired whether or not she could refuse their patronage for the reason they were unsanitary and diseased and thus obnoxious to her regular customers besides requiring an unusual amount of trouble in sterilizing their dishes.... Even the bars would much prefer not to have their patronage.... Therefore we desire to protest their being kept quartered at Ward cove and to suggest they ought to be moved to some suitable location where they would not have immediate contacts with large numbers of people.³

The city council debated the issue and listened to a number of witnesses. One witness argued that the Aleuts should have been left in their island home. Others claimed that most of the charges were false. On a vote of five to one, the council voted to send a petition to the governor to either move the Aleuts from Ward Lake, or provide proper medical attention for them. Gruening left the matter up to the OIA to find a suitable solution.

In response to the council's concerns, Superintendent Hirst told them that based on a medical investigation by the territorial medical director, Dr. J.P. Eberhardt, the Aleuts would not be resettled in other camps away from Ward Lake. However, he promised to improve their health conditions and bring another nurse for the evacuees at Ward Lake and Burnett Inlet.

Despite the public meetings on the matter, health conditions continued to worsen. Medical reports from the camp indicated that many of the residents were sick with the flu. Hirst admitted that medical care for the natives was worse than in the States, but that with their limited funds and personnel, his agency was doing everything possible to meet the situation.

The council's complaints resulted in the removal of 46 Aleuts to Burnett Inlet. This action helped relieve some of the overcrowded conditions at the camp, but in truth, it was the pollution in the Ward Lake recreational area that forced the move. Tests performed on the lake in the early months of 1944 showed that the lake was polluted with high levels of coliform. Fecal waste from the continued use of the inadequate and antiquated septic system drained into the lake, thus preventing the citizens of Ketchikan from swimming or fishing in it.

In addition to the city council and the citizens of Ketchikan, the Aleuts had to deal with an unfriendly police department. The evacuees were arrested on a regular basis, charged with drunkenness and disorderly conduct, and fined for their behavior.

For the next two years, the Aleuts disappeared from the public debates. In a rare appearance in 1945, they sang Christmas carols in Russian and Aleut at the Ketchikan General Hospital and the USO. A number of the city's residents were invited to enjoy a traditional Aleut New Year ceremony and were introduced to a display of church adornments.

The death rate at Ward Lake was one of the highest of all the Aleut evacuation camps. In September, just one month after they arrived, a 13-year-old boy died, and by Christmas, three more evacuees died. In the next three years nearly a quarter of the residents would die from pneumonia and other diseases that plagued the daily lives of the camp's residents. Many were buried in Bay View Cemetery, but some of them rest in forgotten graves in the woods near the camp.

18

Funter Bay

The *Delarof*, with its human cargo, dropped anchor off Admiralty Island on June 24, 1942. Almost 300 Aleuts and FWS personnel from St. Paul went ashore to the devastation of their new home. In their haste to find suitable locations, the Alaska Indian Service selected two sites at Funter Bay, an abandoned cannery and a gold mine. The sites were located about fifty miles from Juneau, and the only way to reach them was by water.

Time was of the essence, and the FWS personnel in Seattle had not investigated the sites. The OIA was aware of the deplorable conditions the Aleuts would encounter. They knew Funter Bay was uninhabitable, but because of the emergency they were faced with due to their lack of planning, this is where the Aleuts would live for the next three years.

On June 16, the U.S. government negotiated a lease with the P.E. Harris Company for use of the cannery site and all living quarters to house the natives evacuated from the Pribilof Islands. The bunkhouse usually occupied by visiting fishermen, the watchman's house, the warehouses, the cannery building, the dock, and the marine float were exempted from the lease. The Harris Company collected a rental payment of $60 a month from the government and was not responsible to make repairs or to maintain the buildings or equipment. A comparable lease was executed with the Admiralty Alaska Gold Mine Company for use of the facilities at the mine.

As soon as negotiations were completed and the Interior Department had obtained the necessary authority, they instructed the captain of the *Delarof* to proceed directly from Dutch Harbor to their ultimate destinations, Killisnoo and Funter Bay.

Prior to the *Delarof*'s departure from Dutch Harbor on June 19, the Seattle office of the Department of the Interior was busy making plans to supply provisions for the two camps. In a written report to Chief Bowers of the Alaska Fisheries Division, Superintendent Johnston wrote that fifteen tons of foodstuffs that had originally been purchased for the Pribilofs was already loaded aboard the FWS *Penguin*. He stated that the ship could be diverted and the provisions unloaded at Funter Bay and Killisnoo.[1]

With the evacuation underway, the foodstuffs were no longer needed in the Pribilofs. The OIA supplied an additional twenty-five tons destined for the islands and the village of Atka to the provisions on board the *Penguin*. Johnston reported that the ship would get underway from Seattle on June 19, and arrive in the vicinity of the camps at about the same time the refugees disembarked from the *Delarof*.[2]

Assistant Fisheries Management Supervisor F.W. Haynes was present when the *Delarof* arrived at Funter Bay. In a brief conference with the ship's captain, Haynes wrote a memo for his department's official records:

> Captain Downey agreed to leave enough mattresses, blankets and food supplies to maintain the people until the PENGUIN arrived with her load of supplies which would be within a day or two at the most. The original plan, according to Mr. [Daniel C.R.] Benson [FWS agent on St. George], had been to take all the white personnel to Seattle and leave the natives to shift for themselves. This was modified, however, and eight whites, including Agent Benson, Shopkeeper Halverson and some of the teachers were to be left to assist with the work, at least temporarily, of caring for the four hundred sixty eight natives from the Pribilofs. Both doctors decided to resign, and this temporarily left the evacuees without medical attention, which was not so serious as it might appear since it was planned to take all of the worst cases to the Juneau hospital on the BRANT upon the completion of unloading at Killisnoo. Dr. White assured Mr. Benson that a doctor would be provided within a few days, together with adequate medical supplies.[3]

As soon as the evacuees from the Pribilofs had disembarked at Funter Bay, the *Delarof* proceeded on to Killisnoo with the villagers from Atka. In a borrowed lighter from the Hood Packing Company, the Magees and eighty-two Aleuts went ashore at Killisnoo. With its task completed, the *Delarof*, along with the *Brant*, departed from the area.

Now that the evacuees were safely ashore at Funter Bay, Dr. White inspected the camp and filed his report:

> Eleven white and 95 native families from St. Paul and St. George Islands were landed at the Funter Bay Cannery. There were 479 Natives and 22 whites in this group.
> I was requested to see nine sick Natives, including five cases of tuberculosis, one tentatively diagnosed as hysteria, one appendical abcess, one infant with phimosis and balanitis, and one uterine fibroid. Five of those patients including a terminal case of tuberculosis, were brought to Juneau for hospitalization.
> Housing facilities at the Funter Bay Cannery are inadequate for such a large group. There are 15 houses suitable for the use of families, which will

accommodate a total of about 75 persons. There are twenty rooms which will accommodate families consisting of the parents and one child, or a total of 60 individuals. The remainder of this group must be housed on a dormitory basis.

Cots and beds were not available to accommodate all, but the supply of mattresses and bedding appeared adequate.

There is a great danger to the health of such a large group of persons living under crowded conditions, especially where adequate facilities are lacking for bathing and sewage disposal.[4]

In the meantime, the *Penguin* arrived with food and emergency supplies for Funter Bay and Killisnoo.

When the Aleuts disembarked from the ship, they were shocked beyond belief. They couldn't understand how their government could force them to live in such horrendous surroundings. The cannery was situated in a clearing on five acres covered with muskeg and heavy underbrush. The buildings sat atop a well-drained ridge, but the knee-deep mud in the swampy area surrounding the buildings required the construction of wooden sidewalks. A dense growth of alder and underbrush that nearly covered the cottages made

Wash day at Funter Bay, circa 1942–43 (National Archives).

them dark and damp. The Indian Service estimated that it would take a minimum of 100 days of chopping and clearing brush, and repairing the existing wood sidewalks to make the cottages livable for their occupants.

At the gold mine, the buildings were located on a narrow beach from the high-water mark to the base of the mountains. Like the surroundings of the cannery, the dense underbrush created an almost impenetrable wall that made it extremely difficult to beat a path to the cottages.

At the cannery site, the buildings had been unoccupied for more than a dozen years and were used for storage. A few cottages were available for some of the families, but most of the evacuees were forced to live in two large barracks-like buildings. They were so old and rotted that people fell through the wooden floors. Space was limited and groups of as many as thirteen people took turns sleeping in ten-foot-square cubicles. Since lumber for partitions and walls was in scarce supply, the residents hung blankets between the families for privacy. It wasn't until late September that the overcrowding was eased.

The two dormitory-style frame buildings, the China House and the Filipino House, were named after the nationalities of the cannery workers who had lived in them. The fifteen cottages adjacent to the dormitories were originally designed with small sleeping quarters for twenty families. The buildings were stripped bare to the walls. Electrical wiring and plumbing fixtures had been ripped out and they were devoid of furniture. Tops, grates, draft doors and venting pipes were missing from the kitchen ranges and there were no utilities for heating water.

The cottages were in worse condition than the dormitories. Doors were missing and the plaster board was torn from the studs. Stoves, plumbing, and heating were also gone. The windows in all of the buildings, including an old warehouse, were broken or missing.

The agent and caretaker for the Funter Bay camps, Lee C. McMillin, was appalled at the conditions the Aleuts were forced to endure. In a letter to his superior, Superintendent Johnston, McMillin expressed his concerns and included comments from FWS Agent Benson:

> Benson says he is writing you a report on the buildings [on the gold mine side] and for this [cannery side] there isn't much to say except they are so old and rotten it is impossible to do any repairing whatsoever. The only buildings that are capable of fixing is the two large places where the natives are sleeping. All other houses are absolutely gone from rot.... We have as many as ten and thirteen persons, large and small, sleeping, or trying to sleep, in one room. The novelty has worn off long ago.... No brooms, soap or mops or brushes to keep the place fit for pigs to stay in.... seems funny if our government can drop so many people in a place like this then forgets about them altogether.[5]
>
> Can you not try to get some of the portable houses that are piled up around

the coast? These could be made into fairly good places to live. Stoves could be used for heat. Mr. Green, the engineer said we would have to put in flush toilets if we stay here and hot water for washing and baths.... We cannot dig clams nearer than a mile from the cannery because of the dumping of all garbage and toilets into the bay.[6]

After he had inspected the water system and the toilet facilities at the cannery site, Green reported that the water system was inadequate to fight fires and was only suitable to provide drinking water in the summer. In the winter, the water mains would freeze and the residents would have to break up the ice, scoop up the water in buckets, and carry it to their abodes. Worse yet, a sewage disposal system was nonexistent. For a toilet, a large outhouse that served ninety percent of the evacuees rested on piles just above the low water mark. It was left to the action of the tide to wash the sewage into the bay.

In his letter to Johnston, McMillin included Green's comments on the water system and toilet facilities:

> The sanitary engineer that was here said this water system cannot under any conditions be made usable for winter and if these people are going to stay here then some other arrangements will have to be made and that should be quick.[7]
>
> He says he cannot build outdoor privies, even though they empty into the water at high tide. The sewage still washes back onto the beach for the flies to walk on and the children to track around.[8]

The generator was too small to provide electricity to light the mess hall and the living quarters. The absence of laundry rooms required the residents to wash their clothes in buckets or streams. There were no bathing facilities and there were few dishes or utensils in the mess hall.

Across the water, about a mile from Funter Bay, 180 Aleuts and FWS employees from St. George were relocated to the Admiralty Alaska Gold Mine, also known as the Funter Bay Mine. Despite the fact that the mine hadn't been worked for many years, conditions were slightly better than those at the cannery.

Ten families consisting of 46 people were housed in a two-story unpartitioned building. Twenty-six single men lived in a low-ceilinged loft above a newer mess hall that was used as a storeroom, canteen, and church. The remaining Aleuts occupied an adjacent two-story dormitory similar to the one at the cannery. Like McMillin, Agent Benson must have felt a modicum of compassion for the evacuees. He reported to his superiors that the crowded, dark, and unheated quarters were definitely out of the question for the natives during the winter months. He recommended that 32 apartments or two-room cottages be built with separate facilities for everything but sleeping.

18. Funter Bay

Even though the conditions of the living quarters were an improvement over those at the cannery, they were unfit for human occupancy in their present condition. Two of the cottages had cots, heaters, and a cook stove, but the plumbing was missing. An old two-story bunkhouse was in barely livable condition. The walls were unfinished and the few cots were ruined by mildew and mold. The old mess hall contained some usable equipment, but lacked a range and heater. Unlike the cannery, there was a one-shower bathhouse with a faulty but repairable hot water system.

Without indoor plumbing, drinking water had to be carried from two small streams. The sewage system consisted of two pit toilets on pilings over the beach. With the large number of people using these facilities, it wasn't long before the area was inundated with human waste and sewage.

Danger lurked around every corner. Bare electric wiring and drop cords hung from the buildings or were stretched across the ground. The assay office and the mill building held large amounts of corrosive and poisonous chemicals that were used to extract gold from the ore. It was necessary to lock the doors and take stringent security measures to keep the children away from these toxic substances.

Cook stoves, furniture, plumbing fixtures, water tanks, other equipment and supplies were all but impossible to obtain. The situation was becoming more desperate for the evacuees every day. On July 2, the *Alaska Fishing News* sent out an appeal to canneries and fishermen to donate gear of all types. Since no supplies had arrived by September, it appeared that the Aleuts were on their own.

In early October the Aleut women from St. Paul signed and submitted a petition protesting their living conditions.

> We the people of this place wants a better place ... to live. This is no place for a living creature. We drink impure water and then get sick the children's get skin disease even the grownups are sick from cold.
>
> We ate from the mess house and it is near the toilet only a few yards away. We eat the filth that is flying around.
>
> We got no place to take a bath and no place to wash our clothes or dry them when it rains. We women are always lugging water up stairs and take turns warming it up and the stove is small.
>
> We live in a room with our children just enough to be turn around in we used blankets for walls just to live in private.
>
> We need clothes and shoes for our children how are we going to clothe them with just a few dollars. Men's are working for $20 – month is nothing to them we used it to see our children eat what they don't get at mess house and then it's gone and then we wait for another month to come around.
>
> Why not take us to better place to live and work for ourselves and live in a better house. Men and women are very eager to work. When winter comes it still

would be worse with water all freezed up grub short do we have to see our children suffer.

We all have rights to speak for ourselves.[9]

In response to the petition, Superintendent Johnston wrote a letter to his division chief, Ward Bower. In the letter, Johnston stated:

> The women were told that under war conditions they could not expect to enjoy the comforts and conditions as they existed on the Pribilof Islands.... Analysis of water samples by the Territorial Department of health indicates the water to be potentially unsafe.... Sickness mentioned in the petition is not due to drinking water. Some of the children have "fish poisoning" which Dr. Smith states is common this time of year and will clear up when the salmon runs are over.... The toilet which has been in use is over tide water and is further from living and eating quarters than any on the Pribilofs was.... The men are satisfied with the food furnished, but the women do not like the community mess. They refuse to help with the cooking which is done by the men.... The food mentioned in the petition which is bought for the children is principally candy.[10]

In the fall of 1943, numerous government officials, including Dr. Berneta Block of the Territorial Department of Health, visited Funter Bay. During her four-day visit, she was appalled that conditions in the camp had not improved since the Aleuts arrived in Funter Bay. Her report was one of the most graphic accounts submitted to the OIA:

> As we entered the first bunk house the odor of human excreta and waste was so pungent that I could hardly make the grade. After a time we did not notice it so much. The buildings were in total darkness except for a few candles here and there which I considered distinct fire hazards since the partitions between rooms were made mostly by hangings of woolen blankets. The overcrowded housing condition is really beyond description since a mother and as many as three or four children were found in several beds and two or three children in one bunk. In the darkness it was difficult to see the details of the state of uncleanliness, but even so we gathered it was deplorable. There were very few beds that were properly covered with sheets and pillow cases were seldom used. Children were found naked and actually covered with excreta. There were only a few rooms into which one could walk with any sense of comfort in the olfactory sense—and I was very careful to commend the women on their neatness and cleanliness.
>
> The next morning we made rounds again in daylight and I was impressed with the fact that very little or no civic pride was taken in the way of disposal of garbage, waste disposal or care of the privies. The garbage cans were overflowing, human excreta was found next to the doors of the cabins and the drainage boxes into which dishwater and kitchen waste was to be placed were filthy beyond description. There were numerous flies in many of the rooms. The kitchen and the screened building in which food was kept were not as clean as they should have been and a dish of fermenting material of some kind gave off a very obnoxious odor.[11]

18. Funter Bay

The conditions in the camps had been developing over several months. Dr. Block's report prompted additional comments to Alaska Fisheries Division Chief Ward T. Bower from Assistant Fisheries Supervisor Haynes.

> It has long been apparent that the camps were not operating successfully, even as temporary refuges, and we are convinced that unless adequate measures are taken to improve conditions before the arduous winter months begin there is more than a possibility that the death toll from tuberculosis, pneumonia, influenza and other diseases will so decimate the ranks of the natives that few will survive to return to the islands.[12]

Medical care was of paramount importance to the evacuees, but was not readily available to them. Treatment was provided by a full-time white nurse assisted by an Aleut nurse. Doctors stayed in the camps for a few days or a few weeks. The infirmary at the gold mine was a three-room bungalow. The infirmary at the cannery was a twenty-foot-square room. There were few medical supplies to treat their patients in either facility.

The medical staff was ill-prepared to handle the epidemics that ravaged the camps. By March 23, nearly every one of the natives was struck down with influenza. There were more than 100 cases at the peak of the epidemic. Just as the residents were recovering, many of the men, senior FWS officials, and the camp doctor departed for the fur seal harvest in the Pribilofs.

According to the camp logs, two cases of measles were reported on September 18, 1943. This was followed by an epidemic that struck the women and children of Funter Bay. By October 1, ninety Aleuts were stricken with the disease. On that same day, Haretina Kochutin gave birth to an infant son. He died three weeks later of complications of measles.

The Aleuts at Funter Bay were virtual prisoners of an uncaring OIA. The camps were extremely isolated and the agency had neglected to provide a two-way radio, so communication with the outside world was limited to a weekly mail boat. Timely treatment of the seriously ill was out of the question, and without a radio, prompt response to emergencies was impossible. If the residents wanted to leave Funter Bay, it was necessary to obtain permission from the FWS. Once permission was granted, it was then up to each person to make his own travel arrangements on supply ships or the weekly mail boat.

Publicity was the last thing the OIA needed. As conditions in the camps worsened, they censored the press to keep them from reporting the truth of the situation to their readers. In his report to Bower, Haynes expressed his concerns regarding this issue.

> Being closest to the scene, this office naturally bears the brunt of criticism and it is becoming more and more difficult to defend our position. Scarcely a day passes that some well-meaning person does not descend upon us with recrimination for

our heartless methods. Censorship has kept the press off our necks thus far but this line of defense is weakening rapidly. A few days ago we were advised by one of the physicians who had inspected the camps and aided in emergency work there, that he was preparing a report to the Surgeon General of the United States and also to Secretary Ickes and had no intention of "pulling any punches." He warned that it was only a matter of time until some publication, such as Life Magazine, would get hold of the story and play it up, much to the disadvantage of the Service and the Department of the Interior as a whole. He pointed out that the value of this year's fur seal take from the Pribilofs would nearly equal the original purchase price of Alaska, yet the people who had made it possible are being herded into quarters unfit for pigs; denied adequate medical attention; lack of a healthful diet and even facilities to keep warm and are virtually prisoners of the Government, though theoretically possessing the status of citizenship.[13]

Like so many others who had visited the camps, Haynes demanded that Bowers provide the services of a competent full-time physician, materials to make the camp habitable, two-way radios, and the installation of an adequate water supply and sewer system.

The Aleuts had now been at Funter Bay for fifteen months, yet the OIA seemed to be indifferent to their needs. In all the many long months since their initial inspection of the camps, the FWS had done almost nothing to correct the problems. It wasn't until the spring of 1943 that the government made any effort to reduce the suffering of the residents. Six additional cottages were built on the cannery site and authorization was obtained to transfer 25 Quonset huts from the Army camp at Duck Creek. Before long, ten of the huts were quickly in place. The assigned physician arrived on December 29, the camps were provided with electricity, and upgrades to the water supply and sanitation facilities were completed.

As the improvements continued, travel restrictions for the evacuees were relaxed and greater numbers of Aleuts were permitted to leave Funter Bay. In February 1944, OIA Superintendent Johnston reported:

> Although not as many natives are living in Juneau this winter as were during the winter of 1943, there are enough to make an appreciable difference at Funter. The number varies with every boat trip. On December 31, 1943, the number of natives temporarily absent from the St. Paul camp was 52 persons including 4 complete families; from the St. George camp, 76 persons including 9 families. These figures include 19 school children attending Wrangell Institute, a school giving advanced education for Alaska Indians.[14]

On the matter of vital statistics, during 1943, twenty-five Aleuts died from influenza, pneumonia and measles. Some of deaths might have been prevented if the recommendations of the FWS inspectors had been implemented and followed with any degree of diligence in 1942 when the evacuees arrived at Funter Bay.

19

Killisnoo

Three miles south of the entrance to Kootznahoo Inlet, the village of Killisnoo was situated on the northwestern side of Kenasnow Island near the shore of Admiralty Island. Because the Tlingit Indians thought the rock formations resembled a "bear's rectum," they named the village Killisnoo. With the exception of the herring saltery, a warehouse, a shed, a store, and machine shops, in 1928, the entire village burned to the ground. Since the village wasn't rebuilt, the inhabitants were resettled at the Tlingit village of Angoon. Built in 1880, the herring saltery went out of business in 1930. According to the Indians, the stench from the fish oil and fertilizer operations drifted north with such potency that the bears who inhaled it grew to gigantic size.

Before the Japanese attack on the Aleutians, transportation from Killisnoo was limited to pontoon planes landing and taking off from the harbor. Weekly passenger service, cargo and mail were provided by the M.S. *Estebeth*.

On May 13, 1942, Virgil R. Farrell, director of education for the Alaska Indian Service, informed Hirst that Killisnoo could be employed as a potential site to house the evacuees.[1]

In his report, he noted that the water supply was limited to a small spring with a maximum capacity of twenty-four barrels a day. He also noted that the water supply needed repairs and that other than three outdoor pit toilets, sewage disposal facilities were nonexistent. Buildings were wired for electricity, but without major repairs, fire hazards were a distinct possibility. A small laundry was available, and bathing facilities consisted of an ancient bathtub. The generator was still installed, but Farrell said "it is very doubtful if the same could be put back in working order."[2]

Based on available accommodations, Farrell estimated that Killisnoo could house 75 to 80 people. One house would be utilized as a residence for the teachers, and large families would reside in the two remaining houses. The five cabins were without furniture and one of the cabins consisted of a single

Aleuts from Atka and the Pribilof Islands arrive at Killsnoo with nothing more than the clothes on their backs or what they could carry in one suitcase, June 25, 1942 (National Archives).

room for small families. The only bunkhouse on the property was home to two large families.

On June 25, 1942, nineteen Families from Atka arrived at Killisnoo with nothing more than the clothes on their backs. When they left home, the Navy prevented them from retrieving their personal belongings. They started life in the camp with the barest of necessities. They were given old army surplus clothing, but the basics for subsistence living were denied to them. The Tlinglit Indians from Angoon Village, three miles to the north, befriended them and donated blankets and mattresses. Fishermen gave them salmon. This much-needed help did little to ward off the cold weather and hunger they faced in their battle to survive.

The skipper of the *Delarof*, Captain Downey, was moved by the plight of the evacuees. He provided the initial provisions for the people from his own ship's stores. In his report to Governor Gruening on the conditions of the eighty-three Aleuts, Hirst wrote:

> Since the Atka group had to leave all of their personal possessions, including food and clothing on the Island, they were indeed very poorly provided for. However Captain Downey was very generous, sympathetic, and cooperative, and furnished these people from his ship's stores a four day supply of food, a mattress for each adult, and blankets in sufficient quantities to assure each person protection against suffering.[3]

Stores from the *Delarof* were supplemented by additional supplies from the *Penguin*.

After he completed his inspection of Funter Bay, Dr. White inspected the facilities at Killisnoo:

> The general health of the Atka Natives landed at Killisnoo appeared to be good, and no one requested medical attention.
> There were 19 Native families in this group consisting of 83 persons. Two white teachers were also landed at Killisnoo.
> Housing facilities are considered adequate as far as space is concerned. There are cots or beds, and stoves in most of the houses, but none of them are supplied with lights or water. Certain repairs are needed to make these houses weatherproof and to prevent injury to occupants, as it was noted that some of the steps and verandas have decayed to a considerable extent. The mortar between the bricks in some of the chimneys has fallen out, and these flues should be pointed to reduce fire hazards to a minimum.[4]

The refugees at Killisnoo were fortunate that the Indian Service school teacher Ruby J. Magee, and her husband, C. Ralph Magee, decided to remain with them during their first year of internment. A caring couple dedicated to the welfare of the Aleuts, they were determined to improve the substandard living conditions imposed on the people. The OIA wanted to transfer the couple to an Indian school on the mainland, but the Magees refused to abandon the natives of Atka.

The Magees described their first few days at Killisnoo, and the efforts they undertook to improve the condition of the camp:

> The Atka people were taken to tiny Killisnoo Island ... across from the southern tip of Admiralty Island. There were some very old flimsy buildings that had belonged to a fish meal factory, and we were told to fix them over to live in "for the duration." The [*Delarof*] gave us cooking utensils, food, and blankets to tide us over until more help came. It was not long before health officials arrived to give inoculations and check-ups, and more clothing and food supplies were sent from Juneau.
> One old building that had been used as a mess hall was fixed over into a schoolroom. Desks and benches were built by our best carpenter, supplies were sent from Juneau, and in September we opened school for the children.[5]

The Magees did their best to ease the suffering of the natives, but their efforts were often frustrated by government officials and endless red tape. They believed that instead of idly sitting around camp, the Aleuts needed some sort of entertainment to fill their time. Ruby asked Superintendent Hirst for money to replace the radios, guitars, banjos, and accordions that had been destroyed when the Navy burned their village. He sent the request on to the Commissioner of Indian Affairs for the radios and musical instruments to be paid for out the emergency evacuation fund. The commissioner questioned the legality of using these funds for this purpose and refused Hirst's request. He in turn suggested that Ruby should contact the Red Cross for the money.

The harsh living conditions the refugees were forced to endure took their toll on the people. They remembered how the climate in Southeastern Alaska damaged the health of the internees and the loved ones who died there.

In his deposition to the government, William Dirks recalled, "Eight people shared my quarters at the cannery and ... a warehouse was built by the people as a community church. My daughter, Margie Dirks, perished at Killisnoo and is buried there." As a teenager at Killisnoo, Vasha K. Golodoff lost her father and brother. According to Vera Nevzoroff, "At least ten people died at Killisnoo, and were buried on the island."

In a letter to their friends, Dr. and Mrs. Berenberg, dated September 20, 1943, the Magees made the following comments describing many of the hardships they saw at Killisnoo:

> We lost the most picturesque of those [Atka] characters—Larry Nevzoroff, the boat builder, who was the best and oldest man of the village.... He was buried the very same day we left. We think he had pneumonia. He took some Angoon Indian medicine which we think poisoned him. We felt bad to think he wasn't able to return to Atka to spend his last days. Another man who died of tuberculosis was buried the same day.
>
> Last winter was the worst in fifty years—so old timers told us. Our people were not very comfortable in their poor houses. Food froze solid during the coldest weather. They had good warm clothing, though fuel was plentiful.[6]

Even under such adverse conditions, the people refused to surrender to despair and defeat. They made the necessary repairs to their living quarters to get through their enforced ordeal. Some men found jobs and others started a cooperative store. The OIA considered it a resounding success and it became the model for similar stores in the other camps. It was supported with funds from the pre-evacuation fur seal harvest of 1942.

Many of the men were skilled carpenters and were able to make repairs to their living quarters and other buildings. Some of them went to work in canneries or for the Forest Service in Juneau and Sitka. The women found employment as babysitters for fishermen on Chichagof Island, while others used their sewing skills to make clothing from castoff garments. The people became self-supporting and as a result did not drain funds from the budget of the Alaska Indian Service.

Cooking was a problem for the women. Since the Magees occupied the only house in the camp that had a stove, the women were forced to cook and eat their meals in the community mess hall. The women continued to complain

Aleut children and dog at Killsnoo (Butler/Dale Collection, Alaska State Library).

about this situation until one of the evacuees, Andrew Snigaroff, scrounged up a stove and installed it in one of their homes.

The Aleuts, like most Indians, had little tolerance for alcohol. The Magees believed that liquor was the curse of the village, and that money spent on strong drink should have been used to purchase necessities like clothing and supplies, or invested in U.S. War Bonds. The Magees tried to dissuade their charges from what they considered the path to destruction, but the evacuees preferred to follow the example of their Tlingit friends from Angoon village.

After months at Killisnoo, the Magees were ready to throw in the towel and move on. In June 1943, after one of the worst winters on record, they were transferred to the Indian school at Port Graham on the Kenai Peninsula.

Potable water was a major problem for the residents of the camp. They drew their brown drinking water from a stagnant pool they described as "a dead lake with bugs in it." Fresh running water was unavailable to them. They were forced to haul rainwater from a source across the bay and boil it before drinking or cooking with it.

The Aleuts blamed poor drinking water, lack of food, and substandard living conditions for the high mortality rate at Killisnoo. Seventeen evacuees died there. Four died from tuberculosis and five from pneumonia. Four Aleuts above the age of seventy, along with six who were over fifty, four newborns and three children under the age of ten, also died.

In spite of the harsh conditions of the camps, the Aleuts were determined to survive their adversity and return to their beloved island homes. Even though the kindness of the Tlinglit Indians eased the trauma of relocation and internment, the Aleuts suffered illness and unnecessary loss of life due to weather, substandard housing, and limited medical support.

20

Employment Opportunities

Unlike the internment camps in the United States and Hawaii, the camps in Alaska did not have guard towers or barbed wire fences, but they were nonetheless prisons for the Aleut people. Except for medical reasons, or to join the military or for possible outside employment, the evacuees required permission from the authorities to leave the camps.

There were numerous employment opportunities available for able-bodied Aleut men. The agents in charge of Killisnoo, Ward Cove, and Burnett Inlet made arrangements for outside employment for the men in defense-related industries. But the agent in charge of the camps at Funter Bay refused to allow them to take outside employment.

The evacuees were looking for any reason to leave the camps. The jobs presented an excellent opportunity for them to earn money to support themselves and their families, but they also required long separations from their loved ones. Once the men left the camps, it didn't take long for officials of the OIS to become aware of their desire to return to their families. They were also aware that the men might not leave the camps and return to work.

> We now have 27 [Aleuts] from Burnett Inlet, 27 from Ward Cove, and 13 from Killisnoo employed at Excursion Inlet [a major defense-related facility being constructed on a peninsula west of Juneau] ... a majority of them wish to return to their camps for [the Russian Orthodox] Easter celebrations. There is a possibility that all of them may not return to Excursion Inlet.[1]

Men who were not needed to maintain the facilities of the camps were permitted to take employment in relatively high-paying jobs in defense-related industries while their families remained behind. Aleuts not employed in these jobs seldom had an opportunity to leave the confines of the camps, although many of them did support themselves with jobs in the private sector. This was a far cry from the experience of the internees at Funter Bay.

Alaska's acting director for the United States Employment Service, R.E. Barnes, believed the Aleuts should not have to depend on the government for their needs. Four days after their arrival in the camps at Funter Bay, he interviewed some of the evacuees, surveyed the labor market in southeastern Alaska, and developed recommendations for gainful employment for Aleuts who wanted to work.

Barnes reported to Fish and Wildlife supervisors that within two weeks, "there will be a need for from six to twelve of the adult male natives in each one of the canneries in the area.... We expect that we can employ about fifty of them in canneries in the immediate vicinity of Funter Bay...." "The cannery work was definitely a contribution to the war effort," Barnes pointed out, and urged that "strong consideration be given to releasing of suitable men from the camp to enter this important work for the season."[2]

Barnes identified numerous suitable employment opportunities. The Director of the Siems-Drake Puget Sound Company in Sitka wanted to hire as many as 200 Aleuts for their facility on Japonski Island. The director stressed that the men were needed for military construction projects that were critically important to the defense of Alaska and the nation. The Alaska Juneau Gold Mining Company offered to try out 12 Aleuts as ore sorters. If they proved satisfactory in their jobs, the company would hire more of them.

Barnes soon realized that a severe labor shortage existed in southeastern Alaska. He believed that by allowing Aleut men to fill these jobs, the shortage would be alleviated and the evacuees would become self-sufficient. Barnes summarized the situation in a written report to Sealing Division General Superintendent Johnston:

> These Pribilof people, or at least the able-bodied men among them, are needed in the labor market in southeastern Alaska and we have made plans to, and are ready to interview, classify, and place them; that we have considered the placing of them from every angle which concerns their welfare as well as the needs of national defense; that the employment referred to above would be suitable to them and that they could adapt themselves to it; that the employment for the most part would not change their mode of living greatly and certainly not permanently.[3]

When the agent and caretaker in charge of the Funter Bay camps, Lee C. McMillin, learned of Barnes's plan to arrange for outside employment for the evacuees, he became alarmed. He knew that some of the Aleuts had openly declared they were going to take their families and look for work outside the camp. He had no intention of allowing his charges to defy him and undermine his authority. To protect his position, he submitted his own report to Johnston, stressing the need for command and control of the camps and the Aleuts:

> [I] have considered nearly all angles in the situation here and urgently recommend every endeavor should be made to keep the Pribilof natives together as a unit and pay them a nominal salary to try to keep them satisfied. Otherwise all the work the Government has put in and the expense would all have to be done over again if they are allowed to roam at will. It would also be a terrific expense to pick them up again because it would have to be in the end. *So far[, I] have denied all request to be allowed to leave to look for work....*
>
> [I] have not made any promises to the natives but something will have to be done to correct the living conditions here [at Funter Bay] or some other diversion or it will be more than any living person can handle. They are over $8,500 in debt [to the government store] now and should not be allowed to get any deeper, but they still have to have tobacco and the things the bureau has stopped furnishing to them in later years.[4]

Military service was another option for the Aleuts. The Army needed men to fill their ranks and the Selective Service board was ready to help. A few days after the evacuees arrived at Funter Bay, they attempted to register them for the draft. McMillin objected and wrote to Johnston asking for clarification of the situation:

> The Selective Service board is asking for registration of the Natives and so far have done nothing towards this as we have been expecting the Penguin now for over a week. As I understand these natives, classed as wards, with no voting privileges will not be drafted but can enlist if they want.[5]

McMillin held power and control over the Pribilovians for eighteen years before they were relocated to Funter Bay. He misinterpreted the status of his charges. He failed to recognize that they were United States citizens and subject to registration and the draft. Sixteen men from the Funter Bay camps were inducted into the armed services, and many of them served with distinction throughout the war.

Like most government officials, McMillin did not consider the Aleuts to be American citizens. When America purchased Alaska from Russia in 1867, the Aleuts were guaranteed American citizenship under the terms of Article 3 of the Treaty of Cession[6]:

> The inhabitants of the ceded territory, according to their choice, reserving their natural allegiance, may return to Russia within three years; but if they should prefer to remain in the ceded territory, they, with the exception of uncivilized native tribes, shall be admitted to the enjoyment of all the rights, advantages, and immunities of citizens of the United States, and shall be maintained and protected in the free enjoyment of their liberty, property and religion. The uncivilized tribes will be subject to such laws and regulations as the United States may, from time to time, adopt in regard to aboriginal tribes of that country.

Russia formally transferred the Territory of Alaska to the United States on October 18, 1867. It was not until June 2, 1924, that Congress officially granted American citizenship to the Aleuts and Native American tribes in the United States.

Until just prior to World War II, the government administered the Pribilofs as a virtual prison colony, as shown in testimony before the Indian Claims commission on June 9, 1978:

> The authority of government agents on the Pribilofs was virtually unlimited. Agents could summarily fine and incarcerate Aleuts. There was one instance in which an agent exiled a Pribilof Aleut from the islands. Agents interfered in the system of Aleut government and even decided the types and quantities of goods Aleuts could purchase. By the later part of the government period, the government agent [i.e., Lee C. McMillin] was the integral part of a system that controlled nearly every aspect of the Pribilof Aleut lives.[7]

Outside employment became nothing more than an unfulfilled dream for the residents of the Funter Bay camps. McMillin had succeeded in keeping them under his control. Within three weeks of its establishment, the refugee camps at Funter Bay had become an internment camp for the Aleut citizens of the Pribilof Islands.

21

Fur Seal Operations, 1943

The Department of the Interior wanted the evacuees to return home, but their motives were not entirely altruistic. They needed the men for the fur seal harvest. The annual fur seal harvest generated tremendous revenues for the U.S. Treasury. Government officials in Seattle and Washington, D.C., were determined not to lose these revenues by continuing sealing operations, if possible, despite the war.

On November 23, 1942, Secretary of the Interior Ickes urged Secretary of War Henry L. Stimson to repatriate the evacuees no later than April or May of 1943. In his letter, Ickes reminded Stimson of the circumstances that led to the removal and internment of the Pribilof natives:

> On June 16, without consulting me or any official of this Department, our armed forces evacuated 468 natives and 20 supervisory employees of the Fish and Wildlife Service and their families from the Pribilof Islands, Alaska, moving them to Funter Bay in Southeastern Alaska, about 1,500 miles away, where presumably they would be less subject to enemy attack.
>
> This action caused great inconvenience and hardship, and resulted in the loss of more than a million dollars by reason of the discontinuance of the operations at the Pribilof Islands, where 95,013 fur-seal skins were taken in the summer of 1941 and 834 fox skins were obtained in the preceding winter.[1]

Less than a month later, under strict conditions, Stimson authorized the repatriation of the entire Aleut community from Funter Bay and the commencement of the 1943 fur seal harvest to be conducted by a sealing gang recruited from Funter Bay and other Aleut communities:

> I have ... agreed to the return, under certain conditions, of about 151 natives and supervisors to the Pribilofs (St. George and St. Paul). The conditions are that, provided the military situation permits, they may return for the sealing season only in order to direct the pruning of the seal herds by military personnel.
>
> With respect to St. George Island, I have no objection to the return of the natives of that place for rehabilitation.

As to St. Paul Island, it is impractical to return its natives for rehabilitation at present. As I stated in my letter of December 4 to you on this subject, there is insufficient housing for both the natives and the military garrison.

Details connected with the rehabilitation of St. George and the temporary return of the 151 natives and supervisors for the sealing season will be coordinated locally between the Army, the Navy, Governor Gruening, and the other agencies concerned.[2]

The OIA had a difficult time convincing the men of Funter Bay and other camps to participate in the sealing operations. Some of the refugees were concerned that the Japanese might attack the islands and they would be killed or taken back to Japan as prisoners of war. Other evacuees knew that harvesting fur seals paid far less than what they earned working in Juneau and Excursion Inlet. If they returned for the summer seal harvest, they wanted a bonus to compensate for the higher wages they now earned.

Superintendent Johnston of the Fish and Wildlife Service was responsible for much of the hesitancy and confusion on the part of the Aleuts. In an effort to justify their anger over the conditions of the camps, he warned them that

Unidentified St. Paul Island fur sealers prepare to harvest seals for the U.S. government, 1944 (National Archives).

with the possibility of military action in the Aleutians, they were much safer away from the islands. Now that he needed workers for the seal harvest, he changed his approach. He informed them it was no longer necessary for them to fear the danger of a Japanese invasion. He withheld permission to enlist in Governor Gruening's guard units. He promised that those who remained in camp would share in the proceeds from the sealing operations, but anyone who refused to go would forfeit any money they might receive from this endeavor.

Johnston's scare tactics included a warning that anyone refusing to work in the seal harvest would be denied a permit to return to St. Paul when it was resettled. St. George residents who refused to participate would not share in the proceeds from the harvest and would never be permitted to return to their homes. Island residents would lose all privileges for all time. Johnston believed that his threats would be enough to convince the Aleuts to return to the islands for the summer seal harvest.

After threatening the evacuees, Johnston decided that his threats might not be legal. Looking for endorsement for his policies and clarification of the legal status of the Pribilovians, he asked his superior, Chief Bower, to validate his position. Bower turned the matter over to government lawyers for a determination of the extent to which the government was legally obligated to the natives and the natives to the government.

Since the lawyers were unable to come up with a definitive answer, Bowers was left with the responsibility to determine a suitable response. He decided that in view of the war conditions, the forced evacuation of the islands, and the designation of the area as a war zone, it was not fair to the natives to force them to forfeit their rights to return to the Pribilofs.

After Stimson authorized the resumption of the fur seal harvest, on May 6, 1943, the sealing crew boarded the *Delarof* for the voyage to St. Paul Island. It consisted of Aleuts from Funter Bay and other camps, thirty-eight Fouke Fur Company employees, and FWS supervisors. As they moved away from the dock into open water, the men lined the rails of the ship and sang a farewell chant in Russian. Crying their farewells, the women stood on the shore and waved to their men. This was the first time they had been separated from their loved ones.

The return to St. Paul was an awe-inspiring moment for the Aleuts. As they gazed on their beloved landscape, they removed their hats and sang praises to God. For the natives of St. Paul, this island was their home.

For the Aleuts who participated in the harvest, the government planned to pay $100 a month for natives from villages other than St. George and St. Paul. The Pribilovians would be paid an additional 90 cents for seal skins on a piece-rate basis. Before operations commenced, the rate for non–Pribilovians was increased to $150 a month.

St. Paul Island fur sealers hard at work, 1944 (National Archives).

The slaughter of the seals on June 10, 1943, went on record as the greatest number of seals taken in the history of St. Paul Island since the U.S. government took over management of the fur seal herd. It was the first time the U.S. military participated in the harvest, and it was the first time since the war started that the Treasury Department received revenues from the fur seal industry.

Treasury revenues were not the most often stated reason for bringing in the Aleuts to resume the harvest. FWS personnel were quite adamant that the production of seal oil, meal, and glycerin-bearing fats were necessary for the war effort. The war in the Pacific had cut off the Asian sources of these commodities and they had to utilize every available source for these vital necessities of war.

The harvest concluded on August 8, with a total of 95,342 skins taken. The Aleuts were paid more money for their participation than they'd ever received before, but they were anxious to return to their families at Funter Bay. With the men gone from the camps, conditions had deteriorated, to the point of desperation. The evacuees from St. George assumed they would be joining their men in the Pribilofs, but Bower decided the time wasn't right for their return.

When Johnston learned that resettlement for the evacuees in the fall of

1943 was impossible, he left St. Paul Island. After his departure, the sealers became dissatisfied. The harvest was finished and they missed their families. They refused to work and demanded to know whether they were returning to Funter Bay or if their families would be repatriated.

Agent McMillin was left in charge. In his entry in the Pribilof Log for September 13, 1943, he called them "mutineers" and described the actions that were taken to resolve the situation.

> Since the departure of Mr. Johnston, Superintendent, the St. Paul natives have become very dissatisfied with conditions on the island; therefore a meeting was called today and the natives asked to air their complaints. Most of the complaints came from the younger men in the gang; all, however said they were promised in a meeting with Mr. Johnston at Funter Bay (agent was not present) that all they had to do up here was "seal," then return to Funter.
>
> After hearing of this today, the "mutineers" were informed by the agent that unless they were willing to work, the cook would be instructed to refuse to prepare food for them; that they were the same as government employees who were expected to work every day, even at Funter Bay.
>
> The natives were given to understand the delay in our departure could not be remedied by this office and that no instructions had been left by Mr. Johnston who laid them off. The junior foreman was instructed to prepare a roll call for the following morning and any man who did not feel he should work could stay at home; he would be given supplies to do his own cooking and the Sealing Division readjusted accordingly.[3]

McMillin's ultimatum appeared to be successful. All of the men showed up for work the next morning, but many of them resented his heavy-handed tactics.

The sealing crew from St. Paul were the first group to leave the island. They loaded the sealskins and seal oil aboard the USAT *Northcoast*, and departed St. Paul on October 4, 1943. After an uneventful voyage, they were reunited with their families at Funter Bay on October 11. Delayed by measles and dangerous winter storms, the men from St. George followed aboard the *Penguin* on November 11.

In their absence, the intolerable conditions at Funter Bay had continued to worsen. The camps were in desperate need of attention. There were four deaths in early December. Dr. Smith was so depressed with the lack of cooperation from the government and its failure to provide even the most basic medical facilities, he resigned after less than a year's service, a disillusioned and broken man. With the doctor gone, the nurse resigned, followed by the school teachers of St. Paul Village. They were frustrated over the government's callous treatment of these Alaskan natives, and since there was nothing more they could do to ease the suffering of the Aleuts, they decided it was time to leave.

22

Home Is Where the Heart is

The stated purpose of the evacuation and relocation was to protect the Aleuts from the possibility of a Japanese attack. They dreamed of the day they could leave the camps and return to their ancestral homes and the life they knew before the war. Even though the war never reached the Pribilofs, the military considered them a combat zone and the Aleuts were not permitted to return.

The first opportunity to return the evacuees to their homes in the Pribilofs came with the resumption of the fur seal harvest. When the director of FWS visited Funter Bay in the late summer of 1943, he became depressed with conditions in the camps. He sent a telegram to Assistant Director Charles E. Jackson in Seattle to inform him that he had "checked [the] Funter Bay situation and under [the] conditions it is desirable [to] make arrangements [to] return natives to [the] Pribilofs this fall."[1]

After receiving Gabrielson's wire, Jackson consulted with General Buckner. He outlined his actions in a memorandum for his files:

> I discussed Dr. Gabrielson's telegram over the telephone with Col. J.K. Tully, of the Alaska unit of the War Department, and he telephoned G-3 at San Francisco immediately. He then reported back that San Francisco had stated they were sending a cable to General Buckner at Anchorage, asking him to report on the feasibility of re-establishing our natives at St. George immediately, and also the possibility of returning our natives to St. Paul Island. Col. Tully seems to be very much in favor of assisting us in returning the natives to the Pribilof Islands. He has promised to contact me again when a reply is received from General Buckner and may at any time request me to specifically state in writing our reasons for wanting the natives to be returned there.[2]

Jackson believed he was close to obtaining high-level approval from the military. In his telegram of September 8, 1943, he informed Assistant Fisheries

22. Home Is Where the Heart Is

Supervisor Frederich Morton that the War Department had given the green light to their proposal, and that they should proceed with plans for returning the natives to the islands:

> War Department telephoned from Washington that we may proceed immediately with plans to rehabilitate natives on St. George Island. Formal written authority will follow. Next week I will see General Buckner in Washington and settle matter whether St. Paul natives may be returned this fall. It seems likely that favorable action will result. Inform Dr. Gabrielson immediately upon his arrival. Begin at once definite plans for returning natives St. George and preliminary plans for returning St. Paul.[3]

With Johnston gone, McMillin was now the agent and caretaker for St. Paul Island. Rehabilitation and resettlement of the Aleuts did not fit into his plans. He was afraid that with supplies running low he would be forced to remain on the island with the Aleuts. On September 8, he sent a strongly worded telegram to Supervisor Morton. He expressed his opposition to the resettlement plan. He further requested that unless assurances were forthcoming that adequate supplies to get them through the winter months, along with medical supplies and a doctor, would be sent to the island, he wanted transportation to Seattle for him and his wife:

> No furniture or cook stoves for native families and natives say they refuse to remain under these conditions. St. Paul rehabilitation impossible this fall. Supplies now on hand will last only to end of October. Recommend that rehabilitation wait until next spring and that you consult Johnston when he arrives.... Please furnish me transportation to Seattle and endeavor to get my wife to Seattle.[4]

McMillin considered the prospect of leaving the Aleuts on the island through the winter and allowing their families to join them to be extremely foolhardy. Mcmilliin's apprehension over spending the winter on the island is understandable. He had exercised control over them for eighteen years prior to his Funter Bay experience and he knew how terrible the winters were without sufficient supplies and adequate shelter.

He called the return of the evacuees a fantasy and warned against the hazards of the landing women and children in the atrocious winter weather of the Bering Sea. In his opinion, if FWS persisted in returning the natives to the islands, he assured them that without proper arrangements, criminal charges could be brought against the persons responsible:

> Whoever pushing Fantastic idea rehabilitate Pribilofs not acquainted with conditions this time of year in Bering Sea.... Criminal charges should be preferred upon person responsible unless rehabilitation plans dropped for present until supplies and equipment obtained to properly equip station.[5]

Even though FWS still wanted to return the evacuees to their homes, they heeded McMillin's warnings and abandoned their plans for resettlement. McMIllin and the sealers were returned to Funter Bay. Supplies intended for the islands were diverted to camps in an effort to improve the conditions of the natives.

Assistant Supervisor Morton attempted to return a few Aleut families to St. George. In the fall of 1943, he advised the authorities at Funter Bay that fifteen Aleut men would remain on the island at the completion of sealing operations. He directed his subordinates to draw up plans to transport the sealers' fifty-three dependents and provisions to see them through the winter on the next voyage of the *Penguin.*

Morton was overruled and his plans fell through. Sadly for them, the men were not reunited with their families on St. George. On November 21, the fifteen men, along with Agent Benson and his wife, were returned to the squalor of Funter Bay.

The fear of adverse publicity, the conditions of the camps, and the financial burdens on the resources of the Alaska Indian Service dictated the necessity to abandon the camps and return the people to their homes. With the seal harvest, the Pribilovians had provided revenues for the government, but this was not the case with the evacuees from Akutan, Atka, Biorka, Kashega, Makushin, Nikolski, and Unalaska. Revenue-producing industries were nonexistent in their villages. As a result of the urgency to restart the seal harvest and generate revenues, they were not resettled until one year after the Pribilovians.

Resettlement of the Aleuts was driven more by government expenditures than by humanitarian considerations. As early as April 1943, the Department of the Interior wanted to end the financial outlays to maintain the camps. In the beginning, they believed the evacuees would find suitable employment and the camps would become self-supporting. This policy was a dismal failure and the department's costs were mounting. In its budget for 1944, the OIA estimated the operating expenses for the camps at $4,500 a month, and outlays for food at $10,000 a month.

Resettlement of the Aleuts became a major issue for the Department of the Interior and the OIA. They had already expended $200,000, and all available funds would be depleted by July 1, 1944. Whether the affected agencies kept operating the camps or repatriated the natives, they would need additional funds.

In an effort to resolve the budgetary crisis they now faced, officials of the Department of the Interior initiated discussions with the War Department. On November 26, 1943, Secretary of the Interior Harold L. Ickes suggested to Secretary of War Stimson that further consideration should be given to the repatriation of all Aleuts who had been relocated to the camps in southeastern Alaska in 1942. One of the reasons for this urgency was that "funds which are available to [the Interior] Department for expenses incident to the maintenance of the natives will probably not be available after 30 June 1944."[6]

Stimson approved Ickes's request for the repatriation and stated that the Aleuts could return to their homes depending on the military situation at that time.

> The War Department concurs in the proposal as outlined in your letter of November 26, 1943 to return Alaskan natives to their homes insofar as the military situation permits. It is thought this would affect reoccupation of villages in the Pribilofs and the Aleutians, as far west as Atka, inclusive.
>
> War Department funds will be made available for their return and the restoration of homes in areas as indicated above except for restoration of homes in Atka, which is believed to be a Navy responsibility.[7]

Even though the War Department had given its approval, resettlement was dependent on financial considerations. By February 1944, FWS began drawing up detailed plans that called for the Pribilovians to participate in that season's fur seal harvest. Superintendent Johnston was directed to provide the Army Transport Service in Seattle with FWS requirements for ships to transport 468 Aleuts and 22 white personnel from Funter Bay to the Pribilofs, along with 2,800 tons of cargo to St. Paul, and 1,200 tons of cargo to St. George, no later than early March.

Johnston sent a message to the owner of the abandoned cannery at Funter Bay that the Aleuts would soon be gone. He apologized for any trouble or inconvenience the evacuees caused. He neglected to mention the FWS admission that the Aleuts had been forced to endure conditions unfit for pigs.

> Arrangements have been made for an Army Transport and plans are under way to move the Pribilof evacuees from Funter Bay about May 1. Both this office and the natives themselves are anxious to complete the rehabilitation at the earliest possible date.
>
> We fully appreciate the trouble and inconvenience our natives have caused you and will do all we can to prevent delay in the departure date.[8]

The Aleuts were ecstatic at the prospect of returning home. After three years of despair, they were going home. On March 31, 1944, the school was closed and the building torn down, the lumber used to build boxes and crates for their personal belongings. The children living at Wrangell Institute returned to the camp aboard the *Penguin* and were reunited with their families. FWS recruited fifty-four Aleut men from Killisnoo, Ward Cove, and Burnett Inlet to assist in shutting down the camp. The USAT transport ship *William L. Thompson* arrived from Seattle to take the people home.

Aleuts from St. Paul line the railings of the USAT *Delarof* to take a last look at their home as the ship sails south to the relocation camps (National Archives).

The Aleuts left Funter Bay for the last time and boarded the ship on May 2. The next day, the stevedores completed loading cargo into the holds, and on May 4, 1944, the *William L. Thompson* sailed for the Pribilofs.

The ship dropped anchor in Village Cove off the shore from St. Paul Island at 6:20 p.m. on May 13. Crew members went ashore to check out the village before allowing the natives to disembark. Their first impressions are recorded in the Pribilof Log of April 1, 1944:

> The village was found in very poor shape—all dwellings, both native and employee had been left dirty and littered; furnaces, radiators and pipes broken through freezing; no water system since the tanks had been burned down; lights off in many buildings because of broken lines.[9]

The next morning, the Aleuts walked down the gangway. The horrendous conditions of the village didn't matter. For the first time in three years, they were home. Almost as if it were an omen of things to come, on that day, at 7:30 p.m. a daughter, Erena, was born to Daniel and Theodosia Shabolin. The Aleuts from St. George remained aboard ship until it sailed for their island on May 24.

The Aleuts were appalled at the utter devastation of their village. The agent who accompanied them vividly described the scene:

Inspection of St. Paul village disclosed conditions which were difficult to believe. Most of the buildings, including the native houses, bore evidence of having been ransacked.... Doors had been left open and windows were broken, and snow drifts were still piled high inside these openings. Snow which had drifted through and melted had flooded the basements of various buildings.... Plumbing, water lines and tanks were broken in all parts of the village.... In many buildings losses could be attributed to actual looting or vandalism. Boxes and chests of personal belongings had been opened by prying off locks and other fastenings, and contents were scattered in the search for things of value. Furniture was marred or broken, overstuffed pieces were torn or rendered unserviceable, and household fixtures had been removed or damaged. Warehouses and storerooms showed that there had been complete disregard for the value of the stores.... The carpenter shop did not contain any tools, and a survey of machine shop and garage showed that a large proportion of valuable tools had disappeared.[10]

From 1942 to 1944, the military occupied most of the buildings, including the supervisors' cottages, office buildings, the schoolhouse, and the community hall on St. George Island. On St. Paul, they took over every home and building with the exception of buildings that were used as storehouses. The log entry for May 24 described the condition of the Aleut homes on St. Paul:

> The native houses were all in an extremely dirty and upset condition, with many doors and windows broken, and much furniture and furnishings ruined and in bad shape. All employees' cottages were in much the same state.... The company houses were still occupied by Army personnel, and very dirty and untidy. The Aleutian bunkhouse was vacant but had been left in bad shape, with all sewers clogged, and most windows broken. All of the buildings had broken doors and windows and were all littered badly.[11]

The FWS budget did not include money for repairs to the homes or replacement of furnishings and personal items lost or destroyed during the military occupation. They requested the Army to make restitution and replace the lost and damaged contents of the Aleut homes. These items included furniture valued at $8,811, and dishes and other kitchenware valued at $713. The Army honored their request.

Money was a major issue in the resettlement of the Pribilofs. On August 7, 1944, President Roosevelt approved a joint request from the secretaries of war, the Navy, and the Interior for an allocation of $200,000 from the President's Emergency Fund. Its stated purpose was "for the return to their villages and rehabilitation of Aleut natives and certain white inhabitants of the Aleutian Islands, Alaska, who had been there during the current war."[12] To compensate the natives and white inhabitants for their suffering, he directed the Secretary of the Treasury to make funds available for limited payment of claims not to exceed $10,000.

At a conference of the representatives of the government agencies involved in the repatriation, it was recommended that the allocations from the President's Emergency Fund be increased to include the Pribilovians' resettlement cost and raise the limitation on payment of claims from $10,000 to $25,000.

Even though Stimson approved the decision to repatriate all Aleuts in December 1943, the natives from the Aleutian island villages were not returned to their homes until the late spring of 1945. Like so many promises that were never kept, it was one year later than promised by government officials and a year and a half after the decision was made that the military permitted repatriation of the villages in the Aleutian chain.

Not everyone agreed that the Aleuts should be repatriated in 1944. Officials of the Bureau of Indian Affairs were reluctant to cooperate, and the citizens of Unalaska were opposed to their return. They knew that the houses the Aleuts had lived in were broken into several times and the contents pilfered or destroyed. They wanted to know where the returning Aleuts would be housed and how their lost property would be restored. Assistant Superintendent Fred Geeslin thought the Indian Service had compiled an inventory of the villagers' belongings which would help in establishing claims for compensation at a later date.

With the blessing of Secretary of the Interior Harold Ickes, Commissioner John Collier fired Hirst as general superintendent and replaced him with Don C. Foster. Collier felt that Hirst and his office staff should have been attending to their duties instead of going fishing every time a problem came up. Ickes was happy to see Hirst go. He believed that he was a disgrace and had left Alaska in very bad shape.

The question of who would foot the bill for the repatriation was once again a major sticking point. Secretary Ickes wanted the Navy to assume the cost of rehabilitation of Akutan and Atka. After a number of meetings, Acting Secretary of the Navy James Forrestal agreed to take responsibility for rehabilitation of the two villages. He directed his subordinates to charge all expenditures to the naval emergency fund and announced that Akutan was now ready for occupancy. Atka would be ready as soon as construction materials for five more houses were available. Forrestal stated that the area commander would arrange and pay for transportation if the Interior Department failed to obtain it.

Despite the Navy's offer, preparations were halted when Superintendent Foster wired his superiors to "please delay further action." He claimed that a survey of conditions in the villages and the needs of the natives hadn't been completed and that despite Forrestal's support for the move, it was opposed by the commander of the Seventeenth Naval District.

Forrestal's predecessor, Frank Knox, had earlier ordered the commander of the North Pacific Force to proceed with the return of the natives to their villages. The commander informed Knox that officials of the Bureau of Indian affairs in Juneau were unwilling to move ahead with the plan. Knox passed the information on to Secretary Ickes.

When pressed for their reluctance to cooperate, the officials claimed the impracticability of hiring school teachers, the difficulty of supplying the villagers, and the impossibility of prevention of intermingling with military personnel, a code word for sexual encounters between Aleut women and military personnel. Rather than repatriating the Aleuts, the Indian service planned to move them from Ward Lake to Funter Bay once the Pribilovians had departed.

Upon hearing the news of the proposed move, Assistant Commissioner of Indian Affairs William C. Zimmerman notified Foster that the move from Funter Bay to Ward Lake was unnecessary and demanded that Foster return the evacuees to their villages at the "earliest practicable date." He told him that the failure to obtain teachers was no excuse and that many villages would be without teachers for a long time. Given Ickes's directives, and the approval of the military, his stall tactics were an embarrassment to the service.

Zimmerman wanted the move to be completed in 1944, but it wasn't to be. Foster was not quite ready to comply. He knew the villages had been badly damaged and how bad conditions would be if the Aleuts were allowed to return home. When Zimmerman pointed out that conditions in the camps were equally bad, Foster appeared to back down. He agreed that the natives should be returned to their homes, but given the horrendous winter storms that often struck the islands, it was imperative that the move be completed no later than September.

Officials of the Department of the Interior continued to debate the issue with no resolution in sight. The director of the Division of Territories and Island Possessions, B.W. Thoron, sent a telegram to Governor Gruening stating that the "Indian Office" had concluded that inability to secure teachers for the communities did not outweigh the advantages of repatriation.[13] Gruening concurred with Thoron and requested that the Aleuts should be returned to their homes in the spring of 1944.

Despite Gruening's approval, Foster had serious misgivings, as did Geeslin, who had previously supported the repatriation. They blamed the delay in planning on the military's misinterpretation of the OIA position on the matter. Foster was concerned that the military presence on the islands and the fraternization with the Aleuts would create social problems for the service for a long time to come. Ignoring Thoron's comment that securing teachers for the communities did not outweigh the advantages of repatriation, Foster argued that he needed teachers and qualified personnel to protect the Aleuts when they returned home, especially at Unalaska.

Foster's protest fell on deaf ears. The Army, Navy, and the Department of the Interior arranged for the resettlement in May of that year. Reluctantly, Foster drew up an agreement between the military and the Interior Department outlining their responsibilities. In July, Stimson, Forrestal, and Ickes signed the agreement.

Throughout the summer months, Foster and Geeslin argued against resettlement. They were opposed to making any commitments against current appropriations until they received the money the military had promised them. If the Department of the Interior and the military wanted to ensure the return of the people by the later part of August or the first part of September, funds had to be forthcoming no later than June 30. By July 20, the Department of the Interior completed a funding agreement with the military.

Adequate funding should have been the final hurdle on the road to resettlement. Even though the money was available, Foster recommended cancellation of the repatriation until March of 1945. He claimed that the Aleutian weather would make it almost impossible to land large numbers of people and supplies on the islands. Reconstruction of the villages would have to be halted due to the constant winds and winter storms.

Foster was plagued with multiple problems that helped to fashion his decision, among them a lack of supplies and transportation. He argued that by delaying the move until March, it would give him ample time to purchase and assemble equipment and supplies. He also reported that he had to deal with protests from the Aleuts that they should not be returned to their homes until the following spring. Zimmerman gave in and agreed with Foster and Geeslin. The Aleuts would not be repatriated until the spring of 1945.

There is no evidence that the Aleuts protested. They wanted to go home. They were desperately disappointed when they didn't follow the Pribilovians in 1944. They were dealt a double blow and felt a keen sense of loss when they were told that they would not be resettled in their home villages, but would be transported to Akutan and Nikolski. Biorka, Kashega, and Makushin would be abandoned.

23

Homecoming

Planning continued throughout the remainder of 1944 and into the spring of 1945. An Indian Service resettlement officer was assigned to join a construction superintendent who would oversee the rebuilding of the burned-out village of Atka. Teachers where hired for Akutan, Nikolski, Atka, and Unalaska. Aleuts would have to pack their belongings, household equipment and Indian Service supplies and report to a central assembly point to be determined by the location of their camp.

The Aleutians were a restricted area. Before the military issued travel permits and allowed the evacuees to return, they required each person to be pho-

The last boat from Killsnoo docks at the pier to take on natives waiting to return to their homes (National Archives 75N-C8).

tographed and fingerprinted. Two enlisted men proceeded from Ward Lake to Burnett Inlet to Killisnoo to complete the task. In mid–April, the Coast Guard transported the entire population of Ward Lake to the Ketchikan Dock. The camp was dismantled and the lumber given to the Tlingit tribe at Saxman Village a few miles from Ketchikan.

April 15, 1945, was not only the day they left Ketchikan for the last time; it was also the holiest day in the religious life of the Aleut people. The night before their long-awaited escape from their internment, they held an Easter worship service, secure in the knowledge that the next Easter celebration would be held in the churches of their beloved villages.

The dawn broke over the horizon and one hundred and thirty-eight excited Aleuts boarded the USAT *David S. Branch*. At Burnett Inlet, the ship picked up 135 natives bound for Unalaska. On April 17, the ship made its last stop at Killisnoo, to pick up 77 Aleut citizens of Atka. Pulling up anchor, the *Branch* headed out to sea and its final destination, the Aleutian Islands.

Total desolation of Atka. The U.S. Navy burned the village to the ground to keep it from falling into the hands of the Japanese army in 1942 (National Archives, 75-N-AL 742).

23. Homecoming

Akutan was the first port of call. Thirty-five Akutans, twenty-one Aleuts from Biorka, and eighteen refugees from Kashega lined the deck and watched excitedly as the ship approached the island. The first building they saw was their beloved Russian Orthodox church. They were happy to be home, but saddened and shocked by what they found when they went ashore.

The ship dropped anchor about one and a half miles from the village and loaded the Aleuts aboard an Army scow for the short trip to shore. The Navy provided three hot meals at cost to the returnees.

Before the war, Akutan village consisted of sixteen homes, the church, the school, several small warehouses, two boat shops, a small fish saltery, a store and post office building and a dance hall. They had been in good repair when the Aleuts evacuated, but after the Navy moved in, the situation changed. The destructive force of the Aleutian winters of the last three years and vandalism at the hands of Navy personnel had taken their toll.

Unidentified Aleuts who were interned at Burnett Inlet wait on the pier for their ship to take them home to their village of Atka, April 23, 1945 (National Archives, 75N-Aleut-C2).

Johnny Gollecf (upper left), Paul Zachneof (left) and other poorly-clad Aleut boys (names unknkown) sitting on snow covered lumber during their first winter at the abandoned cannery at Killsnoo. Winter clothes were scarce. Paul Zachneof died while interned in the camp (National Archives 75-N-AL 742).

On the outside, the houses appeared untouched, but on the inside, they were a disaster. The rooms were filthy and wallpaper was ripped off the walls and strewn all over the floors. Doors and windows were broken and the roofs leaked. Small boats, outboard motors, guns, fishing gear, and personal belonging were missing. Many of the homes were devoid of furniture, bedding, pots and pans, and dishes. What furniture remained was torn and no longer usable. All of their possessions were gone or destroyed.

The commandant at Dutch Harbor directed his subordinates to conduct an inspection of Akutan. Despite Superintendent Geeslin's claims that there was very little damage to the buildings or incidents of looting, the Navy reported "extensive damage to houses and personal property, resulting from acts of vandalism committed by Navy personnel."[1] The inspection report revealed extensive destruction of Aleut property in the village and concluded that "without exception, all rooms in every building of this village clearly gave convincing evidence of looting and ransacking of the very worst kind."

In their report to the commandant, the inspectors employed graphic lan-

23. Homecoming

guage to describe the senseless vandalism and looting by officers and enlisted personnel assigned to island[2]:

> Many examples of inexcusable damage and extreme acts of vandalism were apparent [at Akutan]. Outstanding examples of this being:
> (a) Fixtures torn from walls and trampled.
> (b) China and glassware having been apparently swept from shelves and trampled.
> (c) Furniture and stoves being overturned and damaged beyond repair.
> (d) Window panes being broken from the inside after they were boarded on the outside.
> (e) Locked closets and desks being forced open by ripping the doors from the hinges.
> (f) Locked chests, trunks, and suitcases being forced open and damaged beyond repair; with contents damaged and scattered over the deck.
> (g) Piano keys being ripped from the keyboard.
> (h) Personal effects, consisting largely of clothing being removed from drawers and chests, torn beyond repair and scattered about the deck.
> (i) School supplies being removed from shelves and cupboards, tossed on deck and trampled.
> (j) Ink splashed over schoolroom, bulkheads, and ceiling.
> (k) School books and records mutilated.
> (l) Church records, books, and religious objects mutilated, and in several cases torn from their mounts.
> (m) Church windows broken from inside after being boarded up on outside.
> (n) Church door hacked, probably with an axe or hatchet, in an attempt to break in.

Aleuts boarding the last boat from Killisnoo (National Archives).

In an effort to make amends for the wanton destruction of the community and especially the church, navy personnel repaired doors and windows and completed major renovations. Unfortunately, they were unable to replace personal property or the icons and other items so important to the religious beliefs of the people. The total cost to the government for these efforts was $27,085.26. By January 3, 1946, the government paid out a total of $306 to satisfy claims brought against them by the citizens of Akutan.

Unalaska was the next stop for the *Branch*. On April 22, one hundred and thirty-five citizens of Unalaska and five from Makushin disembarked at Captain's Bay and climbed into waiting trucks. The natives wanted the church to be the first building they saw when they entered the village, but their hopes were soon dashed. They were driven to a remote area, herded into a fenced compound and quartered in Quonset huts. No explanation as to why or for how long they would be required to stay there was ever given.

Everyone wanted to go home, but the homes weren't habitable. They'd been vacant for three years and vandalized and attacked by the weather. Most of the housing was so far gone that the Army bulldozed them and replaced them with 16' × 20' cabanas until new houses were built.

The military command at Dutch Harbor was aware that the Aleuts would be evacuated form Unalaska Village. They had promised to provide patrols to provide security for the Aleuts' homes, but the patrols were never implemented. In a statement by sailors on patrol duty during the evacuation paint a vivid picture of the situation:

> On the afternoon of 18 July 1942 we were instructed by a [sic] Commanding Officer, Captain Copeland, to tell the natives that they were to board the Alaska the following day. They had less than 24 hour notice and were allowed to take with them only such belongings as they could carry, mainly clothing. Such items as rifles, radios, and phonographs were not taken. Except for a few houses having prepared shutters, none were boarded up by the departing residents. A detail from the Post went around later and nailed the doors shut and put slats over the windows. None of us recall having seen signs posted against trespassing.[3]

Nailing the doors shut and boarding up the windows apparently didn't stop military personnel from breaking in and looting the homes. A report describing the vandalism and looting was included in the planning process for rehabilitation:

> Trespassers have come from all branches of the service represented in this locality and from servicemen passing through here on boats. Perhaps the greatest loss to personal property occurred at the time the Army conducted its cleanup of the village in June of 1943. Large numbers of soldiers were in the area at that time removing rubbish and outbuildings and many houses were entered

23. Homecoming

Internees board the USAT *Delarof* for the final voyage from Killsnoo to their villages in the Aleutians (National Archives, 75N-Aleut C12).

Internees wait on the pier at Killsnoo for the boat that will take them home (National Archives, 75N-Aleut C#).

unofficially and souvenirs and other articles were taken. Other occasions when large numbers of men were in the area were during the salmon run in Unalaska creek in the autumn of 1942 and when Naval task forces visited here in the summer of 1943. Unalaska ... is a natural congregating place ... for men off duty. Military Police soldiers have patrolled the village hourly since the evacuation and their presence has prevented more looting.

Most of the native families had rifles, shotguns, small boats and fishing gear. These items along with radios, phonographs, ivory articles and photographs have been most frequently taken. It is probable that some of the furniture found in Army and Navy quarters came from Aleut houses. Damage to houses has consisted principally of broken locks, doors and windows.[4]

A survey of Unalaska Village conducted by the military in April 1944 placed the blame on the military for the looting and vandalism, and its failure to protect the homes and property of the Aleuts during their absence:

> The survey party accompanied by U.S. Deputy Marshall, Mr. Verne Robinson, inspected 34 of the 53 native homes. All buildings were damaged due to lack of

Remains of a kitchen in a residence in the village of Unalaska, 1945. Members of the U.S. clean-up campaign removed debris from the home after vandalism and wanton destruction by occupying Army personnel (National Archives, D.O.I. File 7469 RG 75 ccf AK 123–7469 IA).

normal care and upkeep. The natives were so hurriedly evacuated that they had no time to secure their homes, cover stove pipes and chimneys to prevent rain from blowing in, to turn off water supply, or otherwise protect their homes. The army detailed soldiers to board the windows and nail the doors shut, but this has not prevented breaking and entering. Apparently the buildings and premises were not posted. One home had been destroyed by fire, one razed, and several privies and other outbuildings razed to improve sanitation in the area.

The furnishings, clothing and personal effects, remaining in the homes showed, with few exceptions, evidence of weather damage and damage by rats. Inspection of contents revealed extensive evidence of widespread and wanton destruction of property and vandalism. Contents of closed packing boxes, trunks and cupboards had been ransacked. Clothing had been scattered over floors, trampled and fouled. Dishes, furniture, stoves, radios, phonographs, books, and other items had been broken or damaged. Many items listed on inventories furnished by the occupants of the houses were entirely missing.

It appears that armed forces and civilians alike have been responsible for this vandalism and that it occurred over a period of many months. Policing the area by military police, the efforts of the U.S. Deputy Marshall and of course private citizens to prevent this vandalism have been for the most part ineffective. The necessity of maintain blackouts in Unalaska over a period of months further increased the difficulties of adequately policing the area in which native homes are located.[5]

The houses weren't the only buildings that were in a state of serious disrepair. The school and the hospital needed cleaning and painting and some minor repairs. The Navy contributed enough supplies, equipment, and building materials to complete the reconstruction. Foster planned to hire the Aleuts and pay them fifty cents an hour, but he also planned to charge them thirty-five cents an hour for their food and other necessities they would need for the next year. Geeslin acquired an old panel truck to haul materials for the reconstruction. He employed the Aleuts to dismantle ammunition storage buildings for lumber, siding, and roof materials.

The Aleuts were more concerned about their church than they were about any other building in the village. They asked Geeslin for cedar shingles to replace the roof and a large oil heater. He negotiated with the Navy and before long the natives had the material and equipment they requested. In appreciation for his efforts to rebuild the church, they presented Geeslin with a framed and glass-covered picture. It was a picture of Alaska made of cotton to give it a three-dimensional appearance.

The total expenditures for the rehabilitation of Unalaska Village was $28,837.41, with a large portion of the money going to pay for coal and other supplies for the community. There is no record of any of the Aleuts receiving any of the funds allocated for satisfaction of personal claims for loss of property.

The natives scheduled to return to Nikolski weren't as fortunate as the

Aleuts who returned to Atka or Unalaska. They had a much more difficult time getting home. Instead of sailing to Umnak Island, the *Branch* sailed to Chernofski Harbor on the eastern end of Unalaska Island. With their personal belongings in tow, fifty-nine Aleuts climbed down the side of the ship into a power-driven scow for the eighty-nine-mile journey across the open sea. Upon their arrival they were greeted by the three Aleuts employed by the Aleutian Livestock Company ranch.

The Aleuts were happy to be home, but they were saddened by the destruction of their village. Nikolski was much more isolated than Unalaska, but it hadn't prevented the vandalism that began as soon as the Aleuts were evacuated from the island. Every house was broken into and ransacked. The contents of cupboards, and closets were thrown casually around the rooms. The native store was torn up, the merchandise strewn over counters and floors. The Navy claimed that Army personnel were responsible. The Army claimed the Navy did it. The Navy ordered an investigation to establish responsibility.

Remains of furnishings in the second floor bedroom of the home of Artie Ermerloff in Nikolski Village. The damage is the result of vandalism of Aleut property by U.S. military personnel stationed in the villages during August 1945 (National Archives, D.O.I. File 7469 ccr. AK-123–7469 I.A. APIA P82).

23. Homecoming

The vandalism and damage were so extensive that the Navy convened an Officer's Board to investigate the looting of private property. In their final report, they reported:

(a) Certain property and equipment chargeable to Alaska Indian Service and individuals was appropriated by the Armed forces for use, and that an incomplete accounting was made of property and equipment used.
(b) Extensive pilfering and looting of private property occurred in the homes of the Nikolski natives.
(c) It has been impossible to fix responsibility for such pilfering and looting.
(d) Certain efforts were made to prevent pilfering and looting, such as policing and boarding up homes to prevent breaking and entering, but these precautions were not established soon enough or were in general ineffective.[6]

Before reconstruction commenced, the Navy needed to know the extent of the damage. On April 12, they directed a survey party made up of Navy personnel and two residents of the village, Dan Krukoff and George Charcasen, to evaluate the condition of the village. At the completion of the survey, the members issued the following report.

In many of the homes, pilfering and looting was extreme, very little usable personal property remaining. Much of the contents of the homes was demolished or damaged beyond repair. After cognizance of these conditions was taken by Army officials, some action was taken and orders given to place personal property in boxes. The execution of this order resulted in making of standard size boxes, one for each house, and cramming all sorts of odds and ends into these boxes, without reference to value, so that many materials of considerable value were still left exposed to further damage from pilfering and wanton destruction.[7]

Prior to their return to the island, Resettlement Officer Harvey Coval conducted a hurried investigation. He decided that a majority of the houses weren't in any condition to be occupied. The school and the store would have to serve as temporary quarters until the housing situation was resolved. The school was presently occupied by military personnel and needed a thorough cleaning and some minor repairs before it was suitable for occupancy.

Geeslin visited the village and was convinced that the people were pleased to be back home where they could fish and hunt. Even though they had to rebuild their homes and reestablish their store, he assured them that they would be aided by the government and would receive twenty-five cents an hour for their labor.

By January 23, 1946, the government spent a total of $22,711.54 to rehabilitate Nikolski. Official records indicate that Aleuts of Nikolski received the paltry sum of $519.10 to cover the cost of merchandise left in the village store when they were evacuated in 1942. The residents of the village were never

Remains of the furniture in the home of Alex Chercasen in Nikolski Village after the U.S. Army left in 1945 (National Archives. D.O.I. File 7469, RG 75 ccf, AK-123-7469 IA).

compensated for their lost property as a result of the military occupation of their village.

Atka was the last stop for the *Branch*. The people of Atka were the first to be evacuated and the last to be returned to their village. Their experience was far different from that of the natives from the other islands. They'd watched the flames devour their homes as they sailed away in the dark of night and now they were returning to a burned-out village.

The next day, as the dawn rose over Nazan Bay, seventy-seven Atkans lined the rail and stared in horror at what was left of their village. They had hoped that their church had been spared from the fires, but like most of the buildings it no longer existed. The village they'd been forced to leave was gone forever.

The troops arrived at Atka village aboard the U.S. Army transport ship *St. Mihiel* on September 16, 1942. Aleut homes not consumed by the fire were occupied by military personnel. Navy personnel aboard the seaplane tender

23. Homecoming

Teal arrived at the end of September and set up a weather station in one of the homes. Looting and vandalism were as rampant on Atka as they were on each of the other islands. Contrary to the assertion that the entire village had burned to the ground, an official Army survey in April of 1945 revealed that some of the Aleuts' homes had survived the fires. The report included how the military used the homes and property of the natives during the occupation:

> A medical detachment was established in one of the abandoned native houses. The remaining houses with the exception of two ... were used by troops as offices, mess, kitchen, store rooms and quarters. Certain dwellings were dismantled for building materials. Ranges, dishes, cooking utensils, furniture, tools, and other gear and equipment found in the vacant houses were used by the troops.
>
> Nothing was left in Atka homes. They had been completely stripped of all furniture, personal belongings, and other equipment. Rehabilitation of those homes, in addition to repair of buildings will require replacement of all furnishings, stoves and ranges, tools, gear and equipment.[8]

At the conclusion of its inspection, the survey party recommended that before leaving Killisnoo, the Aleuts prepare sworn statements listing the contents of their homes, plus boats, engines, and any other gear left behind at the time of the evacuation. Inventory lists could then be used to complete the necessary purchase orders to replace lost or destroyed property.

The first problem to face the Aleuts was a lack of housing. Most of the buildings, including the church, were consumed by the fire, but a few buildings still remained standing. To provide temporary living quarters and hot meals for the returnees, the Army set up Quonset huts and a mess hall in a special fenced-off area outside of town. The huts were portioned into rooms measuring sixteen by eighteen feet as living quarters for families. Pit toilets were dug outside the huts. The Army provided food and labor for a few days until the unloading was complete.

For more than a year, the returnees struggled to rebuild their community. They worked evenings and weekends without pay. As each house was completed, it was occupied by one of the families living in the Quonset huts. They rebuilt their church complete with an onion dome and the double cross of the Russian Orthodox faith. It resembled the church that burned down and announced a new beginning for the Aleut people of Atka.

Many of the evacuees believed that their wartime suffering was a sacrifice to be forgotten. The less said about it the better. When the Aleuts left Ward Lake, they burned their temporary church altar and buried the ashes near the site of their newly completed church. In a symbolic gesture to their contribution to the war effort, they brought back and planted a number of trees in the Aleutians.

Lucy Prokopeuff (wife of George Prokopeuff) with her three-year-old granddaughter Annie aboard the USAT *Delarof*. Annie was born in 1942 while her mother was interned in Killsnoo (National Archives, 111 sc 207247).

With the resettlement of the Atkans, there was one more group of Aleuts who waited to come home. The people of Attu were still incarcerated in Japan. It wasn't until August 1945, when Japan surrendered, that they were free to return to the United States. At 8:00 a.m. on September 21, twenty-five Attuans left Japan forever. Suddenly they were free. Three years of sickness, death, and imprisonment had come to an end. For three years they dreamed of going home, but for these former prisoners of war, they wouldn't be returning to Attu. They would be resettled with the Atkans, Aleuts they had little in common with.

On September 22, government officials learned for the first time that some of the Attuans had survived and were coming home. They hadn't been heard from since the Japanese occupation of Attu and no one knew what had happened to them. Even before the Aleuts landed in California on their way home to Alaska, the OIA had decided not to rebuild their village or send them back to Attu.

The military gave immediate approval for the resettlement of Attu, but Superintendent Foster was dead set against it. He knew that the Japanese army had burned Attu to the ground, there were too few survivors, and the island was too remote to justify the cost of rebuilding the village. A return to Attu would necessitate the construction of a new hospital, and the island was still

23. Homecoming

occupied by the military. Geeslin met with Atka's leaders and convinced them to allow the Attuans to settle in their village. The Elders agreed, provided that their people could trap fox and seals on the Islands formally assigned to the people of Attu.

After the elders agreed to Geeslin's proposal, Foster claimed that the Atka natives were more than happy to accept the Attuans, and the Attuans were ready and willing to live with the Atkans, that it was the plan of the OIA to send them there, and that no coercion, force or any other undesirable tactics were employed. Despite Foster's claim, the Aleuts maintained that they were not given a choice. Most of them wanted to return to Attu, but according to the Attuans the government refused to honor the wishes of the people.

The refusal to return the people to Attu was based on economic concerns rather than a desire on the part of the OIA to rebuild the village. Settling the people on Atka saved the Indian Service a tremendous amount of money. They would not only save the cost of reconstruction, but because of the remoteness of Attu, they wouldn't have to transport supplies, build a school, or provide teachers for the community.

Their long journey nearly over, on December 12, the Aleuts boarded the *David S. Branch* in Tacoma, Washington, and sailed for Unalaska Island. On the way they stopped at Adak to unload military personnel and transfer to a small tugboat. They arrived at Atka on December 21, 1945, just in time to celebrate their first Christmas in the Aleutians in three years.

The Attuans disembarked from the tug and climbed into a waiting truck for a ride to the village school, where they were assigned to newly built homes or living spaces in the Quonset Huts. A total of twenty-four homes were rebuilt, eighteen for the Atkans and six for the Aleuts who were liberated from their prison in Japan. Although their arrival placed a strain on both groups, as time passed they overcame their differences, though the Attuans still longed to return to their home on Attu.

The Atkans, who had lost everything in the evacuation, received a credit in the amount of $6,168.48. Of this total, $3,000 was allocated to replace church utensils and $2,216.83 to settle the claim for lost merchandise in the community store. For satisfaction of claims for individual property losses within the community, they received a total of $451.65.

24

Restitution

The evacuation was a harsh experience for the Aleuts. It threatened their survival as a group and nearly destroyed their way of life forever. When there was little hope that they would be resettled in their villages after the war, they were sustained by their faith in God. They struggled to survive and hold their lives together in meaningful ways. As a people, they lost so much, but they learned that through concentrated protest, they had the power to change matters over which they previously believed they had little control.

Life in the camps transformed them forever. From their non–Aleut neighbors they learned the importance of democracy, after which they wanted to participate as American citizens and not wards of the state. The evacuation had given them a new awareness and the power to choose their own destiny.

Many of the survivors wanted to forget the horror of the camps and the damage and loss inflicted on them when they returned to their villages. Like the German, Japanese, and Italian survivors of the internment camps in America and Hawaii, they refused to talk about it at all. They had no desire to relive the memory of their ordeal. Reviving those memories served no practical purpose. They believed the evacuation and subsequent internment were their contribution and sacrifice for the war effort.

There were others who believed that the people should remember everything they lost. As time passed and the people told their stories, they began to wonder how they could receive justice from an uncaring government. Younger Aleuts who heard the stories of the internment from their elders decided that it was an unnecessary insult to the Aleut people. They ignored those who urged them to forget the camps. The evacuation and relocation were an indelible part of their history that must never be forgotten.

How and when would they be paid for their losses? Was restitution even possible? Based on the example of the Tlingit Indians who lived near Killisnoo, they did not believe it was possible. In 1882, on orders of Commander E.C.

24. Restitution

Merriman, the U.S. Navy bombarded, pillaged, and burned the Tlingit village of Angoon. Six children died in the attack. Ninety-one years later, under threat of a lawsuit, the Tlingit won a monetary settlement, but the government and Navy refused to apologize for their actions.

Immediately after the war, non–Aleuts filed claims with the government for their losses during the evacuation. The Fish and Wildlife Service received compensation for a cottage the Army Weather Bureau occupied on St. Paul. The owner of the Aleutian Livestock Company received monetary restitution for his losses and the owners of the evacuation campsites in southeastern Alaska received rental payments or had their properties improved as compensation from the government.

Official military investigations and reports documented the damage and vandalism, and no one ever denied these losses occurred. Somehow the government never got around to paying restitution to the Aleuts, and by the early 1950s it looked like they were never going to. President Roosevelt had authorized a grand total of $25,000 from the Presidential Emergency Fund to compensate all 881 Aleuts evacuated by the U.S. government. Pribilovians, who numbered about half of the evacuees, received approximately twelve dollars each. Aleuts living on the islands along the chain received nothing.

Restitution for the survivors of Attu took a different twist when in October 1945 the Interior Department filed claims through the State Department against the Japanese government. The Attuans wanted to rebuild their church, and they asked for $74,425 for loss of income during their imprisonment and the destruction of their fox-breeding stock. They also wanted $220 for loss of life. The War Crimes Commission agreed that since the Attuans paid such a heavy toll as victims of violations of established principles of international law, they were eligible for compensation. The Attuans were eventually awarded $32,000 from enemy property retained in the United States by the Department of Justice.

A new wind of political freedom was blowing through the Aleut communities. No longer would they sit back and allow the government to control their lives. An emerging group of Aleut leaders came forward, pushed for restitution, and won. In 1988, forty-three years after the evacuation, Congress passed Public Law 100–383, a bill providing compensation for the evacuees and an apology from Congress and the president on behalf of the people of the United States.

This victory was possible because former evacuees Flore Lekanof and Philemon Tutiakoff, and younger leaders like Patrick Pletnikoff, Agafon Krukof, Jr., and Dimitri Philemonof, refused to let the past remain silent. In the tradition of American justice, they fought to right a terrible wrong committed against their people. They wanted restitution and they wanted to ensure that future generations would never forget.

The restitution process had a slow beginning. In 1977, Patrick Pletnikoff, executive director of the Aleutian/Pibilof Islands Association, sought funding from the Department of the Interior to institute legal action against the governments of Japan and America. The Interior Department refused their request. In January 1978, Pletnikoff retained Cook and Henderson, a Washington, D.C., law firm, to pursue their case.

Pletnikoff worked with Alaska Senator Mike Gravel on a project to clean up and remove the war debris from the Aleutians. At one of their meetings, Gravel informed him that the Aleuts might be included in a bill under consideration in the Senate granting civil service retirement benefits to Japanese Americans interned in America in World War II.

By the time he was replaced as executive director, Pletnikoff had contacted the Japanese Consulate in Anchorage requesting restitution for the actions of the Japanese against the Aleuts during the war. He was arrogantly rebuffed. According to the peace accords, the Allied powers waived all claims of reparations against the Japanese as a result of the war.

The Alaska congressional delegation played a major role in the quest for restitution. The Congress had created a special Commission on Wartime Relocation and Internment of Civilians. The original purpose of the commission was to right some of the wrongs suffered by American citizens who were denied the rights of their American citizenship because of their ancestry. At the

Japanese-Aleut Reparations dinner, 1984, with Senator Ted Stevens (center) and members of the committee (names unknown).

24. Restitution

request of Alaska Senator Ted Stevens, Congress expanded the mandate of the commission to include an examination of the government's treatment of the Aleuts during the war.

The commission was faced with the twin task of documenting the losses of the Aleut people, and finding the funding for restitution. A young attorney in the law firm of Cook and Henderson, former naval officer John C. Kirtland, researched the historical context of the evacuation and compiled data on the human suffering and property loss of the Aleut people. The Alaska state legislature approved an appropriation of $165,000 to support Kirtland's work. His research formed the basis for the Aleut section of the commission's report, *Personal Justice Denied*.

The next step in the process was to organize the Aleut testimony. The Aleutian/Pribilof Islands Association appointed a three-member leadership panel chaired by Philemon Tutiakoff to take depositions and to prepare their witnesses for their appearance before the commission. Fifty-three Aleuts gave their testimony and 136 depositions were presented.

Attorney John C. Kirkland (left) and Philemon Tutikof testify before the 98th Congress in Washington, D.C., on June 27, 1984.

In November 1983, legislation was introduced to implement the commission's recommendations[1]:

   (a) A $5,000,000 trust fund established for the beneficial use of the six surviving Aleut villages which were relocated, and for the use of surviving Aleuts and their descendants.
   (b) Per capita payments of $12,000 for each surviving Aleut evacuee.
   (c) The restoration of church property damaged or destroyed by U.S. forces in Alaska.
   (d) The cleanup of wartime debris left on populated islands of the Aleutians.
   (e) $15,000,000 to the Aleut Corporation for the loss of Attu Island.

From 1983 to 1985, Congress failed to take further action on the bill, and there were other problems that had cropped up. The Japanese-Americans were split on the inclusion of the Aleuts. The bill was stalled by budgetary constraints, and the Justice Department was opposed to paying restitution. They argued that victims of war were not necessarily deserving of special compensation. They further argued that restoration of the church under this bill would violate the separation of church and state.

Attorney John C. Kirkland (left) and Philemon Tutiakof meet on June 26, 1984, to discuss their congressional testimony.

24. Restitution

Kirtland, the Alaska politicians and the Aleut leaders addressed these problems the same way that politicians have always done. In the American tradition of political expediency, they compromised and tailored the bill to meet these objections. In 1987, the chairman of the Aleut Corporation, Agafon Krukof, Jr., and the executive director of the Aleutian/Pribilof Islands Corporation, Dimitri Philemonof, submitted supporting statements and testified before Congress on the newly revised bill.

The Aleuts won their victory for restitution and an apology from the United States government when, on October 10, 1988, President Reagan signed the Aleutian and Pribilof Islands Restitution bill into law.

Redress had drawn large numbers of Aleuts into the political process. They fought for equity and fairness and now the hard-won victory was theirs. Unfortunately, many of the survivors died before receiving redress for their loss and suffering. Dimitri was born six months after his parents returned to St. George from Funter Bay. Nevertheless, he felt the restitution issue "very close to my heart."

Dimitri and other Aleut leaders could now look ahead to a brighter future. "Compensation," Philemonof predicted, "will assist in the rebuilding process. It would benefit elderly, disabled or seriously ill Aleuts and students in need of scholarships. The trust fund would help remind everyone of the sufferings caused by severe dislocations of the war years. Its earnings could be used to promote Aleut culture and train new leaders. Restitution would further Aleut community development. Aleuts always held dear their island homes." Dimitri Philemonof expressed his belief in a brighter future for his people when he said, "There is hope in the Aleut heart."[2]

Appendix

The attack on Dutch Harbor and invasion and subsequent occupation of Attu and Kiska by the military forces of the Empire of Japan was a horrendous event in the history of Alaska. The U.S. government and the military saw it as the first step in an invasion of mainland Alaska. In a misguided attempt to protect the Aleuts from the same fate the people of Attu suffered at the hands of the enemy, they evacuated them from their island homes and relocated them in abandoned canneries, fishing camps, and gold mines for the duration of World War II. Unlike the Japanese, German, and Italian Americans who were interned in camps across America and Hawaii, the Aleuts endured substandard living conditions, starvation, illness and death. Forced to harvest the fur seals for the United States government, they faced the loss of their American citizenship and the threat of never being allowed to return to their homes in the Pribilof Islands.

Each letter and document included in the appendix presents a small part of the entire picture of the evacuation and relocation of the Aleut people and the suffering they endured during three long years of internment in Japan and southeastern Alaska. They help to explain the attitudes of government officials and the military in dealing with the native peoples of the Aleutian Chain and the actions they felt were justified to protect them from an invading enemy.

Salt Lake City, Utah
October 19, 1942

Mr. E.C. Johnston
706 Federal Office Building
Seattle, Washington

Dear Mr. Johnston,

   Mrs. Grover has been with us for some little time now and we have learned to think a great deal of her and to have considerable respect for her opinion.

   She has talked many times about Sophie Procopius and her many good qualities, so we decided to see if arrangements could be made to bring her to the states to do housework for us. We would be willing to wire money for her bus and boat fare here and then Sophie could pay it back to us at $5 a month. We would like to have her come down on the next boat if arrangements could possibly be made.

I remain respectfully yours,

Mildred Greenhagan
1415 So. 5th East
Salt lake City, Utah

Letter from Mildred Greenhagan to Superintendent Johnston requesting she be permitted to bring Sophie Procopus to Salt Lake City, Utah, to work as a domestic.

Funter Bay, Alaska
November 2, 1942

Mrs. Mildred Greenhagan
1415 So. 5th East
Salt lake City, Utah

Dear Mrs. Greenhagan:

   We have just received your letter regarding the employment of Sophia Procopius. Sophie Procopius is already filling a position in Juneau at a salary of $50 per month with room and board. She expects to return to the Pribilof Islands when the emergency is over.

   It is the policy of the Fish and Wildlife Service to refuse to allow Pribilof natives to accept work in the states.

Very truly yours,

Edward C. Johnston
Superintendent

Letter from Superintendent Johnston to Mildred Greenhagan explaining the policy of the Fish and Wildlife Service. This letter indicates that like most Federal officials, he considered the Aleuts to be wards of the government and not U.S. citizens.

Appendix

Fouke Fur Company
Thirteen Twenty-Eight Kings Highway
St. Louis
May 12, 1942

Mr. Edw. C. Johnston,
Fish and Wildlife Services,
705 Federal Office Bldg.,
Seattle, Wash.

Dear Mr. Johnston,

Harry May is leaving Chicago at 11 p.m. today on the Northern Pacific, arriving in Seattle around 7:50 Friday evening. The rest of the group are scheduled to leave here next Sunday afternoon, the 17th, and should arrive in Seattle the morning of the 20th. We are giving the boys this day extra in Seattle because of the traffic congestion on the railroads. We were afraid that movement of troops and supplies might prevent them making connections and delaying you if their arrival was left until the morning of the 21st. Unless I hear from you to the contrary we will anticipate the "Penguin" leaving on the 21st.

In a letter to Mr. Fouke several weeks ago you mentioned the probability of using the scorched earth policy in case of an enemy attack on the Pribilof Islands. We delayed answering you specifically until we were able to find out from the insurance companies what the situation would be with respect to insurance that covers the skins. *It now appears that it is not possible to purchase insurance to cover the skins while on land except for some two weeks at Dutch Harbor or other port of transfer.* Now that the insurance problems seem to be cleared up we are of the opinion that the best means of destruction would be dumping the barrels into the sea from the village cliffs. It would appear that the flat area where scorea has been taken could be used to store the barrels of sealskins. Then in case of an emergency it would seem quite practical to use natives for rolling the barrels off the cliffs. We feel that even if the barrels are intact after they hit the sea they should sink and water will gradually filter in, leaching the salt from the skins. The skins would then very quickly deteriorate and the balance of the destruction would come from the sand fleas and other marine life. We doubt the practicability of attempting to destroy the skins in salt and in tanks by acid or other chemicals. We feel that dumping in the sea would be the most effective method for these skins too—presumably trucks would be used to transport the skins to the village cliffs and the dumping take place from that same area. There would almost always be the possibility that these skins could be recovered by the enemy but we feel that sufficient damage would be done and unless the skins were very carefully handled and cured promptly after recovery they would be of very doubtful value for either fur purposes or leather. There may still be a better spot for dumping than the village cliffs, but the proximity to the salt house and the possibility of storing awaiting shipment seem to us to make the village cliffs the best situation.

If there is any further information you would care to have we will be very glad to submit same upon request.

We believe it is your intention to ship the barrels of sealskins to Dutch Harbor on the "Penguin" from time to time instead of holding them on the Islands for the supply ship as in former years. We are wondering what if any facilities there are at Dutch Harbor or Unalaska for storing the sealskins pending shipment to Seattle. If the barrels are not stored under roof it would be advisable to place them where the midday sun would not hit them for any length of time, for we are under the impression that Dutch Harbor and Unalaska get considerably warmer and get more sunshine than the Pribilofs. In view of the fact that most of the ships plying between Seattle and Dutch Harbor would most likely be returning comparatively empty have you thought of transferring the skins from the "Penguin" to any government boats returning to Seattle rather than storing them at Dutch Harbor until the end of the season? One of your recent letters conveyed the information that the supply ship would be going to the Islands earlier than usual. We are wondering if you contemplate sending down on the supply boat all the skins that are available at the time the supply ship is ready to return to Seattle.

Harry will advise you of the changes contemplated in blubbering bonuses for both the Aleutian natives as well as the Pribilof natives, and we trust that the arrangements we have made will meet with your entire approval.

I know you must be frightfully busy at this time so instead of bothering to answer this letter we would appreciate you discussing these points with Harry May if the opportunity presents itself and then Harry can advise us of any decisions you anticipate making. Would however appreciate hearing from you promptly if there is any anticipated change in sailing date.

Hope you are enjoying the best of good health, and with kindest personal regards.

    Sincerely,
    G. Donald Gibbins
    Vice President
    Fouke Fur Company

The loss of the seal skins posed a major financial loss to the Fouke Fur Company. Mr. Gibbins was reluctant to have them destroyed in the event of an enemy attack and was making plans to ship them to Dutch Harbor for safekeeping.

Air Mail   Seattle, Washington
                                                                                     May 28, 1942

Mr. Ward T. Bower, Chief,
    Division of Alaska Fisheries,
        Fish and Wildlife Service,
            Washington, D.C.

Dear Mr. Bower:

In my letter of March 18, 1942 addressed to the Director and marked "attention Mr. Paul H. Thompson," I stated that the Commandant of the 13th U.S. Naval District had asked that we follow a "scorched earth" policy on the Pribilof Islands in case of an enemy attack. All supplies of value including seal skins to be destroyed.

As to the destruction of the seal skins, we know of no practical way to destroy any skins that may be in the washing tanks. Those on hand in barrels could be rolled over the cliff back of the village on St. Paul and to the east of the village on St. George. We believe the fall is great enough to break the barrels, and skins that are not carried away by the sea will soon be destroyed by sand fleas.

Gasoline, diesel, seal oil and kerosene can be destroyed by burning or draining the tanks. Food stuffs will be destroyed, but we are not certain of the extent to which this should apply to general stores.

If the Washington Office has any directions along these lines please advise.

We understand that the take of sealskins is not to be limited to 50,000, but that as many additional seals are to be taken as possible up to the total take of last season. Killing will continue until skins become too "stagy" for commercial use.

Very truly yours,
Edward C. Johnston
Superintendent.

Superintendent Johnston discussing the destruction of the sealskins and his intention to continue the fur seal harvest, thereby preventing a huge loss of revenue to the U.S. Treasury.

Official Logbook, St. George Island, Alaska 1942

JUNE 16 Tuesday
Having received orders from the navy to prepare for an immediate evacuation of all white and native population, the entire village has been mined with TNT; the cattle were rounded up and stanchioned, then shot; pails of gasoline stationed in each house to facilitate destruction, etc. Everyone was limited to one suitcase only; however at the last minute several small boats and outboard engines were salvaged.

JUNE 17 (En route to Dutch harbor) Wednesday

JUNE 18 Thursday
Arrived Dutch harbor yesterday, picked up Atka natives, some of whom were flown in after their village was bombed and machine gunned by the Japs; left Dutch Harbor early this morning.

JUNE 24 Wednesday
Arrived at cannery site, Funter Bay, Alaska.

JUNE 25 Thursday
Due to lack of space at the cannery, all St. George Natives and white personnel have been moved to the Admiralty Alaska Gold Mining Co., just across the bay.

JUNE 29 Monday
Miscellaneous

9 men cleaning up around buildings, etc.
7 removing rocks from boat landings
2 sharpening saws

2 splitting wood
2 assisting with the stores
6 digging for clams, cutting grass, etc.
6 carpenters repairing walks, broken down bldgs.
1 man building bed pan
2 men making a bell (dinner)
1 working in the laundry

Birth

Tikhon, infant son of Constantine and Agafia Mandregan, born 6:30 p.m.

The daily log was discontinued during the internment at Funter Bay.

UNITED STATES
DEPARTMENT OF THE INTERIOR
OFFICE OF THE SECRETARY
DIVISION OF TERRITORIES AND ISLAND POSSESSIONS
WASHINGTON

JUNE 22, 1942

Memorandum for the Secretary:

I attach a confidential message which has just been received from Governor Gruening. You may wish to discuss the subject matter with the secretaries of War and Navy.

Guy J. Swope,
Director

See CONFIDENTIAL message on next page

CONFIDENTIAL
WAR DEPARTMENT
CLASSIFIED MESSAGE CENTER
INCOMING MESSAGE

June 21, 1942
3:15 a.m.

From: Juneau Als
To: Div. of Terr. and Island Possessions
No 212455 June 20, 1942
From: Governor Gruening and the Chairman of the Alaska War Council
For: Secretary Ickes

In pursuance of your executive order of June eleventh, the Alaska War Council holding its first meeting urges immediate unification of the command in Alaska as has been done elsewhere. Enemy has already invaded the Aleutians in force entrenching himself and moving his new bases of operation toward mainland invasion of which is imminent thus operations for major offensive against enemy

Appendix **211**

and unified command indispensable prerequisite as situation clearly calls for such.

Stevenson,
Operator in charge

ACTION: DEPT OF INT.
INFO. COPIES OPD, G-2, A-2, CG AAF, TAG, FILE

CONFIDENTIAL
THE MAKING OF AN EXACT COPY OF THIS MESSAGE IS FORBIDDEN

Confidential message from Governor Gruening to Secretary of the Interior Harold Ickes, informing him of the results of the first meeting of the Alaska War Council.

Untitled Document
UNITED STATES
DEPARTMENT OF THE INTERIOR
DEPARTMENT OF COMMERCE

Bureau of Fisheries
706 Federal Office Bldg.,
Seattle, Washington

Funter, Alaska
Pribilof Evacuation Camp
July 1, 1942

Mr. Edward C. Johnston, Sup't.,
U.S. Fish & Wildlife Service,
706 Federal Office Building,
Seattle, Washington

Dear Mr. Johnston:

Confirming our verbal conversation regarding the payment of some sort of a salary for the Pribilof natives while they are evacuees from the Islands.

There still isn't a doubt in my mind that a salary of some account <u>should be paid them while</u> they are away from their homes. They come in contact with many people here that tell them of all the work that is available around and the money they can make. Some have openly declared they are going to take their families and look for work to make some money. Even saying the Government has to take care of them no matter where they <u>go and give them some pay</u>.

<u>Believe it would not be satisfactory to take part of</u> the men and send them around to other localities for work and some would have to be left behind to look after the women and children and do the necessary work here. Have asked the Superintendent about work at the hawk Inlet plant and he says they are full over there. <u>He also said he could not keep liquor away from them</u>. Have considered nearly all the angles in the situation here and urgently recommend every endeavor should be made to keep the Pribilof natives together as a unit and pay them a nominal salary to try to keep them satisfied. Otherwise all the work the Government has put in and the expense would all have to be done over again

if they are allowed to roam at will. It would also be a terrific expense to pick them up again because it would have to be in the end. <u>So far have denied all request to be allowed to leave to look for work.</u> Have explained to them that their stay here is very indefinite and if they leave they may not be here in case they get orders to go home again.

Last year first class native on St. Paul drew $754.10 or better than $60 a month. Recommend a salary of twenty five dollars a month be paid first class men and graduated down to ten dollars. If they should be returned to the Island this could be deducted from divisions coming to them in the future or paid outright as a salary. Japanese, I believe, are paid a monthly wage in concentration camps and if so the above recommend should not be so far out of line as those are our own people.

Have not made any promises to the natives but something will have to be done to correct the living conditions here or some other diversion or it will be more than any living person can handle. They are over $8,500 in debt now and they should not be allowed to get any deeper, but they still have to have tobacco and the things the bureau has stopped furnishing to them in later years.

For a basis to figure on will give here the number of men in each class last division and the new ones added by graduation from school. Total St. Paul men 84, do not know the number of St. George workmen but all should be treated alike.

```
33 men first class.................$20 .............$660
19 men second class...........17.50 ............332.50
18 men third class ...............15.00 ............270.00
14 men fourth class ............10.00 ............140.00
                                                $1,402.50
```

St. George has about 60 men. The exact figures could be furnished when and if necessary. Entire payroll could not be over $2,500 per month. Any payments or salary should be dated back to May 1, 1942, so much needed supplies and clothes can be purchased that were left behind when the Islands were evacuated.

Yours very truly,
L.L. Mcmillin
Agent and Caretaker.

Superintendent Johnston believed the Aleuts from the Pribilofs should receive a salary. Johnston knew how important the revenue from the fur seal harvest was to the U.S. Treasury. He may have felt that paying them a small salary and keeping them together as a unit and refusing to allow them to take employment outside the confines of Funter Bay would make it much easier to provide the needed labor force if and when the seal harvest resumed.

Appendix

706 Federal Office Bldg.,
Seattle, Washington
July 21, 1942

Mr. G. Donald Gibbins,
　Care of Fouke Fur company,
　　1328 South Kings Highway
　　　St. Louis, Missouri.

Dear Mr. Gibbins:

The St. Paul Island canteen has paid the Imperial Candy Company for the candy ordered by Mr. May. A receipt is enclosed for your records.

The sealing season is almost over and we are way behind on the take. So far, St. Paul has 96 skins in salt and St. George 31. Let's hope we can make it up next year. I am anxious to learn how the St. George fox skins arrived as they were packed by military authorities after evacuation of the Island.

All of our people—whites and natives—are established at Funter Bay on the west side of the northern tip of Admiralty Island. It is about 50 miles from Juneau—20 minutes by airplane. The St. Paul section is quartered at an abandoned cannery on one side of the bay and the St. George section on the opposite side. It is about one mile straight across or two miles around the beach at the head of the bay. The locations are not bad and with some lumber for repairs and partitions in large bunkhouses (and many other things) some degree of comfort may be obtained. We were exceedingly lucky that the evacuation was not ordered in early winter as it takes considerable time to get 500 men, women, and children comfortably settled for the winter. We are greatly indebted to the Forestry Service, and the Bureau of Indian Affairs, as well as the cannery and mine owners, for their fullest cooperation. Everyone has been willing to donate their services and equipment whenever possible.

At the present time, with the exception of 100 natives awaiting transportation, all natives as far east as Akutan have been evacuated. Attu was lost before evacuation.

All of your equipment, which we had for sending on the *Penguin*, we will hold in the dock warehouse. The boxes of toys will be sent to the natives at Funter Bay. Unless, of course you direct otherwise.

As you may be interested in the condition in which the Islands were left, here was the situation. On June 16 St. George was completely evacuated. Pails of gasoline were left in every building and dynamite with fuses set was placed under all equipment including motors, tanks, radio, etc. Cattle were shot. St. Paul was evacuated the same day but no preparations were made for destruction. Roy Hurd, acting as radio man was left on the Island until June 25 when six Army men were landed on each Island to attend to the scorched earth policy. Hurd was brought out. All orders were given by Military authorities.

With kindest regards for all members of the company,

　　　　　　　　　　　　　　　　　　Sincerely yours,
　　　　　　　　　　　　　　　　　　Edward C. Johnston,
　　　　　　　　　　　　　　　　　　Superintendent.

Superintendent Johnston is concerned with the low take of sealskins and hopes for a better take next year. He outlines the status of the natives and believes the various government agencies involved in the evacuation and relocation have done an excellent job. Once the natives arrive at Funter Bay, his description of the camps will come into conflict with the truth of the situation.

UNITED STATES
DEPARTMENT OF THE INTERIOR
FISH AND WILDLIFE SERVICE

Pribilof Evac. Camp
St. Paul Island,
July 24, 1942

Mr. E.C. Johnston, Sup't.,
706 Federal Office Bldg.,
Seattle, Washington.

Dear Mr. Johnston:

Mr. Davis of P.E. Harris made an inspection of this old cannery; he stated that the warehouses now being used for our supplies will have to be vacated by the end of the fishing season which I believe in this district is August 18. All other buildings in the cannery leak so bad that the roofs will have to be repaired, and the building which he indicated we could use is 50' × 150,' and the roof is of ⅓ pitch and should have a complete shingling all over. This building has a large balcony; this in the place Mr. Davis stated we could use for storing our supplies and personal effects.

It will be impossible to heat this building, and only such supplies that can stand being frozen can be stored here. Mr. Davis also stated that he had worked in Funter Bay in years past and that he had seen the weather here as cold as 26 degrees below. It seems to me the best solution of this entire project would be to endeavor to find some place that could be used as a winter camp where we would at least have a place to keep food supplies, have a water supply, and better housing conditions than here at Funter Bay.

If you intend to have school this winter, a place will have to be built of sufficient size to handle all the students. I think some plan should be made to get started on such needed buildings and improvements as soon as possible. If you intend to keep the people at this place without further improvements, then we should be notified immediately so we can begin preparing for winter with what little material we might be able to salvage, otherwise the only thing I can see is extreme hardships and possible deaths under present conditions for cold weather.

The suspense of waiting for material and supplies to make repairs possible with material on hand, would take the heart out of a mummy (if a mummy has a heart!), 90 percent of the buildings leak very bad; we obtained a few rolls of roofing from the cannery after much "talking," but it could be used only on the warehouse to keep the supplies dry. We received additional roofing on the Penguin but *didn't* receive nails or cement to lay the paper- It's things like this which can be so trying.

The work we are doing is looking in the direction of our winter stay, but there must still be many, many improvements made before any of the present buildings could be lived in during extreme cold weather. There isn't a building at this site which is made for winter occupancy—as you know. The canneries are operated only in the summertime.

If you think the attitude of this office regarding this situation is wrong, would you please converse with Mr. Olson—as you know, he has firsthand knowledge of conditions in southeastern Alaska both for winter and summer, and also the condition of the buildings at this and other sites in the territory. He I think is the only person in the government service who really gave this place and the mine site a thorough investigation, before the Pribilof people were landed here.

The health and safety of the people, both natives and employees, should be the first consideration now confronting the Bureau.

There is possibly less than one chance in a thousand of ever returning to the Pribilofs before winter; I feel that the government has a duty to perform in taking care of the people now that they are away from home. Every employee here is doing and will continue to do all in their power to make a success of this evacuation, and I believe the morale of the people is very high under existing conditions. They seem to have faith that everything will be fixed and they will be made as comfortable as possible before long.

Yours very truly,
L.L. McMillin

Burnett Inlet, Alaska
March 26, 1943

Dear Ken,

Received six dollars from you and two letters.

We are all pretty discouraged as we all want to go home. I can't say we are living in good houses. They are all warehouses, and if you heard anything different from Mr. Hope or anyone else just don't believe it. Some people don't mind living off people as cheap as possible. Well, most of us have no way to make our food money, so I think there's some catch to us.

Now I want you to write to Washington, D.C. Ask them why we have to pay for our food and other things when we have no way to make a living. If it's clear, and not so dangerous up at Unalaska, I can't see why we aren't sent there as Jenson's wife is there, but I can't think anyone else is. So if she can stay there well so can we.

They practically treat us as if we were so dumb, or as aliens. So find out, if we can go home. We're practically discouraged here.

Later on, I'll let you know what my plans are, and be sure and do some writing to Washington, D.C. Please.

Love to all,
Martha

Next letter will be written longer—excuse writing—am in a hurry to catch boat.

Unalaska, Alaska
April 30, 1943

Mr. Claude Hirst
Superintendent, I.B.I.A.
Juneau, Alaska

Dear Mr. Hirst:

I wish to express my appreciation for the help you have given to my children in starting them out in life with a good education and now the good work the Bureau is doing in taking care of the Unalaska evacuees at Barnett Inlet and Wrangell Institute.

Herbert, my eldest son, graduated from Kciutua high school, and is now a full-fledged diesel engineer. Lillie, eldest daughter, attended Kciutna high school for two years, and then they changed the school to a vocational school, she left to finish her education at the Seward high school. She graduated the second highest in her class and is now happily married.

I returned the early part of this month from a visit to Wrangell. While there I visited the institute and also spent four days with my wife and two children at Barnett Inlet. Had a long talk with Mr. Barrett, the Superintendent, and he struck me as "being the right man in the right place." All the children are well taken care of, and they are satisfied and happy.

All the people at Barnett Inlet seemed to be happy and satisfied too. They have their own little church and school, and are in need of nothing more. I talked with all the people, and did not hear one complaint. Of course, they want to return to Unalaska as soon as possible, but were willing to stay there for the duration of the war.

Excuse me for taking up so much of your valuable time, but I wanted you to know there is at least one family (and I know of several others) who appreciate the wonderful work you and the Bureau are doing.

Yours truly,
C.H. Hope (Sgd)

HEADQUARTERS WESTERN DEFENSE COMMAND AND FOURTH ARMY—PRESIDIO OF SAN FRANCISCO CALIFORNIA

Office of the Assistant Chief of Staff G-2

9 August 1943

INTELIGENCE MEMORANDUM)
NUMBER ... ... 8)

FINAL REPORT OF REDUCTION AND OCCUPATION OF ATTU
FROM THE COMBAT INTELIGENCE POINT OF VIEW

FOREWORD

1. This report is a summary of all combat intelligence information as it pertains to the enemy operations on Attu, chiefly during the period from 20

Appendix **217**

October 1942 to 31 May 1943, the date on which our forces completed the occupation of the island. This report is based on the following sources: Prisoner of war interrogation reports; translation of captured enemy documents; reports, studies and sketches prepared by the A. C. of S. A-2 Eleventh Air Force; and observors reports.

2. It is estimated that the enemy seized ATTU and KISKA for the purpose of: a. observation in the Aleutians area; b. disruption of lend-lease supply system between RUSSIA and the UNITED STATES and c. establishment of bases for further offensive operations in the Aleutian-Alaska area. The enemy abandoned ATTU from about 20 September 1942 to 20 October 1942 leading to the conclusion that there was a complete change of plans regarding the ultimate purpose of the ATTU base.
3. That the enemy never exhibited any particular determination to improve the ATTU and KISKA bases and was very dilatory in the construction of proper facilities for the basing of Land-based aircraft, coupled with the lack of naval strength in the Aleutian area, leaves to the assumption that the enemy has not given the Aleutian theatre a very high priority. The conclusion can also be drawn that he lacked the necessary equipment, material, planes and naval forces required to adequately exploit his holdings in the Aleutians.

DECLASSIFIED—DOD Directive No. 5200. 9, 27 September 1956

JOHN WECKERLING
Colonel, G. S. C.
A. C. of S., G-2

Deposition of Parascovia Lokanin taken at Atka, Alaska January 10, 1979

JAPANESE INVASION, CAPTURE AND INTERNMENT OF THE ATTU PEOPLE IN JAPAN DURING WORLD WAR II

1. How many people were there on Attu village who were forcibly taken by the Japanese to their internment camps in Japan?
   More than 41 people.
2. What date did the Japanese come to Attu in June of 1942?
   June 6th or 7th, 1942.
3. Approximately how big a force did the Japanese come to Attu in June of 1942?
   Japanese destroyer was first to come.
   Later 1,200 or 1,500 settled.
4. What happened to the teacher who was at Attu when the Japanese invaded your home?
   They tried to commit suicide on June 9th by cutting wrist. Mr. Jones died in afternoon. Mrs. Jones was taken away, with village people.
5. What time of day did the Japanese come ashore at Attu in June of 1942?
   Sunday, after church services, A.M., about 11:00.

6. How did the Japanese transport your people and the teacher from Attu to Japan?
   By boat from Attu, in morning September 17, 1942. Transferred to another boat Kiska, & on September 19, 1942 they took us away to Japan.
7. What day were you taken away from Attu?
   September 17th, 1942.
8. What kinds of personal belongings were you permitted to take with you?
   Clothes, Basket Weaving Grass, Salmon (dried), Blankets, Holy Water, Icons from Homes.
9. What day did you arrive in Japan and placed in the internment camp?
   October, 1942 early weeks.
10. Was the teacher also placed in the same internment camp with you throughout the entire World War II? Were you or your people at any time questioned by the Japanese before being placed in an internment camp?
    (1) No.
    (2) Yes, In school house at Attu, interrogated and questioned. Teacher and wife were also questioned. The entire village was roped, so no people would not try and escape.
11. Were there more than one camp where your people of Attu were kept in Japanese internment camps?
    1st—Shomisu-Cho & transferred to Hokkaido City—Our people were together at all times, not separated in two camps.
12. Where in Japan was the internment camp where your people were located?
    Otero City, Hokkaido, Japan.
13. How were the meals served to you, was there sufficient amounts per serving?
    No. Sometimes people didn't eat. 1 day or more.
14. Did the Japanese feed you varieties of food for balance of diet?
    Rice & a piece of salt fish, milk in scarce supplies, bread. Small growth of vegetables while they were there, kept by the Aleut people. Carrots, turnips, small other things.
15. What was the main source of diet at the internment camp?
    Rice & Fish, Bread.
16. Did everyone in the internment camp get to see one another regularly?
    Most of the time, some were in the hospital.
17. Were the men used at any time for any hard labor?
    Yes. For care and feeding.
18. Were you allowed to prepare any meals at any time for those of you at the Japanese internment camp?
    Yes.
19. Was there very much sickness among your people at the Japanese internment camp?
    Yes. Many from Tuberculosis & some died.
20. Did the Japanese provide medical services for care of your sick people at any time?
    Yes. Only rest, there was no proper medication for TB.

21. How was Tuberculosis confronted with at the internment camp?
    Dr. Fujimo, They put sick People in sanatorium. Dr. Moriita, Matsuda (assistant).
22. Did the Japanese hospitalize any of your sick at any time while you were in Japan during the second world war?
    Yes.
23. Did the children receive any schooling while at the Japanese internment camp?
    No.
24. Were you permitted to hold church services at the Japanese internment camp?
    No.
25. Have you ever seen any of your people having been brutally, unfairly harmed at the Japanese internment camp during the period you were at the internment camp?
    Yes. If they did not listen to the police in charge & orders.
26. Were your people allowed to have any kind of entertainment while at the Japanese internment camp?
    Only on holidays to Japanese dancing.
27. If there was any life lost to any of your people during the Second World War at the Japanese internment camp or at any medical establishment that you may know about, will you give us some information to this matter?
    The sick with TB & old people, some because of malnutrition.

RETURN OF THE ATTU PEOPLE TO ALASKA

1. How many of your people survived who were able to return to Alaska after having been kept in the Japanese internment camp during the entire second world war?
   Mostly fair. 5 people were admitted to Tacoma, Washington hospital for tuberculosis.
2. Health wise, were all of you who came back from Japan in good or bad health?
   Mostly fair. 5 people were admitted to Tacoma, WA Hospital for tuberculosis treatment.
3. How many of your people returned from the Japanese internment camp with Tuberculosis?
   5 people were still sick with TB when we reached Atka.
4. What date did you and your people arrive to Atka from Japan?
   Shinizu-Cho in Otaru, September 17, 1945 to Chitose by bus, September 20 from Chitose by plane to Atsugi. September 21, 1945; by plane to Guam & Philippines. Nov. 20, 1945; by train to Seattle from San Francisco. We got to U.S. in Navy ship.
5. How were you and your people transported back to Alaska?
   Boat from San Francisco.
6. When you were being taken to Atka, how did you and your people feel about not being returned to Attu?
   We were sick about it.

7. Who made the decision not to return your people to Attu?
   The U.S. Government transferred the people to Atka. There weren't much people to return to Attu village. Village was burned. What was left when the Japanese left they burnt its remains.

8. After arriving at Atka from Japan, was there a medical person provided for physical examinations?
   Yes. Military Drs. Found TB.

9. Where were the tuberculosis striken people taken for treatment after your arrival from the Japanese internment camp?
   Tacoma, WA., Manila, Philippines.

10. Has anyone from the group of people from Attu who are now living in Atka been allowed to see their home village since your return from Japan?
    Yes, with Bob Reeves.

11. What condition did the war of the Aleutians during the Second World War leave the village of Attu?
    No Village.

12. Were homes built or provided by any group or government for your people at Atka after having settled there?
    Yes. They built homes for the people returning there. 4–5 homes were built.

13. Were you able to recover any valuables (guns, radios, etc.), artifacts and church relics or records from Attu since your return from Japan?
    No. Church burned. Japanese may have records of church. Guns were taken. Radio. Never recovered.

14. After having lived at Atka since your return from Japanese internment camps in Japan, do you still have hopes of someday going back to live at your Attu village?
    Yes. It's our home. Yes. If land claims gave us second chance.

15. What types of boats and engines not recoverable had been lost at Attu and how many were lost?
    5 Dories & Johnson Motors.

16. Can you give us a list of names of those who are survivors of this mishap and give us locations as to where we may reach them?
    See attached census.

ATTUANS WHO RETURNED ALIVE FROM INTERNMENT IN OTARU, HOKKAIDO, JAPAN

1. Alfred Prokopeuff — Atka
2. Elizabeth Prossoff — Atka
3. Willie Golodoff — Atka
4. Julia Golodoff — Atka
5. Mike E. Lokanin — Atka
6. Parascovia Lokanin — Atka
7. Olean Prokopeuff — Atka
8. Nick Golodoff — Atka

9.	John Golodoff	Atka
10.	Gregory Golodoff	Atka
11.	Elizabeth Golodoff	Atka
12.	Innokanty Golodoff	Hospital
13.	Juliana Prokopeuff	School
14.	Angelina Hodikoff	Dillingham, Washington
15.	Steven Hodikoff	Atka
16.	Marina Hodikoff	School
17.	Marth Hodikoff	School
18.	Anges Prossoff	School
19.	Anna Hodikoff	Died in Hospital, Tacoma, Washington
20.	Mary Golodoff	Died in Hospital, Tacoma, Washington
21.	John Hodikoff	Died in Hospital, Tacoma, Washington
22.	Alex Prossoff	Drowned in Sea Up North
23.	Alfred Prokopueff	School

ATTUANS WHO DIED DURING INTERNMENT IN JAPAN IN WORLD WAR II
1942–1945

1.	Mike G. Hodikoff	Adult
2.	George M. Hodikoff	Youth
3.	Ann A. Borenin	Teenager
4.	Garman S. Golodoff	Adult
5.	Laventy M. Golodoff	Adult
6.	Feodosay G. Hodikoff	Adult
7.	Helen J. Golodoff	Teenager
8.	Marva E. Artumonoff	Teenager
9.	Peter J. Artumonoff	Youth
10.	Velerian L. Golodoff	Boy
11.	Lianty L. Golodoff	Boy
12.	Maria H. Parkopeuff	Adult
13.	Gavriel M. Lokanin	Infant
14.	Aneaia A. Hodikoff	Infant
15.	Mike W. Golodoff	Infant
16.	Latiana P. Lokanin	Child
17.	Maria J. Golodoff	Child
18.	Mike G. Golodoff	Infant
19.	Marth A. Prassoff	Adult
20.	Anecia Prokopeuff	Adult Died underway from Japan
21.	John Cutumauoff	Adult
22.	Blademer M. Prassoff	Boy

Author's Note: The list of names was difficult to read due to the age of the material. I apologize for any names I may have inadvertently misspelled.

Ted Stevens
Alaska

UNITED STATES SENATE
WASHINGTON, D.C. 20510

November 14, 1988

Mr. Dimitri Philemonof
Aleutian/Pribilof Islands, Assn./ Inc/
1689 C. St.
Anchorage, AK 99501

Dear Dimitri:

I was pleased you could join me for the signing of the Japanese-Aleut Reparations Bill in August. I enjoyed having lunch with you and the others from the Aleut community during your visit. Enclosed is the Photograph taken at the time. It is always a pleasure to meet with fellow Alaskans, and I hope your stay in the Washington area was enjoyable.

With best wishes,
Cordially,
TED STEVENS

Notes

Introduction

1. Letter, Mildred Greenhagan to Superintendent Edward C. Johnston, Fish and Wildlife Service, October 19, 1942.
2. Letter, Edward C. Johnston to Mildred Greenhagan, November 2, 1942.
3. Dean Kohlhoff, "It Only Makes My Heart Want to Cry: How Aleuts Faced the Pain of Evacuation," in *Alaska at War, 1941–1945: The Forgotten War Remembered* ed. by Fern Chandonnet (Fairbanks, AK: Alaska at War Committee, 1995), p. 291.

Chapter One

1. "Report of Fleet Captain Vitus Bering on his Expedition to the Eastern Coast of Siberia," *National Geographic Magazine* 2, No. 2 (1890).
2. "Extract from the Log of the First Expedition of Fleet Captain Vitus Bering," *National Geographic Magazine* 2, No. 2 (1890).
3. C.L. Andrews, *The Story of Alaska* (Caldwell, ID: Caxton, 1938), p. 26.
4. Ibid.
5. Ibid.
6. Stephen Haycox. *Alaska: An American Colony* (Seattle: University of Washington Press, 2002), p. 72.

Chapter Two

1. Andrews, pp. 59–85.
2. Ibid.
3. Ibid.
4. Ibid.
5. Ibid.
6. Ibid.
7. Basil Dmytryshn and E.A.P. Crownheart-Vaughn, *The End of Russian America: Captain P.N. Golovin's Last Report, 1862* (Portland: Oregon Historical Society, 1979).

Chapter Three

1. Frederick Seward, *Seward at Washington as Senator and Secretary of State*, vol. 3 (New York: Derby and Miller, 1891), p. 348.
2. Ellis Oberholtzer, *History of the United States Since the Civil War, 1865–1868* (London: McMillan, 1917).
3. Official Report of General Jefferson C. Davis in Cession Papers, Russian America, Doc. 177, Fortieth Congress, Second Session.
4. Andrews, p. 127.
5. T. Ahllund, "From the Memoirs of a Finnish Workman," translated by Panu Hallaman, *Alaska History* (Fall 2006). Originally published in Finnish in *Suomem Kuvalahti*, 1873.
6. Andrews, p. 127.
7. Ibid.

Chapter Four

1. Andrews, p. 165.
2. Ibid.

3. Pierre Berton, *The Last Great Gold Rush 1869–1899* (Toronto, Canada: Anchor Publishers, 2001).
4. Frances Backhouse, *Women of the Klondike* (Vancouver, Canada: Whitecap, 1995).
5. Ibid.
6. Ibid.
7. Berton.

Chapter Five

1. Theodore C. Hinckley, *The Americanization of Alaska 1867–1897* (Palo Alto, CA: Pacific Publishers, 1972).
2. District Organic Act, 23 Stat. 24, May 17, 1874.
3. Homestead Act of Alaska 30 Stat. 409, March 3, 1903.
4. Treaty of St. Petersburg ,1825.
5. Evangeline Atwood, *Frontier Politics: Alaska's James Wickersham* (Portland, OR: Binford & Mort, 1979).
6. Ibid.
7. Andrews.
8. Ibid.

Chapter Six

1. "Remembering Our Heritage," Office of History, Elmendorf Air Force Base, Anchorage, Alaska.
2. Anthony J. Diamond, Congressional Delegate, Alaska, Comments to Congress, 1937; Brian Garfield, *The Thousand-Mile War* (New York: Ballantine, 1969), p. 54.
3. Ibid.
4. Joseph Driscoll, *War Comes to Alaska* (Philadelphia, PA: J.B Lippincott Company, 1943), p. 18.

Chapter Seven

1. Intelligence memorandum, Office of the Assistant Chief of Staff G-2, Headquarters Western Defense Command and Fourth Army, Presidio of San Francisco, California, August 9, 1943.
2. Ibid.; Message from Admiral Nimitz to Admiral Theobold, May 1942; Garfield, p. 15.

3. Ibid.
4. Ibid.; "He Survived Japanese Invasion," *Seattle Times,* August 9, 1981.
5. Ibid.
6. Ibid.
7. Ibid.
8. Ibid.
9. Ibid.
10. Ibid.
11. John C. Kirtland and David P. Coffin, Jr., "The Aleuts in Japan," in *The Relocation and Internment of the Aleuts During World War II* (Anchorage: Aleutian/Pribilof Islands Association, Inc.), September 15, 1981, Evidence, Vols. I to VII, p. 119.

Chapter Eight

1. Mikizo Fukuzawa, *Attack on the Aleutians* (Tokyo: n.p., 1943), p. 43.
2. Olean Prokopeuff (Golodoff), "An Account of the World War II Attu Captivity," 1981.
3. Ibid.
4. Tomoya Tsuruia, *Attu Island* (Tokyo: n.p., 1943).
5. Garfield.
6. Tsuruia, p. 65.

Chapter Nine

1. Barbara Sweetland Smith, "Restitution for Aleut Churches Damaged and Lost During the Aleut Relocation in World War II," in *Alaska at War 1941–1945, The Forgotten War Remembered.*
2. Prokopeuff.
3. Komiya Mayumi, *World War II Nurses Who Were Interned in Yokohama*, Canberra Seminar of P.O.W. Research Network (Japan, 2006); translated by Yuka Ibuki with assistance by Anthony Walsh.
4. Ibid.
5. "Australian Women Released from Jap prison Camp," *Canberra Times,* Canberra, Australia, September 3, 1945.
6. Jack Percival, "Guard Stretched Up to Slap Nurse P.O.W.," *Sydney Morning Herald*, Sydney, Australia, September 3, 1945.

Chapter Ten

1. Prokopeuff.
2. Kirtland and Coffin, "The Aleuts in Japan," p. 125.
3. Ibid., 127.
4. Prokopeuff.
5. Ibid.

Chapter Eleven

1. Memorandum, Scheurman, Navy Department to Paul W. Gordon, January 16, 1942; Personal Justice Denied, Report on Wartime Relocation and Internment of Civilians, December 7, 1982, p. 7.
2. Ibid., p. 7.
3. Ibid., p. 8.
4. Ibid.
5. Ibid., p. 9.
6. Letter, James C. Rettie to Harold D. Smith, May 7, 1942; Personal Justice Denied.
7. Executive Order 9181, Administration of the Federal Government Services in Alaska, June 11, 1942, FR, DOC. 42-5528; filed June 12, 1942.
8. Letter, Alaska Territorial Governor Ernest Gruening to Secretary of the Interior Harold L. Ickes, June 4, 1942, Evidence, Vol. II, p. 7
9. Letter, Secretary of the Interior Harold L. Ickes to Alaska Territorial Governor Ernest Gruening, June 22, 1942, Evidence, Vol. II, p. 8.
10. Letter, Alaska Territorial Governor Ernest Gruening to Secretary of the Interior Harold L. Ickes, June 22, 1942, Evidence, Vol. II.

Chapter Twelve

1. Dean Kohlhoff, *When the Wind Was a River* (Seattle: University of Washington Press, 1995), p. 70.
2. "During Times of War as Told by Larry Dirks, Sr.," written by Mr. Bergsland, a linguist from Norway, translated by Michael Lekanoff, Sr.
3. C. Ralph Magee and Ruby Magee, "Our Atka Island Experience 1940-1942," Evidence, Vol. II, pp. 13-17.
4. "During Time of War as Told by Larry Dirks Sr."
5. Log Entry, USS *Gillis*, Atka, Alaska, June 13, 1942.
6. Magee and Magee, Evidence, Vol. II, pp. 13-17.
7. Ibid., pp. 14-15.

Chapter Thirteen

1. Letter, Edward C. Johnston to Ward T. Bowers, May 28, 1942.
2. Flore Lekanoff Sr., "Aleut Evacuation: Effects on the People," in *Alaska at War, 1941-1945*.
3. John C. Kirtland and David P. Coffin, Jr., "When Airplanes Are Seen Coming," in *The Relocation and Internment of the Aleuts During World War II*, Index to Evidence, Vol. I.
4. Kohlhoff, p. 71.
5. Lee, Jeanette J., *Aleuts remember, Alaska Natives Recount Their Internment During World War II*. www.juneauempire.com
6. Kohlhoff, p. 72.
7. Letter, Daniel C. R. Benson, Resident Agent and Caretaker, St. George Village, to Edward C. Johnston Superintendent Sealing Division, Fish and Wildlife Service, July 8, 1942.

Chapter Fourteen

1. Letter, Chief, Division of Alaska Fisheries, FWS, Ward Bowers to F.G. Morton, FWS, Seattle, Washington, December 30, 1943, Evidence, Vol. VII, p. 130.
2. Fredericka Martin, "Personal Narrative," March 1965, Evidence, Vol. VII, p. 25
3. Deposition, Haretina R. Kochutan, Evidence, Vol. VIII, p. 25.
4. Testimony, Philemon Tutiakoff, Unalaska, Alaska, September 17, 1981.
5. Debra McKinny, *Anchorage Daily News*, www.aaanativearts.com/article1269.

Chapter Fifteen

1. Joseph Driscoll, *War Discovers Alaska* (Philadelphia: J.B. Lippincott, 1943), p. 37.

2. Ibid., p. 37.
3. Ibid., pp. 38–39.
4. Ibid., p. 49.
5. Ibid., p. 49.
6. Ibid., p. 34.
7. Ibid., p. 38
8. Ibid., pp. 39–40.
9. Ibid., p. 51.

Chapter Sixteen

1. Statement, "The Aleut World War II Relocation and Internment: An Overview," by Philemon Tutiakoff before the National Coalition for Redress/Reparations, Los Angeles, California, November 15–16, 1980.
2. Letter, Martha Newell to her husband Kenneth, March 18, 1943.
3. Letter, Claude M. Hirst, General Superintendent Alaska Indian Service, to Anthony J. Diamond, Congressional Delegate, Alaska.
4. Letter, Edythe J. Long, school teacher at Burnett Inlet, to Superintendent Fred Geeslin, Alaska Indian Service, Juneau, Alaska, May 6, 1943.

Chapter Seventeen

1. Gilda Shelikoff, untitled article, 1996.
2. Letter, Harry G. McCain, Mayor of Ketchikan, Alaska, to Alaska Territorial Governor Ernest Gruening, May 19, 1943.
3. Ibid.

Chapter Eighteen

1. Telegram, General Superintendent Claude M. Hirst to Indian Affairs Commissioner William Zimmerman, June 22, 1942, Evidence, Vol. II, p. 94.
2. Letter, Superintendent Edward C. Johnston to Alaska Fisheries Division Chief Ward T. Bowers, June 19, 1942, Evidence, Vol. II, p. 88.
3. Memorandum for file, F.W. Hynes, Assistant Fisheries Management Supervisor, FWS, June 25, 1942, Evidence, Vol. II, p. 161.
4. As quoted in letter, General Superintendent Claude M. Hirst, Evidence, Vol. II, pp. 164–167.
5. Letter, Agent and Caretaker Lee C. McMillin to Superintendent Edward C. Johnston, Sealing Division, July 11, 1942, Evidence, Vol. III, p. 8.
6. Ibid.
7. Ibid.
8. Ibid.
9. Letter, Superintendent Edward C. Johnston to Fisheries Division Chief Ward T. Bower, October 10, 1942; includes petition by Aleut women.
10. Ibid.
11. N. Bernita Block, M.D., Report on trip to Funter Bay, October 2–6, 1943, Evidence, Vol. III, pp. 34–37.
12. Entry, Pribilof Log, September 18, 1943.
13. Ibid., September 27 and October 1, 1943
14. Ibid.

Chapter Nineteen

1. Memorandum, Director of Education Virgil R. Farrell for General Superintendent Claude M. Hirst, May 13, 1942, Evidence, Vol. II, p. 141.
2. Ibid.
3. Letter, General Superintendent Claude M. Hirst, Alaska Indian Service, to Alaska Territorial Governor Ernest Gruening, June 29, 1942, Evidence, Vol. II, p. 163.
4. As quoted in letter, General Superintendent Claude M. Hirst, Evidence, Vol. II, pp. 164–167.
5. Magee, Evidence, Vol. II, p. 16.
6. Letter, C. Ralph Magee and Ruby J. Magee to Dr. and Mrs. S.R. Barenberg, September 20, 1943, Evidence, Vol. III, p. 65.

Chapter Twenty

1. Letter, Fred R. Geeslin, Acting General Superintendent Alaska Indian Service, to Sealing Division Superintendent Edward C. Johnston, March 20, 1943, Evidence, Vol. V, p. 33.
2. Ibid.
3. Ibid.

4. Ibid., pp. 120–121.
5. Letter, Agent and Caretaker Lee C. McMillin to General Superintendent Edward C. Johnston, Sealing Division, July 11, 1942, Evidence, Vol. III, p. 8.
6. Article III, Treaty With Russia, March 30, 1867, American Historical Documents.
7. *Aleut Community of St. Paul Island v. United States*, 42 IND. Cl. Comm. 1, 54 (1978).

Chapter Twenty One

1. Letter, Secretary of the Interior Harold L. Ickes to Secretary of War Henry L. Stimson, November 23, 1943, Evidence, Vol. IV, p. 2.
2. Letter, Secretary of War Henry L. Stimson to Secretary of the Interior Harold L. Ickes, January 2, 1943, Evidence, Vol. IV, p. 12.
3. Entry, Pribilof Log, September 13, 1943.

Chapter Twenty Two

1. As quoted in Letter to Alaska Fisheries Division Chief Ward T. Bower to Assistant Fisheries Supervisor Frank G. Morton, September 6, 1943, Evidence, Vol. VI, p. 13.
2. Ibid.
3. Telegram, Acting Director Charles E. Jackson, FWS to Assistant Fisheries Supervisor Frank G. Morton, September 8, 1943, Evidence, Vol. IV, p. 14.
4. Telegram, Agent and Caretaker Lee C. McMillin to Assistant Fisheries Supervisor Frank G. Morton, September 19, 1943, Evidence, Vol. IV, p. 15.
5. Telegram, Agent and Caretaker Lee C. McMillin to assistant Fisheries Supervisor Frank G. Morton, September 20, 1943, Evidence, Vol. IV, p. 17.
6. Memorandum for the Chief of Staff, U.S. Army, Return of Natives to their Alaska Homes, December 7, 1943, Evidence, Vol. IV, p. 41.
7. Letter, Secretary of War Henry L. Stimson to Secretary of the Interior Harold L. Ickes, December 13, 1943, Evidence, Vol. IV, p. 43.
8. Letter, General Superintendent Edward C. Johnston Sealing Division to Hans Floe, P.E. Harris Company, March 17, 1944, Evidence, Vol. IV, p. 168.
9. Entry, Pribilof Log,, May 13, 1944.
10. Dorothy Kane Jones, *Century of Servitude: Pribilof Aleuts Under U.S. Rule* (Milburn, NJ: University Press of America, 1980).
11. Entry, Pribilof Log, May 24, 1944.
12. Letter, President Franklin D. Roosevelt to Secretary of War Henry L. Stimson, August 7, 1944, Evidence, Vol. IV, p. 185.
13. Telegram, B.W. Thoron, Director of Territories and Island Possessions to Alaska Territorial Governor Ernest Gruening, May 14, 1944, Evidence, Vol. IV, p. 172.

Chapter Twenty Three

1. Memorandum, U.S. Survey of Akutan, April 26, 1944, Evidence, Vol. IV, p. 184.
2. Memorandum for the Commandant Naval Operating Base, Dutch Harbor, undated, Evidence, Vol. II, p. 191.
3. Ibid.
4. Letter, Alaska Indian Service General Superintendent Don C. Foster to Commissioner of Indian Affairs William A Brophy, undated, Evidence, Vol. II, p. 244.
5. Memorandum for the Commanding General, A.P.O. 939, Seattle, Washington, Statement Concerning Housebreaking and Thievery in Unalaska Village, January 12, 1944, Evidence, Vol. II, p. 197.
6. Ibid., pp. 197–198.
7. Survey Report on Nikolski Village, April 26, 1944, Evidence, Vol. II, p. 187.
8. Ibid., p. 188.

Chapter Twenty Four

1. Dean Kohlhoff, "A Matter Very Close to the Aleut Heart: The Politics of Restitution," in *Alaska at War, 1941–1945*, p. 299.
2. Ibid.

Bibliography

Andrews, C.L. *The Story of Alaska*. Caldwell, ID: Caxton, 1938.
Atwood, Evangeline. *Frontier Politics: Alaska's James Wickersham*. Portland, OR: Binford & Mort, 1979.
Backhouse, Frances. *Women of the Klondike*. Vancouver, Canada: Whitecap, 1995.
Berton, Pierre. *The Last Great Gold Rush, 1869–1899*. Toronto, Canada: Anchor, 2001.
Breu, Mary. *Last Letters from Attu*. Portland, OR: Alaska Northwest, 2009.
Chandonnet, Fern, ed. *Alaska at War, 1941–1945: The Forgotten War Remembered*. Fairbanks: Alaska at War Committee, 1995.
Dmytryshyn, Basil, and E.A.P. Crownhart-Vaughn, trans. *The End of Russian America: Captain P.N. Golovin's Last Report, 1862*. Portland: Oregon Historical Society, 1979.
Driscoll, Joseph. *War Discovers Alaska*. Philadelphia: J.B. Lippincott, 1943.
Garfield, Brian. *The Thousand-Mile War: World War II in Alaska and the Aleutians*. New York: Ballantine, 1969.
Haycox, Stephen. *Alaska: An American Colony*. Seattle: University of Washington Press, 2002.
Hinckley, Theodore C. *The Americanization of Alaska, 1867–1897*. Palo Alto, CA: Pacific, 1972.
Jones, Dorothy Kane. *Century of Servitude: Pribilof Aleuts under United States Rule*. Milburn, NJ: University Press of America, 1980.
Kohlhoff, Dean. *When the Wind Was a River*. Seattle: University of Washington Press, in association with Aleutian/Pribilof Islands Association, Anchorage, 1995.
Oberholtzer, Ellis. *A History of the United States Since the Civil War, 1865–1868*. London: McMillan, 1917.
Robertson, Frank G., and Beth Kay Harris. *Soapy Smith: King of the Frontier Con Men*. New York: Hastings House, 1961.
Seward, Fredrick. *Seward at Washington as Senator and Secretary of State*, vol. 3. New York: Derby and Miller, 1891.

Index

A'Court, Holmes 55
Adak 83, 118
Admiralty Alaska Gold Mining Company 150, 154
Agency for POWs and Noncombatants 102
Akutan 185–86
Alaska at War Symposium 124
Alaska Fisheries Division 150, 157
Alaska Indian Service 113, 137, 159
Alaska JUNEAU Gold Mining Company 166
Alaska Native Allotment Act 72
Alaska Pioneer Home 75
Alaska Railroad 75
Alaska Road Commission 71
Alaska Syndicate 73
Alaska War Council 115–16
Alberta 79
Alcan Highway 79
alcohol 50, 163
alcoholism 69
Aleut Homes Inspection Report 187–88, 195
Aleutian Livestock Company 146
Aleutian/Pribilof Islands Association 1, 99, 200–1
Aleutian/Pribilof Restitution Bill 203
Alexander (czar) 41, 45
Alexander (emperor) 44
Alexander Archipelago 18
Alutiq Indians 20, 24
Amchitka 22
Anahootz, Chief 54–5
Anchorage 78–9
Army of the Columbia 51
Army Transport Service 177
Army Weather Bureau 199
Atka 112, 114, 118–19, 120, 122, 130–31, 160
atrocities 101

Atsugi Air Base 111
Attu 11, 80–81, 83, 88, 98, 112, 114, 116, 118–19
Australia 81–83, 104
Avacha Bay 17

baidarkas (boats) 12, 26, 29–30, 35, 38
Ball, W.D. 68
Ballenger-Pinchot Scandal 74
barabaras (houses) 11–12, 22, 36
Barber, Henry 35
Barnes, R.E. 166
Baronov, Aleksander 25, 28–31, 33–36, 39–41
Baronov Hill 47
Baronov Island 37
Battle of Midway 119
Battle of the Coral Sea 82–83
Bay View Cemetery 149
Beardslee, A.L. 56
Benson, Catherine 137
Benson, Dan 137, 153–54
Bering, Vitus 15–19
Bering Island 20
Bering Sea 35, 42, 46, 123
Bering Strait 15
"birthplace of the winds" 11
Bodega Bay 38
Bower, Ward 123–24, 127, 130, 150, 156, 158, 171–72
British Columbia 44, 46, 51, 55, 57, 59–60, 71
British East India Company 32
Buckner, Gen. Simon 84, 113, 116, 120, 126, 174–75
Bureau of Indian Affairs 58, 180–81

California 23, 33, 37–39
cannery 150–51, 155, 158, 162, 166, 177

Index

Cape Addington 17
Carmack, George 60–61
Catherine (czarina) 28
Catherine (empress) 24
Catherine the Great 31–33
Checkout Barracks 78
Chichagof 90, 109
Chichagof Island 37
Chichagof Village 91, 93
Chilkoot Pass 62, 64–65
China House 153
Chirikov, Alexeii 17–18
Chirikov Island 18
cholera 101
Chukchi Coast 16
Church of England 59
Cleveland, Pres. Grover 69
Colcheka 52
Commissioner of Indian Affairs 161
Committee for Wartime Restoration and Internment of Civilians 200
Committee on Police, Health, and Sanitation 148
communicable diseases 147
con men 63
contagious diseases 101
Cook Inlet 17, 20
Copper River 31

dance halls 65
Davis, Gen. Jefferson C. 50–52
Dawes Severality Act of 1887 72
Dawson 64–67, 69
Dawson, Charley 60
Deady, Mathew 70
Deady Code of Oregon 70
USAT *Delarof* 125–26, 150–51, 160, 171
Department of Agriculture 144
Department of the Interior 89, 150, 176–77, 180–82, 199
Diamond, Anthony 78
Dinks, William 162
diphtheria 109
Dirks, Larry, Sr. 119, 121, 162
Division of Territories and Island Possessions 113, 181
Doolittle, Gen. James 81–82
Driscoll, James 78–79, 134–37
drunkenness 50, 56, 149
Dutch East Indies 81
Dutch Harbor 35, 78, 83–84, 113–14, 118, 129, 131, 133–34, 150, 186, 188
dysentery 101

Elizabeth (Czarina) 21
Empire of Japan 80–81
England 44

Eskimos 49, 76
espionage 89–90
evacuation 98, 122–23, 127–28, 130, 132–33, 138

Fairbanks 75, 78
Filipino House 153
Fish and Wildlife Service 112, 123, 125–27, 129, 131, 169–70, 172, 174–77, 179
Fletcher, Adm. Frank J. 82
forced labor 107
Forrestal, James 180–81
Fort Mears Army Hospital 128
Fort Richardson 97, 126
Fort Ross 38, 42
Fortuna 15
Foster, Don C. 180, 182, 196–97
Fox Island 22
fraud 69
funeral rites 110

Gamaland 14, 17
gambling 50, 57, 63, 65
Garfield, Brian 96
Geeslin, Fred R. 140, 143–45, 147, 148, 180, 182, 186, 191, 193, 197
Geneva Convention 102
USS *Gillis* 118, 120–21
gold mines 153
gold miners 61–64, 67
Gold Rush of 1896 60, 66, 69
"Golden Steps" 65
Golovon, Pavel 33, 42
Government Census of 1880 68
Gravel, Michael 200
Great Circle Route 77
Great Depression 77
Great Northern Expedition 16
Greenland 46
Greenwich Observatory 13
Gruening, Ernst 78, 113–14, 116, 134, 171, 181
Guggenhiem, Stephen 73

Hagemeister, Leontii 41–42
Hagerty, Donald 130–31
Harrison, Benjamin 68
Hawaii 39–40
Hawaiian Islands 39
Haynes, F.W. 151, 157–58
Henderson, Robert 61
hepatitis B 147
Hirst, Claude 115, 130, 143, 159, 161, 180
Hodikoff, Annie 92, 105
Hodikoff, Fred 109
Hodikoff, Mike 87
Hokkaido 7

Holtz Bay 90
Homestead Act 70
Homesteaders 71
hooch (native brew) 51
Hood Packing Company 151
House, Charles 86–87
House Judiciary Committee 45
houses of prostitution 57
Hudson Bay Company 32, 51
USS *Hulbert* 118, 120–21
Hutchinson, Howard M. 47, 50
Hutchinson-Khol Company 47, 50

Iceland 46
Ickes, Harold 114, 116, 169, 176–77, 180–81
Imperial High Command 88
Imperial Russia 46
Indian attacks 20, 22, 33–34, 54
Indian Claims Commission 168
Indian River 35
Indian schools 60
Indian Service Hospital 145
influenza 67, 76, 157–58
Ingersoll, Charles 75
inspection reports 187
International Fishing Commission 90
International Red Cross 103, 161
intoxicants 50
intoxication 58
Isaof, Achimandrite 25, 30
Ivannovna, Anna 16

Jackson, Sheldon 57–58, 60, 69
Japanese Americans 202
Japanese Civil Defense Force 103
Japanese Combined Fleet 119
Japanese Consulate 200
Japanese High Command 9
Japanese Imperial Army 77
Japanese Invasion 7
Japanese Northern Army 9
Johnson, Andrew 45
Johnston, Edward C. 123, 130, 150, 154, 156, 158, 166, 170–74
Joint Chiefs of Staff 84
Jones, Etta 93–97, 100
Jones, Foster 93–97
Juan de Fuca 37
Juneau 58, 68, 70, 90, 124, 162
Justice Department 202

Kamchatka 14–16, 23, 27, 30
Kamchatka Peninsula 14
Kamchatka River 15
Kamehameha, King 39–40
Kanagawa Internment Camp 86–87, 100
Kanleika (hooded robe) 12, 15

Kaumualii, King 39, 40, 42
Kenai 51
Kenai Bay 32
Kenai Peninsula 163
Kenai River 28
Ketchikan 75, 90, 145, 147, 149
Ketchikan General Hospital 149
Khlebnikov, Kirill 34, 41
Kirtland, John C. 201, 203
Kiska 80, 83, 98, 100, 118–19, 123
Klondike 60–62, 64, 67
Klondike Fever 60
Klondike River 60–61
Kodiak 29–30, 32–34, 51, 78, 85
Kodiak Island 17, 20–21, 24–25, 30–31, 57
Kohloff, Dean 9
Kolash Indians 33–36, 39, 42
Koniag Indians 33
Kotzebue 69
Kotzebue, Otto 201, 203
Krukof, Agafon 203
Kurile Islands 14, 23–24, 31–32, 80

Lebedev-Lastochkin, Pavel 28, 30–31
Lekanof, Flore, Sr. 124
lend-lease 84
USS *Lexington* 82
liquor 50, 76
looting 186

Magee, C. Ralph 120–22, 131, 136, 161–62
Magee, Ruby 120–22, 131, 136, 161–62
mail service 69–70
Makarii, Hieromonk 25
Manifest Destiny 5, 46
Marshall, James 39
massacre 33–34
Matanuska Valley 31
McArthur, Douglas 103
McKinley, William 73
McMillin 153–54, 167–68, 173, 175–76
measles 21, 67, 157–58
medical equipment and supplies 128–29
medical treatment 87, 107–9, 157, 161, 141, 151–52, 157
Medvyednikof 34
Michael of Irkutsk (bishop) 26
Midway Island 80, 82–84
Minimoto-Cho 108
Mission Indians 56
Mission Schools 57
missionaries 25, 57
missionary teachers 58–59
Mitchell, Gen. Billy 77–78
Morgan, J.P. 73
Morris, William 68
Mt. Edgecumbe 36

Mt. St. Elias 18

National Coalition for Redress/Reparation 140
National Planning Board 115
National Resources Planning Board 115
National Tuberculosis Center 107–8
naval inspection reports 186, 193
naval inspectors 186
Nazan Bay 118, 121
Neva 36
New Arkangel 37, 59
New Metlakata 59
New Zealand 81
Newell, Martha 141–42
Nimitz, Adm. Chester 82–84, 119–20
Nippon Around the World Goodwill Flight 88–89
Noguchi, Satorii 108–9
Northwest Canadian Mounted Police 65, 71

Oahu 40
Oar City, Hokkaido 7
occupation of Attu 91, 94
Office of Indian Affairs 113, 122, 131, 137, 144, 146, 148, 156–58, 161–62, 170, 176, 181, 197
Okhotsk 24, 30
Old Metlakla 59
Old Siyka 35
Omori, Santara 90
Organic Act 68
Otaru 110

Pacific Northwest 41
Partov, Egor 30
Paul (czar) 32
P.E. Harris Company 150
Peter the Great 13–16
Petroff, Ivan 68
Philemonof, Dimitri 1, 2, 199, 203
Phoenix 30
Pletnikoff, Patrick 200
pneumonia 21, 158
Point Barrow 69, 76
poliomyelitis 109
potable water 154–55, 164
Presidential Emergency Fund 199
Pribilof, Gavril 23
Pribilof Islands 23, 35, 46, 51, 116, 123, 130, 134, 136–37, 166, 172, 174, 178
Pribilof Log 173
Prince of Wales Island 17, 58
Prince William Sound 20, 28, 30
Prokopeuff, Olean 91, 93, 100, 105, 110–11
promyshlenniki (fur traders) 20–22, 24, 30, 37, 42

prospectors 63–64, 66–67, 69, 75
prostitutes 65

racism 8
railroads 75
Reagan, Ronald 203
Reconstruction 193, 195
Redoubt Archangel Michael 37
Reznov, Natal'ia 31–33
Reznov, Nikolaii 31–33
rookeries 23
Roosevelt, Franklin D. 115, 179, 199
Rousseau, Lovell 42, 50
Russian American Company 28, 32–33, 44, 48
Russian Orthodox Church 24, 26–27, 57–58, 124, 185
Russian River 38

St. George Island 123, 125, 137, 171–73, 175
St. Lawrence 16, 123
St. Paul Island 46, 51, 67, 123, 125–26, 131, 137, 171–73
St. Petersburg 15–17, 25, 32, 42
San Francisco 38, 47, 62, 80, 111
Sandwich Islands 39
Schafer, George 40, 42
Scorched Earth Policy 122–23
Sea of Okhotsk 15
Seal Islands 32, 39, 58
Second Organic Act 74
Seims-Drake Puget Sound Company 166
Selective Service Board 167
Setka Presbyterian Industrial School 58
Seventeenth Naval District 180
sewage 147, 154, 159
Seward, William 43, 45–47
Sheldon Jackson School 58
Shelikov, Grigory 20, 23–25, 28–30, 32–33, 40
Shelikov, Natal'ia 20, 24, 31
Shigeyoshi, Inoue 82
Shikani, Takeshro 106, 111
Shimizo-Cho 106–7, 110–11
Siberia 15–18, 84
Skagway 62–63, 71–72
Skagway Trail 64
Skookum, Jim 60–61
smallpox 21
Soapy Smith 60
Steller, George 18
Stevens, Ted 201
Stimson, Harry 115, 169, 171, 176–77, 180
Stoeckl, Eduard 45, 47
Strong, John 75
Sumner, Charles 45–46
Surgeon General of the United States 158

Index

survey parties 190
survey reports 191
Sutter, John 39
swamps 145, 151

Taft, William Howard 74
Tagish First Nations People 60, 64
teachers 72
Territorial Department of Health 156
Territory of Alaska 74
Theobald, Adm. Robert 35, 84, 119–20
Third District of Alaska 73
Three Saints Bay 24
Three Saints Island 30
Tlingit Indians 26, 35–36, 49–50, 52, 64, 159, 164
Tojo, Hideki 81
Tokyo 81
Totuska-Ku Prison Compound 101
Treaty of Cession 167
tuberculosis 21
Tutiakoff, Philemon 131, 140–41, 198, 201

Unalaska 25, 58, 131–33, 188, 192
Unangan (We the People) 11, 20, 22
U.S. Employment Service 166
U.S. State Department 198
U.S. Treasury Department 68
U.S. War Department 175–77
Updegraf, William N. Captain 132

vandalism 185–86, 188, 190–93, 195
venereal disease 21, 145, 148
Veniminov, Ioann 26

village devastation 178, 185–86, 194
violence 22, 101
Virgin Islands 46

Wacker, Eugene 146
Wakatake-Cho 100, 105, 107
War Crimes Commission 199
Waskey, Frank H. 73
Weckerling, John 80–81
Western Defense Command 80
White Pass 62, 64, 76
Whitfield, Barbara 131
Whitfield, Samuel 131
Wickersham, James 73–75
William III (king) 13
Williwaw 18
Winfrey, Walter 86
winter storms 19, 29–30, 39
Witsen, Nicholas 14
World war I 76

Yakutat 33
Yamazki, Yasuyo 95
Yamomoto, Isoruki 81–83, 88
Yasak (tribute) 21
Yokohama 87, 100
Yokohama Yacht Club 100, 104
USS *Yorktown* 82
Yukon 76
Yukon Basin 69
Yukon River 65
Yukon Territory 65
Yukon Valley 58

www.ingramcontent.com/pod-product-compliance
Ingram Content Group UK Ltd.
Pitfield, Milton Keynes, MK11 3LW, UK
UKHW041941140426
5217IPUK00014B/598